A Brighter Tomorrow

Memories of A South Africa Childhood

Edna May Walker Booth

OLD RUGGED CROSS PRESS

Cover photo:
The author, Edna May Walker, December 1926,
just shy of 18 years old; probably inscribed to
Archie Richardson, her first husband.

Library of Congress Cataloging in
Publication Data:
Edna May Walker Booth
A Brighter Tomorrow
94–067140
ISBN–1-882270-19-3

Published in the United States of America
by Old Rugged Cross Press.
Inquiries should be addressed to:
Editor: Old Rugged Cross Press
1495 Alpharetta Highway, Suite I
Alpharetta, Georgia 30201

Foreword

This is Edna May Walker's story. It is about her childhood in South Africa during the years 1909 until 1920 when her mother, sister, and brother emigrated to the United States. *A Brighter Tomorrow* is the postumous fulfillment of her dream to leave to her extensive family a record of her early life and her recollections of a very large agricultural family. Throughout her pages we discover a remarkable woman who as a girl was very bright, curious, and sometimes perhaps somewhat devilish. While aging for most of us smooths out the devilishness, Edna May never lost the bright curiosity that seemed to have been hers from birth.

Edna May begins her story in Omaha, Nebraska, in September 1930. This beginning, however, simply prompts her to recall her childhood in the Transvaal and along the Indian Ocean coast of the Cape Province of South Africa. Her story unfolds from her birth at the Premier Diamond Mine, Cullinan, the Transvaal, where her father was a stationary engineer and—what would come to be seen as unfortunate for the family—a labor organizer at the mine. Her family, now including her sister Jessie, moved to the parental Green's family farm at Smiling Valley between the Kwelagha and Bulugha Rivers to the east of East London in the eastern Cape Province. The Walker family then soon included brother Leonard, born after his father's departure in early 1914 for the Great War.

Edna May suffered from a goodly number of illnesses throughout her long life. She was deaf from her high school years onward, the result of various mastoid infections beginning in 1921. She lost one eye in August 1974 at age 65. Some three years before she died, having struggled with glaucoma in the remaining eye, she lost it to macular degeneration, a severe and crowning blow to one who so enjoyed reading and her life-long correspondence with her relatives in South Africa and her many friends there and in this country. It was also a blow to the completion of this, her story. We, her sons, inherited no fewer than three versions of her manuscript and it was no longer possible for her to help us carefully to determine which was the one she preferred. We have made our decisions, choosing from among them as much of her story as we can and in her words and style to the fullest extent possible, lacking her counsel. We have retained many of her British spellings. We have, however, in her text changed the word "Kaffir," which she and the British of her day customarily used for the black people, friend, servant, or villain, with whom she and her family came into so frequent contact. Perhaps inaccuratey, we have used the word "Xhosa" most of the time and "Zulu" on a few occasions when this seemed a more likely choice. It may well be in our ignorance and distance from the events that we err in these important ethnic designations and we apologize to those who may have difficulty with the change. As language changes, words we use for one another sometimes take on different and sometimes pejorative meanings; we choose to be sensitive to this matter.

The footnotes are our addition, believing that many of her family will wish to have the information provided. We take full responsibility for inaccuracies, with apologies to Mother for any damage they may do to her text.

Her family and friends know that Mother was very interested in accumulating the genealogical history of her family, being herself justifiably proud in being able to trace her ancestry through the maternal line to the 1820 British Settlers in South Africa. Such work is difficult ever to "complete," as information believed impossible to acquire graciously appears through the efforts of other interested parties. The tables provided in Appendix D: Genealogy are not presented as a complete and thorough description of the Greens, and certainly not of the Walkers. Perhaps the interest of those who read this book will be piqued, old papers will be shuffled through, and absent—or corrected—information will be found to fill in the blanks. We, her sons, will welcome such information and will see to the best of our ability that someday we may issue a Second Edition with those updates.

Leonard C. Richardson
Petaluma, California
Eastertide 1994

Andrew MacAoidh Jergens
2374 Madison Road
Cincinnati, Ohio 45208
Eastertide 1994

Chapter 1

Memories Stimulated

My husband, Archie Richardson, and I lived in a bungalow on North 19th Street and Carter Lake Boulevard, Omaha, Nebraska, in the home owned by my parents. It had been purchased by father while mother, Ivy Green Walker, and we three children were en route to the United States from our native South Africa. My parents and siblings lived in Milwaukee, Wisconsin, where father was employed at the Omaha Printing Company. He was in the printing trade until the end of his life.

Mother came to Omaha to see her first grandchild, Leonard Charles Richardson, who, born 13th March 1930, was six months old that September 1930. The three of us were at the train depot early as I was eager to see her after a four year absence. This was a joyous occasion and Mother quickly took charge of "such a bonnie boy." She was English but often used the Scottish vocabulary, perhaps because her husband's speech was the burr of a Highlander. When we arrived home, I ushered her into a guest bedroom that had been hers previously. She refreshed herself, then went through the house room by room.

"I'm much surprised to see everything so clean and you still have the furniture your dad purchased before we arrived. I never expected you to be a good housekeeper as you were so adept at escaping household tasks I assigned to you." I did not tell her that I had made a supreme effort toward this effect, as I knew she was very particular about cleanliness, and I was secretly glad she had not arrived unannounced!

While I prepared our afternoon tea, Mother was ah-ing and cooing to Leonard. He was indeed a bonnie boy, as he enjoyed her attention and responded with appropriate gurgles and talk.

"Tea is ready Mother," I called.

After putting the infant in his crib, she came into the kitchen saying, "Oh there is nothing so pleasant and satisfying as a good cup of 'tay,' and I realize I'm hungry, too, so thanks for the sandwiches and biscuits." ("Tay" was Mother's playful designation for tea; all cookies were called "biscuits.")

"I have been curious to learn why you were hospitalized so long when Lennie was born," she said. (I noticed the "Lennie" and smiled, because this was the name she used when speaking of my brother, also named Leonard.) I explained what I knew about that situation then asked, "Did you have any such problem with any of us three?"

"No. You all were born at home; you and Jessie were born on the Cullinan and Dr. Lister attended me both times. Your brother was born in Grannie Green's home on Smiling Valley Farm near East London. Grannie took care of us then. In those days women never thought of going to a hospital for childbirth."

"Tell me about Dr. Lister. Aunt Alice[1] sent me many newspaper clippings about him. I had no idea my life had been touched by such a famous person.[2] The paper's account of his death listed such a variety of medical accomplishments. He apparently was a brilliant doctor."

"Well, all I know is what everyone in Cullinan knew. He cared deeply about the blacks and their working conditions. They were prone to contract lung diseases from the dust and digging so far underground. Many died before help could be given." I interrupted by asking, "What connection did Lister have with the mine workers? Did the Mine hire him?"

"Oh yes. Dr. Lister worked for Cullinan Mine. Because your dad was working there, I was entitled to his services when you girls were born. He took care of all the Mine employees and the families. And when he was able to check the lung diseases, even other diamond as well as gold mines wanted his services.

"It was because of Dr. Lister's deep interest in bacteriology,

---

[1] Most likely, Alice Elizabeth Green Gager; see Chapter 5.

[2] Joseph Lister. 1827-1912, was an English surgeon who introduced to surgery the principle of antisepsis, itself an outgrowth of Louis Pasteur's theory that bacteria cause infection. There is no record of Baron Lister's travel to South Africa. It is likely that this is another Dr. Lister.

immunizations, and the use of antiseptics that help came to so many. All these medical approaches and especially for his research in lung diseases, was reason for Dr. Lister's being knighted by the King of England, George V, in 1920. It must have been been a great day for him to receive such recognition."

"I wonder if our antiseptic, called Listerine was named because of him? You said he promoted antiseptics during childbirth, didn't you?"

Mother laughed, "I really don't know about the Listerine! It could be true. I do know that many fewer deaths occurred from childbirth after the use of antiseptics."

Mother appeared in deep thought, then continued. "I recall when you were born. You were so tiny, he remarked, 'It is a doll you have, Mrs. Walker. I'm sure she will survive, even though she weighs only three pounds.'"

"Three pounds," I exploded! "Is that all I weighed? It is a wonder I survived, or did you have an incubator?"

"Never heard of incubators and don't know if any existed then. Jessie weighed four pounds and brother was a big boy of five."

"Heavens! No wonder you had no problems! My Leonard was nearly nine pounds."

Mother went on talking. "Your Aunt Alice was present to help and care for us. The clothing I had prepared was too large, so Auntie just wrapped you in nappies (diapers) and laid you upon a pillow beside me and covered you with a beautiful shawl she had made. You were born a few minutes before eleven that night, so we knew no visitors would arrive.

"Next morning I awakened to the enticing odors from the kitchen and knew Alice was baking for morning tea. We both expected several callers, as the neighbors were always interested in any new arrival, especially babies. Most of my neighbors were Boer families. Actually they had little interest in me, an English person, but all babies were special. As their lives had little of glamour or excitement, these Boer women made much of marriages, births, and deaths. These events were considered milestones in life to them.

"They were a hard-working people, used to many trials. They suffered much during the Boer War and after. Many loved ones were killed on the battle fields, and worse yet, thousands of women and children starved to death in the concentration camps."

"Good heavens, do you mean to tell me women and children were held in concentration camps! Why? I thought such camps were a product of World Wars I and II and the later conflicts."[3]

"Oh no!" Mother exclaimed. "In fact I think it was the British who first considered the idea of concentration camps, especially for women and children. You see the Boer fighters were a stronger force than the British expected. The war was becoming too costly, so Britain wanted it ended. They made offers that the fighters rejected, particularly when their women urged them to fight. The British had no concept of the unity among these men and women and were dismayed when they learned the war was to continue because of the women's declaring their decision.

"Every Boer fighting man soon learned his farm was burned, women and children rounded up and taken to the prison camp. The British were positive the Boers would surrender, but they did not. If one reads the story of what the women endured, one finds this a very sad story indeed!"

Mother was silent for a time and I did not intrude, but quietly watched her expressive face. I realized she was remembering something. Finally she said, "I was just remembering Tante Marie. She was the only Boer woman I personally knew who had lived through the experience of the concentration camp. She was a strong woman both in character and in physical strength. She lived through the long months in that camp under the most unbelievable conditions; almost as if in sheer defiance, to prove to the British she would survive."

After sipping more tea and taking another biscuit, she smiled and said, "I never could blame those men and women for their attitudes toward any Britisher and I respected their attitudes toward me. We were neighbors, but we never visited often. She was highly respected by all who knew her. The younger women often consulted with her about household and personal matters, knowing she had a depth of understanding and much compassion. She could be, and often was, very stern, but also kind and gentle especially to those in

---

[3] An anachronism. Obviously the time of writing this story postdated World War II and probably the Korean War. Edna May's later knowledge of concentration camps is brought earlier into this 1930 event.

trouble. She was my first visitor. Alice had noticed groups of two or three women on the street, talking together; out of deference to Tante Marie, they did not come calling first. Everyone called her 'Tante,' which means 'Auntie.' It was the custom, then, to call every older woman 'Tante' or 'Auntie' as a title of respect.

"I was pleased to see her and knew it was indeed a compliment to me, although I also recognized her visit was meaningful in other ways. She prided herself on setting an example to the younger Boer women and her strong religious feelings would dictate over any personal ideas.

"After greeting me, she came closer to the bed and bent over to look at you. I removed the shawl and suggested she might want to hold you. She beamed her pleasure and picked you up, fondling your hands and feet. Joking at me with her piercing brown eyes, she exclaimed, 'Ach! You call this a baby, this little doll? We Boer women bear big strapping children. Our husbands would be most unhappy if we produced dolls!'"

"She carefully placed you on the pillow and again exclaimed, 'A teacup in bed! Why is this?' picking up the cup.

"'Oh I had forgotten that,' I said, as I reached for the cup, gently placing it over your head. 'See how her head fits into the cup? My sister had the idea,' gesturing toward Alice who came into the room.

"'Ach! This is unbelievable,' Tante Marie muttered, shaking her head as she turned to leave, bidding me good day.

"'Won't you stay for morning tea?' asked Alice, as they both moved toward the front door.

"'No thank you, Mevrou. I have another engagement.' She turned again to nod goodbye and bid Alice farewell too.

"I then remembered it was her custom to have a special tea for the Boer women of the community the first Tuesday after the New Year. It was a happy social event that they anticipated, then savoured in memory. The party over, they would all return to the usual routine, each day having its special tasks."

We had become so engrossed in our conversation, the cries from the bedroom brought us back from memory lane to the present. "Oh the bonnie boy!" Mother exclaimed as she hurried to take charge. Hearing her loving sounds, her cooing to my infant and his gurgling responses, brought a smile to my face as I cleaned up the kitchen and made some preparations toward the evening meal.

It was with regret that I watched Mother repack her suitcase for her return to Milwaukee. We arrived at the train depot early. Mother suddenly laughed aloud, saying, "Now I know why you insisted we get here early! Do you recall our experience of December 1927 when the children and I first went to Wisconsin?"

"Mother, I will never forget how you delayed leaving the house when I knew a snow storm was due. We barely made it to the station, then you stopped to chat with the ticket agent while Dick [husband Archie Richardson] hurried [sister] Jessie and [brother] Leonard to the train. 'All aboard' had been repeatedly called and the trainman on the last car was helping Dick get the kids aboard and here you came running. 'Hey wait for me,' as you waved the tickets. How you managed to climb into that moving car, I'll never understand. All I could think of was the kids aboard and your being left behind with the tickets! I was a nervous wreck."

"Well it was a bit thoughtless of me. The truth was, I did not want to leave Omaha. Dad had been gone so long, I really dreaded having to live with him again."

After the train departed, I thought of her final remark. Somehow I began to understand more of her feelings and the trauma of her life. Little did I know then, how parallel her life and mine would be.

After Mother's departure, I gave much thought to what she told me. My memory was stimulated and I began to recall incidents almost forgotten. In particular, I recalled my overnight stays with school chums who were Boer children. In memory I relived some of those experiences.

Staying overnight or for a weekend was a time for fun and sharing. I was an observant child and noticed that homes were spotlessly clean. The wooden floors had been scrubbed so often they almost gleamed. Our English homes had linoleum covered floors. Linens, clothing, and all window curtains seemed to smell of fresh air and sunshine. They were crisp and ironed to perfection. The table settings were not elegant but always their best possessions graced the table. Breaking bread, eating together, was not just to feed the body but also to feed the soul. It was a time to share ideas as well as food. These families would be considered poor by today's values, but they were rich in customs and history.

I was much impressed by the family manner during meals. Family members stood behind their respective chairs until the mother had placed the food bowls and platters in front of the father. She then sat down, as did the father. The children were invited to be seated. Each head was bowed and hands clasped, while the father gave a verbal blessing for the food. He then began to serve, the first plate's being passed to the mother. Each child was served, and finally the father served himself. All began to eat the regular meal, after which the eldest child, boy or girl, went to the kitchen to bring the dessert. The mother served this. General conversation began. Each child was asked to report the happenings at school; questions were asked and answered. I was much surprised to be included in this procedure. It was difficult to express, as I was never permitted to speak during meals at home. Grandfather [Robert Frederick Green] was a kind person but his motto was, "Children should be seen and not heard," and this was strictly enforced. When dessert was finished and conversation seemed to lag, the mother and family again bowed their heads while she gave an overall thanks-blessing. Each child carried his or her soiled dishes into the kitchen.

This seemed to me a very disciplined way of life. I enjoyed it all, mentally contrasting procedure at home where food was served family style, each helping self and the clearing of the table always done by Mother. I never heard any prayer at home.

I sensed a closeness and harmony among the parents and children in those homes. It was obvious that love was the binding force. Perhaps in later years, the children came to realize meaningful values had been formed that were carried into their own homes. These life patterns were well ingrained.

It was in one particular home that I began to realize mothers were many faceted. Besides caring for children, being manager of households, or flower and vegetable gardens and sundry farm animals, she was teacher too!

Every daughter was a potential wife and mother. She had to be taught the multiple household duties and learn the skills needed for being a well-trained housewife. It was important to be a good needlewoman, as all the clothing had to be handmade. Few homes had sewing machines then.

One had to know how to form clothing and patterns must be made from any available paper. The underclothing was usually fashioned from flour or sugar sacks. This entailed the careful unravelling of the threads that were seams in these sacks, and saving this thread for future use. These sacks had to be well bleached to remove all the printing or marks that would be on them.

Daughters had to work in the farm lands, especially if no older brothers were available. She had to know how to take care of the animals; perhaps even to do the milking and butter making! Managing finances was needful. Although money was a scarce commodity, it had to be carefully hoarded and spent only after family consultations. The lesson of frugality was learned early!

Fathers taught the sons all the basic skills of animal husbandry; especially how to handle the cattle that was a greater facet of wealth than money. Oxen were the farmers' means of transportation, whether they were hauling produce to market or the family on long treks. His oxen were treated with respect for all their inability to be speedy. They were given ample time to rest and chew their cuds. They were never overworked and never mistreated. Boys also had to learn carpentry and other needful tasks in order to be a successful farmer. Discipline and love were the key words of the families I personally knew.

How different was my life! I was disciplined, but not taught domestic skills. Our mother was so busy doing all these household tasks herself, in order to complete the total needs of the family, including her parents and three younger brothers. She was never free to teach us in our younger years. In contemplating this, I realized it was the circumstances in which she found herself that precluded this instruction.

How different our lives would have been had Dad been a better provider, a kind loving husband and father, as my uncles were. He had to leave us the first time because of employment circumstances he himself brought about. This in turn threw mother into the role of sole support for her three children and caused her to feel like a servant for family members. I learned years later that she often did not know for certain just where Dad was!

Chapter 2

Earliest Recollections

My thoughts carried me to my earliest recollections when we lived on The Premier (Cullinan[1]) Diamond Mine near Pretoria, Transvaal, which is today the administrative capital of the Republic of South Africa. I would then recall our journey to the Cape Province, the city of East London's being our destination by train. We would then travel twenty miles out of the city by ox-drawn covered wagon to the former home of my mother. Her parents lived on their farm called "Smiling Valley," situated between the Kwelegha and Bulugha Rivers.

In memory I lingered longest on my first home, in an area called Hallsdorp on the Cullinan Mine. It was there that my awareness of others and myself as a person developed. My life centered around the person of my mother. It was not until I was nearly three that I saw the man in our home was my dad. He was an employee in the Mine and belonged to the rugby team that was competing on the occasion of some local celebration. I was seated beside Mother with many women, children, and some men on something called benches, watching the game. I watched the game, having no idea of what it was all about.

There was much shouting and cries, some happy and others anguished at times. I did not know what was the reason and was startled when everyone stood up, saying "Hurrah" and clapping; talking so excitedly! Men in white shorts, wearing red and white blazers came over. Everyone seemed happy. These players were slapped on the back when others would say, "What a great game!

---

[1] For Edna May's description of Cullinan and its diamond mine history, see Appendix B.

How wonderful, we won." I began to understand some reason for all the commotion.

One of these players, dressed in white shorts, wearing a red and white blazer, came to Mother and greeter her, then lifted me above his head, saying, "And how is Daddy's girl?" I did not recognize him and was silent. It was the first time Dad had ever done that. He lowered me to the ground when a gentleman said, "Are you Sidney Walker?" Excitement again as these two embraced. He was introduced to Mother as "My old college chum, Mac."

After greeting Mother, he bent low, looking intently at me. "Did you enjoy seeing your Daddy play? He was always a good rugby player." I barely nodded as I searched his brown friendly eyes.

This Scotsman, whom I'd never see again, was soon to befriend Dad in an unusual way. They both traveled together to Scotland in January 1914; both would then go to the United States. Mac to locate in New York, while Dad went to the mid-West. Six years later, Mac would be asked to assist Mother and her three children who would be detained at Ellis Island.[2] The authorities never permitted this, so we spent five miserable days in what I later would choose to call a Federal Prison. Mother protested. It was "stay, or be deported," so we endured.

As we left the playing field, Dad talked and walked beside Mother and she held my hand. I could not understand the situation at all, but began to realize this man was my dad! How could he be laughing to me at the game and be so uncaring at home?

Dad was never fatherly and showed no affection toward Mother. I early learned not to disturb him in any way. He was taciturn and Mother often cautioned me to be quiet or put fingers to her lips, which I learned was caution, when he was home. He sat in his special chair in the front room, near the window reading a paper or book and it was then I dared not disturb him. I did not like to hear him say, "Stop disturbing me. Don't make so much noise!" It was a revelation to know this was, indeed, my daddy!

We had two regular visitors in our home. One was the owner of the Mine, Mr. Thomas Cullinan, who was Dad's senior by about

[2] See Chapter 28.

ten years. I never knew how Dad and he became friends. The other was a friend of my parents and I was told to call him "Uncle Billy Baker," quite a mouthful for a small child.

Mr. Cullinan's family lived in Johannesburg, which was about sixty miles southwest of Cullinan, situated in the Transvaal area of South Africa. As the business of establishing the Mine required his constant attention and supervision, he lived on the premises, first in a tent, and later in a lean-to shack. Several of his employees invited him for evening meals and this is how Dad and Mr. Cullinan became friends.

Mother and I often discussed our life in Cullinan, as there was much I wanted to know. I vaguely remembered Mr. Cullinan as being a big man, with a moustache. He was always so loving to me and held me on his lap. I recalled his delight when I walked toward him for the first time and how we used to talk, together. I basked in his gentleness.

"He missed his family very much and always fussed over the children in the homes where he visited. He was a very polite man, a real gentleman!" so Mother said more than once.

Transportation between Johannesburg to Pretoria was by train, but from Pretoria to Cullinan one had to travel by oxcart drawn by two oxen, later by horse and buggy. Eventually Mr. Cullinan was able to make the journey back and forth more frequently by automobile. It was then that his business affairs became more complex and his visits to our home stopped. I often wished I had known him when I got older, but he became only a memory.

Sometimes Uncle Billy Baker would be a guest at the same time, and these two had a great time talking and laughed gaily at each other's jokes. I never knew if they met each other before meeting in our Hallsdorp home.[3] Uncle Billy was a delightful person, slim, blond, with very blue eyes that sparkled with fun and mischief, especially when he and I played together. He always squatted on his heels so he could see eye to eye with me; then he

---

[3] Hallsdorp was a housing area south of the center of Cullinan. The houses have long since returned to nature. Young South African policemen were not able to point out where it was during a 1991 visit.

would lift me up and toss me toward the ceiling, and always caught me as my body came downward. I was delighted and laughed loudly, much to Dad's annoyance. This fun was almost always stopped when he would verbalize his irritation.

Uncle Billy had his piano stored in our home. When I got tall enough to reach the keys, I was instantly told "don't touch." This was my first lesson in life; how often I was told not to touch things! I had a curiosity that often was squelched.

Most of the times when visiting, Uncle Billy would sit at his beloved piano and play. I was enraptured by the lovely sounds that issued forth. Often he would sing as he played and this delighted me. Through this dear man, I was introduced to music and song. I seldom hear a pianist without recalling the happy times with my Uncle Billy. He was not really a relative, but he was my favorite Uncle.

We usually had our meals in the very large, spacious kitchen. Today the dining room table had been extended with all its leaves and covered with snow white table linens. Mother placed her best china, glassware, and silver around, indicating several people were to be seated. She had arranged a flower centerpiece, something she had never done before to my remembrance. I was much impressed! Such a beautiful table setting, I thought and questioned, finally had courage to ask.

"Mommy, why are you making so many places around the table and why are you hurrying so fast?"

"We are having guests, child, and there is much to do yet so please be patient and we will talk later on!" was her reply.

I was used to two guests and Mommy never had fussed before. She had spent hours in the kitchen and began to look so tired and flushed. Her responses to my questionings were vague and sometimes none at all, I observed. It was pleasant being in the kitchen with all the delightful smells, but I could not comprehend the many dishes on the table that were being filled. She had never prepared so much food for our regular guests.

Dad came home and brought some people I did not know. Soon Uncle Billy arrived. I was joyful until I saw he had a pretty lady with him. I felt shy and some disappointment as he did not give me the attention I was used to from him, and there was no indication we would have our usual fun time.

More attention was given to the lady and much conversation and laughter went on. I looked closely at the lady as she was dressed all in white. I thought her very beautiful with her wide brimmed hat, trimmed with a large white ostrich feather and pale pink flowers. I could see she wore her hair in a pompadour style, as did my mother, but her hair was so light, while Mother's was a dark brown. I had never seen hair so like pale honey and wanted to touch. Her white lacy dress had a flower arrangement pinned to one shoulder. This was a strange way to have flowers! I noticed she wore white gloves and carried a white parasol which had a frilly edge in light pink.

I began to realize this was a special occasion, and by listening I heard someone say, "it was a nice wedding." Of course I was too young to understand the meaning of "wedding."

My curiosity changed to gladness when Uncle Billy began to play and then to sing. He looked at the lady all the time he sang *You Great Big Beautiful Doll*! then went on to sing *Only a Bird in a Gilded Cage*. I wondered what a gilded cage was and why he called her a beautiful doll when she was a lady.

Mother announced that dinner was ready at which Uncle left the piano and, putting his arms around the lady, kissed her. I was astonished! I had never seen Daddy kiss Mother. The lady's face got red and her eyes shiny. This was something I could not understand.

Everyone sat down and Mother put me on a chair beside her. I was higher than the others in my special chair and began to observe all. At that moment I began to make comparisons, although I was not consciously aware of doing so. When Mother's face got red, she was usually crying. I was so used to seeing her in a black skirt and white blouse that I began to wish she too could look really pretty and wear all white.

I looked at my dad and wondered why he seemed happy now, because he laughed a lot, something he never did when we were alone. I wondered why he seemed so interested in the guests, but never showed this interest to Mother and to me. Why does he never hold me on his lap and talk to me? There was no answer. I decided that Uncle was better because he made me laugh, made nice music and I felt glad inside. I realized I never felt glad inside when Dad was home, and I wondered about that, too, as I quietly ate what Mother gave me and watched the people,

I thought it strange that they held up their glasses when someone said, "A toast to the newlyweds"—toast was bread! I wanted to say something to Mother about this "toast" but knew I was not to speak. I watched another lady seated across the table from Dad. She looked at me with keen brown eyes and so often smiled. I experienced a nice warm feeling and suddenly felt something happening. I felt quite old and looked at her and felt very wise.

She looked up and nodded her head but seemed to be looking above my head. I did not know it then, but she must have had what is called a "sixth sense" and probably "saw" someone with me who was not visible to others. I was only two years old, but had a sense of "strangeness" for a brief time. I did not become aware then of all this happening, but by the time I was seven a similar occurrence was experienced, more than once.

In view of personal experiences years later, I recalled this incident in the Cullinan home dining room and realized that it was the beginning of my own psychic ability. I never spoke of this to Mother, for I had no words to relate it and by the time the dinner was over, had totally forgotten the whole incident.

About a year later, Uncle Billy came to our home alone. He looked sad and I sensed tension. Daddy was grave and put his hand on Uncle's arm, and said, "I'm so sorry, old chap." Mother kept wiping her eyes and blowing her nose.

I wondered what was wrong, as Uncle Billy was not smiling this time. I was a bit hurt because he had not yet spoken to me. A nameless fear struck my being as I heard him say, "So I will not be seeing you any more. I have sold the piano and it will be picked up this week." Sold the piano! I was speechless.

I was aware of an odd tightness in my chest, a strange feeling in my tummy. My anxiety was alleviated when Uncle Billy bent down to talk to me. His blue eyes were no longer smiling, no sparkle of amusement, but a little moist as he hugged me to him and said I should be the big brave girl when he was gone and to remember him sometimes. He lifted me up and held me but did not toss me toward the ceiling. Instead he placed me on the floor, giving me another hug as he did so, then shook hands with my parents, went out of the door and out of my life. I never saw him again.

I did not understand the situation, although I overheard my parents talking about a "funeral" and "childbirth," but I did not know the terms and no explanation was given to me.

My sister Jessie was born[4] a few days after this episode, and I felt a bit better and less lonely. The baby was not to replace Uncle Billy in any sense of the word, but her arrival at this time of crisis in my life did something to assuage my sense of pain and loss.

At times a great sadness would envelope me and a deep longing or wishing that someone would love me. I would think of Uncle Billy at these times. He loved me, yes, but had been gone a long time. I frequently felt there was something I knew or should know; some moments I would experience a vague remembering of another someone who loved me. How could this be? A part of my mind seemed to open and I would get a glimpse of some past experience. I strived to remember but always gave up because this door closed too soon. I was to experience this knowing and feeling many times as a child, especially when I was seven.

This has been part of my feeling nature often as an adult especially since my understanding enlarged through spiritual and metaphysical studies. I was a lonely child even though I now had a sister, about a year old, but not a companion yet. I had a deep need to understand the strange feelings and ideas that I experienced, but there was no one to whom I could talk. There were no other children close to our home at this crucial time of my life.

Therefore a few months later, when a new family moved next door and I saw their little girl, I was happy with anticipation. Christine was my first child playmate, a lovely child with pretty long golden curls and she too had blue eyes. We were much alike in appearance; she was, however, much more assertive and had an air of knowing all there was to know about her world. I was shy

---

[4] 30th March 1911.

and rather silent except when Mother and I were alone. It was nice to have one my own age to talk to, although Christine was three months older.

One day Christine brought a box to show me the contents. In this was a small doll house with doll furniture, a doll and extra dresses. I had never had a doll, although I was now four. Christine showed me how the arms and legs moved so she could sit the doll on its tiny chair. In this box were several flat objects, covered with dark and silver wrappings.

"What's those?" I asked as I reached for one. Quickly she prevented me from taking one. "Hershey bars, sweets. You cannot have one. These are mine! My Uncle sent them all the way from America," Christine said with much emphasis.

She began to put the doll and doll house away. I observed this with regret as I was trying to get courage to ask her to let me play with them a short time but then she was so firm about the Hershey bars, I refrained. I stood up when she did, as tall as I could make myself and with great dignity announced, "I will get my own Hershey bars when I get to America."

"You cannot go there! It is a long way away and you have to take a boat and be on it a long time. You would be seasick, my mother said so, when I asked her to take me to see Uncle."

I was somewhat puzzled. I tried to imagine a boat and seasick, but it was too much for me. I again firmly stated, "I will too go to America." Christine looked startled, picked up her things, and went home without another word!

(Was this childish imagination or a bit of prophetic insight. Seven years later Mother, siblings, and I were on a steamer, headed for America!)

We had a large back yard where Mother had planted flowers. It was my joy to visit these each morning, watching how they seemed to talk to each other when a breeze caused them to move their flowery heads. I observed all the bugs that moved and when something really excited me, I would call, "Mommy, come quick."

She always came on the run, a bit anxious at first until she realized I just wanted my curiosity satisfied. She would explain what was the bug, or worm, I had been pointing to.

One morning I saw small mounds of dirt, unlike any I had

seen. This was not sand, not clods or lumps, but tiny grains that formed a peak. Again Mother came running and laughed when she saw what I was pointing to.

"Oh that is the soil from the ant home under the ground. Watch what happens when I move it with this stick."

I was delighted to see ants run hither and yon. They were not the red or black ants I had seen but were grey or whitish. Mother explained that the ants had pushed up the dirt as they needed more room in their homes beneath the soil. I was very self-satisfied as I knew something new now. I came to recognize this feeling of self-satisfaction whenever I learned a new word or had enlightenment in other ways. A thirst for learning stayed with me all my life, but later I came to realize I had a smattering of knowledge of many studies, but never had mastered any one subject!

We had a grape vine trained over the yard fence. It was the fall of the year, I went over to the fence anticipating finding a stray grape or two. I noticed how dry the leaves were and many were on the ground. As I reached for one tiny grape still hanging on to its parent frond, something moved! I looked closely, a stick moving? I stood still, it moved again.

"Oh come quick, Mommy, come quick!" I exclaimed. She ran to me as usual as I excitedly pointed and tried to explain, "the stick moved."

"That is a praying mantis, honey. It is a long time since I have seen one. They eat bugs and sometimes eat their mates. This one is almost gray but you might see one very green. They take on the color of the leaves about them. Now stand still and I will tickle him with this stick. Watch what he does."

I stood on tiptoe so as not to miss a thing. Its front legs went up and folded like hands at prayer. I laughed in delight. This seemed very funny to me.

"Step back now and we will watch him quietly." As the mantis began its strange walk along the vine, Mother said, "We will leave him alone now and I must get back into the kitchen. Please do not touch him again and stay in the yard." I stood watching the mantis while Mother moved toward the house then my attention was attracted to a colorful bird.

There was much to see and to learn in this back yard. I had

an excellent and patient teacher in Mother, for she had been a farmer's daughter. She knew much about plants, birds, animals and insect life and always came when I yelled. I think she enjoyed teaching me and probably was pleased her child was so inquisitive and observing.

This gift of observation was something I had all my life; often I would stand still and watch some bird or tiny animal and thus noticed its colorings and habits. My curiosity stood me in good one special day. Mother had sent me out into the yard after an afternoon nap, and I bent down to watch something moving in a different way. Its back went up at each step. It was black, fuzzy, and not too pleasant to look at. Soon I saw a reddish-brown one, then a different color. I called Mother again and when I pointed to what I was seeing, she looked startled, looked beyond me and quickly picked me up, ran to the house, and shut the door behind. She put me down on the floor without ceremony, rushed to the windows and front door, closing all. I was quite upset and a bit bewildered at this strange behavior. She sat down a bit breathlessly and held me on her lap. I was mollified for it was rare that Mother sat down to hold me.

Pointing toward the window, she said, "Look!" and we could not see any daylight, only the tummies of many, many fuzzy caterpillars crawling up and over—a whole army of these creatures. We looked at other windows and saw only these fuzzy worms and of course had no idea if they covered the whole neighborhood. Perhaps our house was the only obstruction in their path as they migrated.

It was an unforgettable sight, and, I think, an unusual phenomenon. This was the only time Mother had seen such a large number of caterpillars. If there was an explanation for that horde, I was never told about it.

Chapter 3

Aunt Agnes Robinson Walker

Mother spent many hours in the kitchen, as she worked hard with household tasks: heating water for washing clothes, baking bread, ironing, sewing, and many tasks just being a good house-keeper, mother, and wife.

Her sewing machine was in the kitchen, making it easier for her to watch whatever she was baking or cooking. In fact, most of her waking hours were spent in this room. I was curious about the sewing machine and asked many questions as to what she was doing and why. When she and I were alone, I could ask questions without feeling naughty as Dad referred to my questioning.

Now I watched intently as Mother moved the pieces of cloth that she was making into recognizable garments for Jessie and me. I enjoyed the sound of the sewing machine. Soon the garments were set aside for what Mother called "the finishing touches." These turned out to be the embroidery, laces, and tucks, all done by hand.

The day arrived when Sister and I were dressed in these new fineries. I was dressed first with bloomers. These had hand-cro-cheted lace at the leg bands. Then the underneath petticoat made of soft flannel, with fancy stitching around the armholes and neck-line. Another petticoat with a few tucks just above the hem line, to be let out later as I grew taller, and then came the third one, beau-tifully fashioned with lace, frills, or flounced, made of fine nainsook.

Finally the lovely white dress was on! How proud I was to have a new dress with smocking all through the bodice, tied with a wide blue ribbon sash.

All the years of my childhood I was bedecked with this kind

of clothing. As I grew older, a pinafore was added to this ensemble. Mother also created a very fancy pinafore to put on me should she be expecting guests. She was an excellent seamstress, as were most of the women in those days. They all had learned to sew by hand before the sewing machines became available.

Now Mother dressed Sister in her new long dress, also white. Jessie was not quite a year old[1] and still wore long dresses. Then Mother went to put on her own new skirt, a white one, and her usual plain white blouse. It was the first time I had seen her all in white, and I thought her even prettier than the lady who had come with Uncle Billy Baker. Mother's hair was done in pompadour style and she wore her pretty hat trimmed with a white ostrich plume.

This was my first remembered walk with Mother and a happy occasion for both of us. It was a change from her daily routine and she was pleased to be carrying her younger daughter to show relatives and friends. We had a long walk, our only mode of transportation.

Soon we approached a small, white frame house and Mother said, "You will meet your Aunt Agnes and cousins, so I want you to behave."

Before Mother could knock on the door, a pretty lady welcomed us into her parlor, as she called it, but it looked like a dining room to me. It could have been both, as I recall its being the length of the width of the house, much larger than our dining room.

As Mother introduced me she said, "This is your dad's sister, your Aunt Agnes." I responded to the warm embrace with which she enveloped me, then she reached for Jessie who was nearly asleep. Aunt Agnes was apparently pleased at her name, for she said, "Oh, you named her for Sid's and my sister."[2]

---

[1] This, then, is the end of 1911 or early 1912.

[2] Agnes Robinson Walker was born 12th July 1871, the sixth child of Alexander and Catherine Robinson MacKay Walker. This "Robinson" is likely the Anglicized version of the maiden name of Catherine's mother, Christian Robertson, of Glasgow, Scotland, who married James MacKay. The sister mentioned, Jessie Walker, was probably the fourth child; she died before August 1903.

As the two women talked, I was observing how Auntie rocked back and forth. Such a funny chair, I thought; it moves! We didn't have such a chair. I began to wish I could sit on her lap when suddenly Auntie exclaimed, "Why, the little dear has fallen asleep. I'll lay her on my bed."

Soon she returned and smilingly asked me to sit on her lap. I did so with a surge of happy feelings.

Soon the door opened and three older children entered. After the two girls embraced Mother, Aunt Agnes introduced the three to me.

"This is your cousin Edith and our little girl Gladys.[3] And this is your cousin, Alfred.[4] We all shook hands, each child stepping over to me where I was still sitting on their mother's lap. They all seemed warm and friendly.

Then Aunt Agnes turned to Edith and said, "Will you make the tea for us, please. Gladys can help you bring it in." Both girls left the room, while Alfred stayed to talk with Mother.

These cousins seemed to know Mother well. I learned that she had known them long before I was born. At one time Aunt Agnes had lived next door to my parents, in a different place. She was a widow and my Dad had supported her, at least contributed a sum of money all the days of her long life. She lived to be 97.

All too soon it was time for us to depart. I was so happy sitting on Auntie's lap that I was reluctant to forsake this delightful luxury of being held. Mother had very little time to sit and hold either Sister or me.

As we were saying good-bye with hugs and kisses, Aunt Agnes suddenly said, "Just a moment, Ivy. I want you to take something."

While we waited on a little bit of lawn soon Alfred came out and gave me a package, as Auntie said, "Take those home for your daddy." I felt very important carrying this and wondered if it contained some of the dainty little cakes we had eaten with our tea. (In fact, it did.)

As we walked toward home I was chatting happily about our

---

[3] Edith was born circa 1901; Gladys, circa 1902

[4] It is not clear who this is.

visit when, to my disbelief and consternation, Mother fell flat on the ground beside me. With Jessie in her arms she had not noticed a small stone in the path.

This upset me greatly. I had fallen at times, but to see Mother in this position was very distressing!

"Mother! Get up!" I was trying to lift her. "You will hurt the baby!" I kept tugging. It never dawned on me that she might be hurt. My concern was for my little sister. Mother must have been very tired. She had worked hard getting us ready. She had carried Jessie all the way for the visit and now she was carrying her home. I heard her give a deep sigh as she struggled to her feet, still holding the baby, and I noticed she limped a bit as she moved forward. She stood still for a moment as I brushed the dirt from her lovely white skirt. I found out later that not only was her ankle painful, but she also had a bruised elbow and she was less talkative the rest of the way home. It was never her way to let anyone know when she was in pain.

I recall my delight when Jessie began to walk at fifteen months.[5] When I once asked why she did not walk sooner, Mother told me I had not even tried to walk until I was eighteen months. She said I was such a crying baby and, because Dad could not stand the noise, she carried me on one hip while she used the other hand to get the meals on the table. As he thought babies were women's work, he never held me or helped in any way to give her any relief.

One Sunday Mother dressed me in my best as she told me that Edith was coming to take me to Sunday School. As Edith was the cousin who served the tea and cakes on our visit, I thought I knew her and awaited this new adventure with joy and little anxiety. I kept asking Mother what "Sunday School" was.

"You will be with many little girls like yourself," was all she said. "I hope you will be well-behaved." So I continued to wonder what was going to happen, as this would be my first trip away from Mother.

---

[5] About June 1912.

Actually, my recollection of that experience has always been a blur of much conversation and music. Nothing meaningful happened except a gift was given to me for attendance. It was a four by six card, brown background, with a design of green leaves and pink flowers all around the edge. In the center in white letters were the words, "Let not your heart be troubled."

This had no meaning for me then but often throughout the years I have thought of these words. I still possess this little treasure; one of the few I brought from that far-away home. It proved to be a sort of prophetic decree, as I've had many trials and tribulations and my heart has often been troubled.

After the service was over, instead of taking me directly home, Edith took me to her home where I saw Aunt Agnes Walker again and the other cousins, and again I had the happy experience of sitting on her lap and being rocked.

I felt a closeness with this aunt, probably because of her loving consideration of me; perhaps because we had the same birth month; most likely it was because she held me on her lap when I was in her home. Being held and rocked was a unique experience for me. She was the only person to hold me this way after I was two years old. Mother was always overworked and had little time for just sitting.

About 1889 when Aunt Agnes was a teenager, her mother (my paternal grandmother, Catherine MacKay Walker) suffered a stroke, and Aunt Agnes took care of her for the three years preceding her death on 12th December 1892. She became the housekeeper, caring for her father, Alexander, and the two little brothers, Sidney and Ivan.[6]

After her mother's death in 1892, Agnes continued in the home to care for her father and brothers, although married and having her own two children. She had married a former Norwegian fisherman, a Jon Svendsen, who decided to go with a group of trekkers to Southern Rhodesia. By the time all arrangements were made, they were married and their three children, Agnes, Thelma, and Percy, were born.

---

[6] Sidney Arthur Walker was born 10th July 1886; his older brother, Ivan Lawrence Walker, was born 7th November 1883.

Many covered wagons set out from the Transvaal with the new pioneers going to Southern Rhodesia. On the way, their scouts hurried back one day to order them to go into laager because a large army of Matabeles were seen in the distance. These were a highly organized, well trained army of blacks whose chief, Lobengula, was a despot for obedience and his army was ruthless.

Their strong shields were as long as the bodies were tall. They were made of well treated animal hides, but they were no match for the gunfire from the white pioneers. The Matabeles' assegeis were needle-pointed in sharpness, sometimes the tips were dipped in poison and the men, totally fearless, carried short, double-edged, razor-sharp daggers for close combat.

It was a terrible experience for the few white men, women, and children against so many hundreds of warlike humans attacking so viciously—yelling, screaming, and chanting war cries. The gun holders made every bullet count, and as the black dead bodies, with the dying, began to pile around the wagons, the Matabeles left, taking all the cattle, horses, and sheep that were not in the center of the laager. No one ever forgot the seventeen long, agonizing weeks it took to arrive near Salisbury, the capitol.

The Jon Svendsen family was finally established in a place called Enheldoorn, situated at least sixty miles north of Salisbury, where they built an inn and trading post. Aunt Agnes baked bread to sell and cooked for a few inn customers who arrived from time to time.

Jon took care of the shop itself, but, as he was not well, she often had to help. They had an East Indian servant who called Agnes "Mother" and helped in many ways. This left her free to do business in Salisbury when it was necessary.

They had not lived in Enheldoorn long when their business licenses had to be renewed. Leaving the Indian in charge of her sick husband and the children, she rode horseback the sixty miles to Salisbury to purchase the licenses.

On her return she was within twenty miles of home when she saw a figure running toward her. It was their Indian servant.

"Oh," he gasped. "Mr. Jon very sick man. Hurry, hurry!"

Auntie had him climb up behind her on the horse and together they finished the trip at a gallop. But they were too late.

When they reached the trading post, Jon and Thelma were dead and Percy was dying. The most horrible experience for her was to see big rats nibbling at the body of her dead daughter! Agnes was the only child left. This was the year 1898.

A severe form of malaria called "black water fever" was the cause of this tragedy. As it was extremely infections, the dead had to be buried immediately and precautions taken against becoming a victim.

Together the Indian and Aunt Agnes tore out the bar and the counter in the store and made two coffins. It was a difficult burden to dig the graves and to bury these loved ones under a thorn tree on the veld.

Soon after this experience a more distant neighbor came for supplies. Learning of the situation, he suggested that Aunt Agnes return to the Transvaal to recuperate. He would take care of the shop until her return. Upon her return, however, she discovered he was not a friend! He had maneuvered matters somehow, and the property was now his.

After that she went to Salisbury to find employment in the hotel kitchen. While at the hotel she met a Scotsman named Alfred William Anderson, a tobacco farmer, and they were soon married. In 1901 Edith was born and in 1902 Gladys; then a third child [the above-named Alfred] was expected.

Anderson was considered an expert on target shots. Shooting matches, called "bisley meetings," were often held, enabling all the men to keep up their shooting skills. One day in Salisbury at such a match he became suddenly very ill and died, apparently of pneumonia. No one seemed to know where he came from. So, because of the heat, he was buried immediately.

When he did not return home on the expected day, Aunt Agnes said to her eldest daughter, "Agnes, I'm going into Salisbury to look for your dad. Stay home and watch the children. I'll return as soon as possible."

Even though she was almost seven months pregnant, she rode horseback into town and there she learned that her husband had died and was already buried. She was given the few things they found in his possession and then went sadly home to continue supervising the tobacco farm until her son Alfred was born two months later.

She continued on for another month, then suddenly decided she had enough sorrow in this land she had helped build as a pioneer. She left everything except the clothing they would need. She and the children returned to Pretoria where she lived for a time with her brother Ivan.

In 1906 Aunt Agnes and her family moved from Pretoria to live in Cullinan and she took in laundry and ironing to earn a living. At that time women were not allowed to live alone in Cullinan without a male in the house. So her brother Sidney, my father, went to live with her and began his working on the Mine.

After all these tragedies she never remarried. When she was well into her seventies, however, fate struck her a greater sudden blow. She had a stroke that robbed her of her speech, sight, and ability to walk. Eventually she was able to get around in a wheelchair and her sight began to return. It took longer for her to regain her speech, but she was never again able to walk. Her determination to live and be self-reliant was strong to the end of her days. She lived 21 years after that stroke, dying at the age of 97 on 26th December 1954. When Mother told me this sad story many years later, I marveled at the courage, stamina, and fortitude of this pioneering aunt. She was indeed amazing!

Chapter 4

New Horizons

I had often gone with Mother to the small grocery shop near our home, about a block away. There were no traffic problems, so Mother felt it was safe for me to walk alone on this particular day.

"You are Mother's little helper, so I want you to go to the shop and get some eggs," she said. "Here is the money. Give all of it to the lady."

I felt very important as I skipped on my way. It gave me pleasure to see my red button high-top shoes as the sun flashed upon them and to feel the bounce of my flared skirt so stiffly starched, with my equally starched petticoat beneath. The greatest satisfaction was the lovely new pinafore Mother had elaborately embroidered and tucked. It was also starched and felt nice beneath my hands when I smoothed its satiny surface.

To get to the store I had to pass the prison that was on the opposite side of the street. No one had explained that to me. I knew nothing of a "prison," nor did I realize there were men behind those strange windows, strange because they had iron bars over them and were unlike any other windows I had ever seen.

Arriving at the shop I asked for eggs as I put the coins on the counter. When the lady asked where my basket was, I said, "Oh, I forgot. It is at home."

I hadn't even thought of that. There were no paper sacks then. Mother must have been so busy that she didn't think of a basket.

Finally the lady decided I could carry the eggs in my pinafore by holding up the edges with both hands. This seemed to work all right and I went on happily, walking carefully as instructed.

I was imagining Mother's "good girl" greeting when I heard voices. Someone was saying, "Hello. Hello, there!"

I turned around but no one was behind and certainly no one was in front of me. The voice continued. Then I looked across the street to see black arms waving out of the window and a black face grinning. I had no recollection of seeing a black face before. We did not have servants and neither did our close neighbors. I hurried my steps, keeping an eye on the window instead of watching my feet, when suddenly I fell flat.

Oh, the eggs! I wailed in dismay, fortunately still holding tightly to the pinafore. Laughter of the man or men rang in my ears as tears streamed down my face.

It was a tearful child who walked into the house, my pinafore full of scrambled eggs. I do not recall the reaction of my mother, but I am sure she was understanding and could salvage some of those eggs.

Mother then explained what the prison was and why the black men were there. Many blacks were hired to work in the Mine. They came a long distance from their kraals and so had to remain at the Mine and live in a place called a compound while they were working. Only when a group of men were to be sent home were they placed in the prison during the time before leaving.

She went on to explain that they worked deep in the Mine to dig the dirt containing diamonds to load into little metal carts that ran on a track. The men were confined for a time before going home so their bosses could be certain no diamonds were being taken out, too. The men could not get out of the prison, therefore they could not catch me. I did not understand all this, but I did feel better.

One evening friends of my parents brought their ten-year old son to care for Jessie and me while they and Mother and Dad all went to the ball. I noticed my dad was all dressed up and so was the other gentleman; both ladies dressed in white with sashes around their waists and wearing white gloves. Both looked very pretty. I also noticed the lady was the same height as her husband, both as tall as Mother, but my father was shorter than Mother by three or four inches, and he was broader than the other man. I wondered about that. It was strange that grownups were so different in size.

Our mothers admonished us to be good and to behave and the boy was told to take care of us girls.

We had a jolly time playing with toys provided for us when suddenly a strange noise sounded outside; a siren, but as we never heard such a thing we were frightened. The boy suggested we hide under the bed. All three of us crowded together far back against the wall, speaking only in whispers and wondering what it all meant.

At last we heard our parents' voices. They did not see us immediately and became alarmed and wondered aloud where we were. I peeked from beneath the overhanging bedspread and was so glad to see Mother that we crawled out and they gathered us up in their arms.

The cause of all this furor was a fight among some of the blacks in the prison. It was feared that a man or men had escaped, hence the sounding of the sirens. The ball was suddenly unimportant, as the parents rushed to their individual homes.

A few days later a time of new activity seemed to arrive and Mother began bringing many boxes into the house. Naturally, I was curious and when I asked her why she said it was time for a "brighter tomorrow."

"Never look back, my child. There is always a brighter tomorrow, you know." That was Mother's philosophy that kept her going. How many times I was to hear her say that, even though not all our tomorrows were bright.

She explained that we were going to live in a new house up on the hill within sight of our back yard. She did not tell me the reason for the move. Perhaps Dad was more affluent now and could afford a better house. I felt unhappy about this change, with a premonition that something was not quite right. Time proved my feelings to be correct; we were in the new home less than a year.

Until the age of twelve, I experienced times of presentiment, and this "knowing" was often correct. When these experiences occurred, I was not surprised or alarmed, but seemed prepared to accept whatever happened. This could not be attributed to any religious training, for there was no such training in our home and I knew nothing of church, dogma, or creed. I just felt this was the end of some good we had enjoyed.

When big things had been packed, Mother set aside some smaller items we could carry by hand to the new home. Each time we were ready to do this, Sister was taken to the house next door, then Mother and I went on to the new home with our packages. I felt important helping in this manner.

On our final trip we took our cat Tabby. I found this to be an interesting procedure, as Mother put butter on his paws before she put him into the gunny sack.

When I asked why, she explained that it would prevent him from running away after she let him out. Tabby made very un-happy sounds en route. When we arrived at the house, Mother carefully closed the door before opening the sack, and out sprang the unhappy cat. It was funny to see him try to run, only to slide on the linoleum covered floor. His buttered paws prevented good traction and he finally gave up his efforts to escape, crawling un-der the stove. He completely disdained the saucer filled with milk.

It was only a short time later that Tabby was missing. We never found him. I wanted to go back to our old home to look for him, but Mother explained there were new people now living in that house so we could no longer go there.

One clear morning Mother called me while she was on the back stoep (verandah), She lifted me up and, pointing to a distant place where smoke was coming from a tall chimney, told me that was the Mine where Daddy worked as stationary engineer. She made some explanation about the Mine which I forgot because I did not understand. We could see the train as it emerged from the Mine and went along the tracks below. Mother explained it was loaded with dirt, called ore, and was being taken to a place where it would be washed so the diamonds could be found.

I wanted to know what a diamond was. She pointed to her ring finger and explained that stone was a diamond but they didn't look like that when first found. Her explanation of the steps taken to make the stones found into beautiful diamonds was beyond my understanding at that time. It was enough to know that Daddy worked there.

I thought about this often and tried to see the Mine each time I was on the back stoep but was too short to see that distance. I determined that some day I would go there and see him. Would he be surprised? I didn't know. He was a person with whom I was never comfortable. I certainly did not like to see him angry; he could quickly become very angry!

When Daddy was home Mother always seemed to be quieter. I wished she would sit down and talk but household duties kept her too busy. It was a long time before I connected her quietness with Daddy's sternness.

A new task developed for me. Mother was digging soil to plant a garden. She asked me to help by giving her the things she needed from where she had placed them. Some were plants and others were small packets that she called "seeds." She called some of the plants "tomatoes," but I could not see any tomatoes. So she explained they would appear later after the plant took root and grew and the little yellow flowers had a chance to grow and become tiny green tomatoes, which in turn would grow into big red ones. I had eaten tomatoes and became excited to realize I could see them grow.

There were other things planted. Some of the seeds were to become vegetables while others would become flowers. It was difficult to understand how all these things could happen because seeds were planted. Mother's remark was to "wait and see."

Life was interesting here. Each morning we would make the rounds of the new garden and one morning we saw little green things barely coming through the soil. Mother patiently explained that the seeds were now beginning to be plants. As time went on, some would be peas or beans, others would be flowers; but again I had to wait and see.

Before long the flowers and vegetables were taking on their distinctive robes. I learned how each grew and how the different petals were shapes. As I was a curious child, I asked many questions, some of which Mother could only explain in a vague way.

Why did some plants grow tall, others close to the ground? Why did all colors come from the same ground. Why did roses have thorns and marigolds did not? These daily visits in the garden were a delight to me.

Eventually the tomato plants bore their fruit and then had other growing things on them—fat caterpillars. Mother said these were tomato worms. They interested me greatly as they inched their way up or down the stems and on the leaves. I noticed their green bodies seemed to have rings around them, dividing sections which were black and tummies were yellow. Some had black spots on them; I discovered that they spit black stuff when squeezed. I wanted Mother to see, so I picked some from the plants and put them carefully into my pinafore, taking them into the house.

"Oh, Mommy, see how they spit when I squeeze them!"

Expecting to hear a happy reply I was astonished to hear her exclaim, "Oh! Look at your pinafore! That black stuff does not wash out and I worked so hard making you a pretty pinafore."

Something in her voice made me feel guilty, a new feeling for me. I went sadly out into the garden and lost interest in those interesting worms. After that I did not pick up anything, as I could not bear to have Mother unhappy. But I still observed the tenants of the garden.

One morning when I went to make my usual rounds, a delightful surprise awaited me. The seeds planted by the steps had grown into plants and this array of buttercups had burst into yellow blooms. I bent over to smell and heard an odd sound. Parting the plants, I saw a strange sight. Once again Mother came quickly at my call. Pointing excitedly I asked, "What's that?"

She smiled. "Oh that is a Plotty! A special kind of frog called a plotina. See the lumps on his back. It looks lumpy because of the black and brown spots on it. Don't touch! He will jump away. We want him in the garden because he eats bugs."

After that each morning I would look for him and a ritual developed between us. "Hello, Plotty," I would say and he would answer, "Croak, croak!" The eyelids would come part way over his protruding eyes, the throat would swell, and he seemed to get fatter and fatter as he made noises. I wanted to touch his white throat and tummy. Was he really wet or did he just look that way?

I never knew because I did not touch. I noticed how his feet seemed to spread far out. Were his toenails sharp? Mother called them claws. Would his back be scratchy? It looked so. Would he bite if I picked him up? These many questions remained unanswered, as I never had the courage to pick up Plotty, remembering Mother's admonition that we must keep him in the garden.

"Oh, I could not bear it if you went away. I love you so," I said. I'm sure he answered, "I love you, too," because he gave an extra loud croak, puffed up larger, then suddenly gave what seemed a big sigh. He got thinner and thinner and finally looked flat!

This was a strange "love story" for a little girl not yet five. For some unknown reason, this communion with a frog has been one of the bright memories of my childhood,

My sister, now not quite three, had become more interesting to me. She could talk and walk and we played well together. No other children played in our neighborhood, so we spent much time together. A patch of grass was a good play area, so Mother often had us outdoors. As there was a four-foot fence around three sides of the garden, with the house in front, she felt we were safe. Jessie enjoyed being in the garden, but I don't think it was in the same way I did.

Chapter 5

Father: Sidney Arthur Walker

My paternal grandfather, Alexander Walker,[1] a baker by trade, married Catharine Ann MacKay. They lived in Edinburgh, Scotland for some years. Nine children were born to them there. With this large family, he felt opportunities would be better for them all in South Africa. They arrived in Port Elizabeth about the time of the gold rush,[2] but Grandfather had no inclination for gold, "bread" being of more importance.

Locating in Uitenhage, a short distance from Port Elizabeth, he started a bakery business. He was a trusting person and let several customers charge their purchases. One of these was a sailing captain who bought large quantities of breads when in port, but did not pay as promised. Some time passed and Grandfather heard that the vessel was in port once more, so he went down to collect what was owed him. As he walked on the dock near the ship, someone hit him on the head. He woke up to find himself in strange surroundings and learned he had been shanghaied onto the very ship whose captain owed him for the bread! As it was impossible to notify his family what had happened, he made the

---

[1] Alexander Walker was born 18th February 1838 at Fort Augustus, Scotland; he died 26th August 1903 in Port Elizabeth.

[2] As will be clear in her story, Edna May had little contact with her father, and so had little opportunity to learn the Walker family history. This much of the paragraph is her consequently inaccurate understanding of the Walker family history. A more accurate version will be found in Appendix D: Genealogy.

best of the unhappy situation. There was no recourse but to work, as this was why he had been shanghaied.

In the meantime his family wondered why he never returned, as he had always been a steady, sincere worker and family man. They kept the bakery operating, however, as it was their livelihood. Many months passed when suddenly one day there was their father and husband, safe and sound. What a story he had to relate![3]

Eight more children were born to the Walker family, and Sidney, born 10th July 1886, the last, was destined to become my father. His brother Ivan, born 7th November 1883 was two years older; the two of them had a sad beginning, as both mother and father died while they were small. Their eldest sister Alice Walker Acker had a son Percy the same age, seven years, as Sidney, and apparently these two became great friends. The two of them, along with Ivan, sold newspapers in the streets of Uitenhage and had to give every penny to Alice. She, suspicious-minded enough even to go through their pockets while they slept, demanded all they earned. Ivan finally had enough, and at age thirteen years became an apprentice in a printing shop.

Sidney and Percy also were unhappy because Alice was so wrathful if she found that the boys had not given her all their earnings. They felt justifiably that any tips given to them were theirs to spend. Finally her harsh attitude caused the two boys to leave as well. They walked the few miles to Port Elizabeth and found a kindly woman who took them in and whom they called "mother." Once again they earned money selling newspaper but this time had no money problems.

While in his early teens, Sidney got a job working on the wharf. An uncle, George Gordon MacKay,[4] was a wharf master there but he did not keep Sidney long as an employee because,

---

[3] This information was in a newspaper clipping sent to the author by one of her mother's sisters who often sent such clippings she thought would be of interest.

[4] George Gordon McKay, brother to Catherine Ann Robinson MacKay Walker,was the second child of James MacKay and Christian Robertson MacKay. He was born in Buenos Aires in September 1827.

fearing the boy might fall into the bay, he decided he was too young for that responsible job.

With his formal education at the Marist Brothers School completed, Sidney became a carpenter. His education was equivalent to two years of college and he apparently was a bright student because he was given a prize for scholastic record when in the third standard.[5]

While working at his trade in Port Elizabeth he met another Sidney, also a carpenter. This was Sidney Victor Green[6] from East London. Perhaps it was the similarity of names and occupation that drew these two unlike persons together to form a strange friendship. Sidney Green was friendly, outgoing, jovial and one who loved to joke in a good-natured way. He smiled easily.

Sidney Walker was dour, silent to the point of being withdrawn, and saw little to laugh about. He was not known to be "good-natured."

Sidney Green, a farmer at heart, soon tired of the big city and announced he was returning to East London to the first love of his life, fruit growing. He invited Sidney Walker to go along and visit, as the latter also was tired of being a carpenter.

Together they left for East London. Once there Sidney Green knew where to find transportation to the farm and to his parents' home, because he knew his brothers, Clement and Leonard, would have a wagon load of produce at the Farmer's Market. This was Sidney Walker's first travel in an oxen-drawn covered wagon. It was also his first experience at camping all night at the rendezvous and seeing these many wagons form into a laager.

When the two men arrived at the Green homestead, the country man Sidney introduced the city man Sidney to the former's

---

[5] *Theology in Science; or The Testimony of Science to the Wisdom and Goodness of God*, by The Rev. Dr. Brewer, Trinity Hall, Cambridge. The book is inscribed "Marist Brothers School, Port Elizabeth, III Standard. 1st prize for Geography, 3rd prize for Grammar, awarded to Master Sidney Walker 22nd Dec. 1897."

[6] Sidney Victor Green was the tenth child of Robert Frederick Green and Louisa Jane Nash Green, and was born 17th September 1887 at Bufflesfontein, Cape Province. See Chapter 11.

sister Ivy. Thus it was that Sidney and Ivy were destined to become the parents of the author.

Ivy Green[7] had been engaged for three years to a man she dearly loved, John Sievert, a mounted policeman who lived some distance from the Green farm. This meant he had more than twenty-five miles to travel on horseback when he got off duty in East London and wanted to visit his fiancee. Riding home one evening, just two weeks before their wedding, the rider and horse stepped into what usually was a dry river bed. As it was dark, he had no way of knowing there had been flash floods in the mountains, as it had not rained in the city nor during his ride homeward. When Johnny did not return, his mother alerted neighbors nearby. Knowing about the flash flood, the men searched and found Johnny and his horse dead.

This was a horrible shock to his family and also to Ivy Green. With a great effort Ivy went with her brother Sidney to visit Mrs. Sievert, Johnny's mother, an Austrian who could not speak English well. She had previously met Ivy and the two liked each other very much. Now she motioned both Ivy and her brother into what had been Johnny's bedroom. Without saying anything she slowly opened a cedar chest, took out a gift-wrapped package, and presented it to Ivy. A card read, "To my Darling Wife on Our Wedding Day," a day that would never come!

Ivy opened it and found a precious piece of jewelry so unique it gave one an excellent picture of Johnny as a man of sensitivity and artistic talent. It was a breathtakingly beautiful brooch he had designed and had made in the form of an anchor. In the center was a silver shaped ivy-leaf, engraved with a Mizpah from the Old Testament, "The Lord watch between thee and me while we are absent one from another." At the three points of the anchor was a heart made of gold; on the other end of the anchor that would hold the rope was her name "Ivy," also in gold. This lovely and unexpected gift triggered Ivy's emotions so that she suffered a complete nervous breakdown that only time could heal.

---

[7] Ivy Green was the ninth child of Robert Frederick Green and Louisa Jane Nash Green, and was born 19th October 1885 at Bufflesfontein, Port Elizabeth District, Cape Province.

Years later, after I heard this story from Mother's lips, I wondered if she had married Sidney Walker on the rebound, although there was a three-year lapse between the two events. Perhaps it was more to escape her own father, for whom she had bitter feelings because he would not permit her marriage at the age of eighteen but had insisted she wait until she was twenty-one. This was something I could not understand, because he had married Grannie when she was sixteen.[8] The other sisters were married by the time they were eighteen. Why, then this seeming discrimination against his daughter Ivy?

She stayed home the longest of any of the five daughters. She was a great help in the home, doing all the domestic chores and thus Grannie was free to rest. Also, Ivy's working in the home eliminated the need to hire domestic servants.

Contrary to the beliefs of many, especially in the United States, the Xhosas who worked in homes and in the fields, or on the farms in any capacity, were paid for services. True, the sums of money were not large. All the Xhosas, however, working for farmers, were allotted an area of the farm, for building their kraal (also known as a "rondeval"), space for raising corn or whatever they wanted. They had free grazing for their livestock.

Grannie often provided lunch, especially in harvesting, times and would give food items for evening meals. She gave gifts of cloth for the Xhosa women and treats for the children. These Xhosas usually stayed with the same white family for generations. They were reliable and trustworthy, so much so that the older men were trusted to take wagon loads of produce to market and bring back the money collected.

In about 1905 when the Cullinan Mine was beginning operations, Sidney Walker, then nineteen years old, finally left the farm and went to Pretoria where his brother Ivan was employed in a printing trade. As Sidney was qualified for this type of employment, he went on to Cullinan from Pretoria and applied for and received employment as a stationary engineer in the Mine.

His sister Agnes had been living with her brother Ivan after

---

[8] The marriage date was 18th November, 1870; Louisa Jane Nash was then seventeen.

the death of her husband Jon Svendsen, but she also moved to Cullinan. She discovered the ruling in the newly-formed town of Cullinan that made it impossible to live in a house without a man. So Sidney went to live with her. She was then able to take in laundry and ironing and thus support her three young children. Her eldest daughter, also named Agnes,[9] married a William Miles, called "Willie."

Mother often spoke of "dear Willie, he was such a nice man." I never met him but she spoke so warmly of him I felt he must have been fun to be around.

Mother's sister Alice Elizabeth Green Gager[10] invited her to visit in Pretoria and once again Sidney and Ivy met. The two were married in March 1908, with his brother Ivan and his wife as witnesses. They never, however, accepted Ivy as a member of their family. In their opinion she was only "an ignorant farm girl," as they were so much better educated. Unfortunately, Dad came to look down on Mother for the same reason, although he knew her as being "all right" when he married her.

This was the cause of my standing up to him in a "verbal battle" some years later when he actually stated his feelings. It was the only time in my life that I ever expressed my personal feelings to him. He listened without comment, although I was surprised he did not slap me, as he was prone to do this when angered.

During the time of his employment at the Mine from 1905 to 1913, he was a good worker, but unrest swept the ranks and Dad became an agitator for a closed shop union.

He had kept his carpenter tools from his previous work, as he sometimes needed them in this job. One day when the weather was inclement and Mother was busy in the kitchen, I wanted some-

[9] This, now, is a third Agnes Walker.
[10] Alice Elizabeth Green was the twelfth child of Robert Frederick Green and Louisa Jane Nash Green, and was born 29th October 1891 at Smiling Valley Farm, East London District, Cape Province, the third of the Green children to be born at Smiling Valley. She later married Horace Albert Gager.

thing different to do. Sister was able to crawl, sometimes even trying to walk. Mother told me to watch her, so I followed Jessie until I tired of this and began looking for something different. I spied the toolbox on the floor in the bedroom. As it was open, I inspected its contents and, finding a small hammer, I gave it to Jessie to play with. She had crawled into the bedroom and now she had fun pounding the floor. For some reason, Mother never once came to investigate the noise.

In the meantime, I managed to get the plane out and pushed it on the wooden floor. I was delighted to see it make curls. As I turned it over to see what did this, Jessie touched the blade and screamed as blood spurted from her finger. Mother came running and quickly began bandaging the cut finger, all the time talking and saying, "Naughty girl!" which I did not realize at first was meant for me. Then who should walk into the house at this moment but Dad! He needed his tools at the Mine, which was within bicycling distance. He always had a temper and now he was just furious because we got into his tools.

Oh, what a scene followed! I recall the tone of angry voices, but not all the words. This was my first experience in seeing a display of anger and loud talk between my parents!

"Cook, why did you let those kids play with my tools? You have to watch them more closely!"

"If you had kept the box locked as I have repeatedly told I you, this would not have happened!" I never heard Mother raise her voice in this way before. "I did not let them play with them! Had you been more helpful this would not have happened!"

As he had to return to work, he had no further time for arguments then. This was just a prelude to a worse display of anger that evening. When he came home he examined the bedroom floor. To him, the scars seemed enormous! This was a rented home and he was responsible for it, so he verbalized his thoughts.

"Cook, I don't know what you do all day, to be so careless and let the kids do this much damage."

Mother maintained a silence. How often I was to hear her say, "It takes two to quarrel."

Although Mother's name was Ivy, Dad never called her anything but "Cook." This made her feel she was beneath his dignity and that he considered her only a legal housekeeper. It was the only sore point she ever spoke of repeatedly and about the only criticism she voiced to me. All her emotional pains were deeply repressed and she never condemned our dad to any of us.

It took time for the understanding of that phrase, "Naughty girl" to sink into my consciousness. I brooded over it for a long time. It was not the words so much as the way they were voiced that pained me. This was a second lesson in my childhood, "not to touch" being the first. Now there was anger and this caused unhappiness.

We had many visitors in this new home, with whom I never felt comfortable. They were men who laughed too loudly and used words we'd never heard before. Mother seemed quiet and unhappy when they were there and she entered the living room only to serve tea and cakes. As far as I know, she never did more than bid them a polite good evening.

Dad was not his usual silent self but became very talkative and laughed often and loudly with the men. This was not the father and husband with which we were familiar. After his guests departed, there often were heated words between my parents. Dad seemed on the defensive and I heard the words "strike" and "demands for a Union," but I had no concept of what this meant.

One time he invited these men, with their wives, for an evening dinner. This meant a lot of extra work for Mother without any help from him. Kitchen work, in his opinion, was woman's work. She had a little helper in me, as I was able to put the silverware in the right order around the table and do a few other helpful things, but it could not have been as much help as she needed. I felt very important that evening.

When the meal was about ready, Mother surveyed the table and noticed the serviettes (napkins) were missing. I knew which drawer these were in, so she told me to get them. Dad apparently overheard her request. To enter the darkened bedroom I had to pass through the living room, where these guests were seated, but I did not look at them. As I bent over to open the bottom dresser drawer, a loud voice said suddenly, "The bogie man has got you!" and hands grabbed me. It was Dad! It was unbelievable that he would play such a joke, as he was not given to doing such things. I went into hysterics and Mother came running to see what had happened. Loud and angry words flowed and flowed while I screamed and screamed. Complete bedlam was the result! Mother had a long period of getting me quieted down. The guests quietly left and the meal was never eaten by anyone. From that day to this, I cannot bear to go into a darkened room.

Home conditions never seemed the same after that. Dad went through with his strike agitation and became, finally, very involved as the working men went on strike. This was probably necessary for the benefit of future workers but had dramatic results for Sidney Walker. He became one of the banned, meaning he would never again find employment in the Transvaal, perhaps not anywhere in South Africa.

I'm positive Dad never once thought of such results from his agitating for a union shop, that it would have such drastic results for himself. In time this became the cause of much family up-heaval.

Perhaps he got some ideas of strikes from his brother Ivan who had been active in strike activity while just a boy and was connected with Labour and the working man's problems. Uncle Ivan never visited in our home. Perhaps this was because he thought Mother an unsuitable wife for his brother Sidney, or perhaps his responsibilities took all of his time and, of course, transportation was difficult. Travel between Pretoria and the Cullinan was by oxen-drawn cart or horse and buggy.

Both brothers achieved entirely different stations in life. Ivan was politically minded, Sidney was not. Ivan had earned his own living and worked himself up the scale in social ways necessitated by his political connections. His name became a byword, as he later became Secretary of Labour, a high position in the Executive Branch of the South African government. He was a devoted family man and had the means to support his family with ease.

Dad never achieved the publicity nor the renown his brother did. He did achieve membership in the United States Typographical Union and was considered "one of the best experts in repairing monotype machines." He was in demand in any printing shop in any city where such a machine broke down.

I know little about the Walker family, as Dad was not communicative, except when relating the meanness of his red-headed sister Alice.[11] He never cared about a woman who had this name nor if she had red hair. He spoke of a brother, James William Walker, who was stationed in German Southwest Africa during World War I. While on guard duty one night, James was dragged by a lion away from his post. All that was ever found was some shreds of the uniform and lion spoors around. Dad was almost emotional the few times he mentioned this. He was silent about the others, even his sister Agnes whom he cared about and with whom he shared part of his earnings all the days of her life. This, of course, meant less for his own family.

When I consider, however, that he was the youngest of all these twelve children, some of whom never reached adulthood, he really would not know much about them. The older ones were married and away from home; his parents had died when he was young, so he never learned about his siblings from them. He was basically secretive. We shared the same roof over our heads only five years of my total life, so there was not much time for conversations. The few times I did ask questions, his reply was "Mum's the word," his way of saying he did not know or that it was unimportant.

Uncle Ivan became a person of influence[12] and my Mother's sister Alice later sent me many newspaper clippings, as she lived in the same city and thought I should have them.

Pretoria is the seat of the Executive Branch, one of the three seats of South African Government. Cape Town is the seat of the Parliament, while Bloemfontein in the Orange Free State is the seat of the Supreme Court. Uncle Ivan was in the Executive Branch.

---

[11] Alice Walker Acker was the third child and first daughter of Alexander Walker and Catherine Ann Robinson Walker. She was born 8th July, 1865 at Port Elizabeth.

[12] In addition to his leadership role in the formation of The South African Typographical Union, he became Controller of Manpower during World War Two and Secretary for Labour during the Post World War Two government of Jan Smuts.

The first time I saw a photo of him, when he was middle aged, I thought it was Dad because they looked so much alike. Both had white hair. (Dad became very gray at age 23.) They were tight-lipped, having mouths that seemed like straight lines, and both had square jaws. They had the same large, almost square shaped heads. I never saw Uncle Ivan but I'm sure he had the same steel blue eyes that my father had, eyes that could bore right through a person when he was displeased.

I often wondered what Ivan thought about his brother's being banned, as it put Ivan in a rather peculiar position. He cared for Sidney, but also realized his position as Secretary for Labour was a public responsibility. A banned person was supposed to be totally ignored.

Ivan Walker had a friend, Ben Weinbren, who had the same deep interest in trade unions which was a facet of Ivan's whole life. He persuaded Ivan to become co-author of a book, *2000 Casualties*,[13] on the history of trade unions, strikes, and the welfare of the working man. Ivan held a number of offices in the Union until he became Secretary for Labour, a post he served for nearly fourteen years.

Uncle Ivan lived a full, colorful life and career and his obituary mentioned how he always kept the interests of the working man in South Africa. Feelings of sadness welled within me as I read the tribute for the first time because I knew no one could say such words for Dad. He was all for self first. He wanted to emulate his brother but failed in this trait.

---

[13] Ivan L. Walker & Ben Weinbren, *2000 Casualties: A History of the Trade Unions and the Labor Movement in the Union of South Africa.* Johannesburg: The South African Trade Union Council, 1961.

Chapter 6

Journey to Smiling Valley

One morning after our breakfast, Mother said to Jessie and me, "Girls, it is a lovely morning and I want you to play in the yard. I am going to be very busy in the kitchen and when I am finished there I'll come out to be in the yard with you. In the meantime, please do not interrupt me. And be sure to stay in the yard; don't go out of it."

We obeyed; but after playing awhile, I began to think of her words, "Don't go out." We had never gone out of the yard except to go into or out of the house, but now my mind began to work overtime. I examined the gate, to which I had never paid attention previously. The latch opened and the gate swung open! I took Jessie by her hand and we walked. It was not my intention at first to go anywhere, just have the adventure of being free to explore. I heard the sound of the bell ringing on an engine as it crossed from the Mine to wherever it was going. Suddenly I decided we would go to see Daddy!

We trudged along the uneven path and Jessie began to get tired. I began to think it was a long walk, but then I soon saw the rail tracks ahead of me." Come on, Jessie; we are almost there and Daddy will be surprised." All was well until Jessie's foot became wedged between an imbedded stone and the track. I tugged at the foot, I tugged at her waist, but I could not get the foot free. Jessie began to cry and I began to scream. I could hear the slow rumble of a train approaching and I could sense danger to both of us. Suddenly a pair of hands roughly shoved me aside. With one arm around Sister's waist, the other unbuttoning her shoe, a young man pulled her free just as the train came into view. We stepped back and watched the wheels crush that shoe! How close we were to a terrible tragedy!

This young man took us to the nearby home of his parents who were sitting on the stoep and had seen us walking alone. When they heard us crying, they sent their son to rescue us. We did not know the people and I doubt that they knew who we were. We girls were sitting contentedly on the steps of these good parents, eating cookies, when we heard the garden gate creak. There was Daddy, a very angry and irate man! He stepped over to a bush, broke off a long, slim branch, tore the leaves off, and same striding over to us. Without even a greeting to the elderly couple, he picked up Jessie from the man's lap, noticed the one shoe was gone and asked for the other. It was then he received an explanation of what had happened. Dad was furious toward me. "Get down and march!" His words were biting as he pointed toward the gate. He did not even thank the people for their kindness.

Hurrying as fast as my little legs would carry me, I reached the gate before he caught up with me. The switch stung my legs and I began to howl. Jessie howled in sympathy. I howled all the way as he switched me back and forth every step of the way. I tried to run ahead but he caught up with me. He switched harder! I cried all the way home and as we came closer to the house, Mother heard and came running.

"Sidney! Whatever has happened?" I ran to her and she started to pick me up but Dad forbade her from touching me.

What a terrible display of temper! I'm sure Mother was embarrassed because her few neighbors heard and saw what was happening. They usually had their afternoon tea while sitting on their stoeps. Mother begged Dad to stop hitting me but he was unreasonable in his anger. As we entered the house, he took me into the bedroom, stripped off my clothing, reached for the hairbrush, and applied this with much harsh anger on my little behind.

Mother had put Jessie into her crib and was trying to rescue me, saying over and over, "Sidney, stop! Stop it!" This added to his anger, until the brush landed on her as she tried to protect me. This seemed to sober him a bit but he forbade Mother to comfort me when she tried to pick me up. I had stopped crying from total exhaustion, but could not stop my sobbing. Mother was so upset that she cried, and of course Jessie added her wailing to the confusion.

Dad brought Jessie a glass of milk and a couple of biscuits. She offered me one and as I reached for it, he snatched it from her and said, "She cannot have any and I will sit right here until you eat both." To me he said, "You will have no supper or anything until morning and don't ask your mother to give you anything." He glared at her. She left the room in silence and I sobbed myself to sleep.

I often wondered what transpired between my parents that late afternoon. I know this beating was a factor in my fearing Dad more. It was a shame, as events later proved to change our lives to such an extent that Dad and I never shared the same roof until almost seven years later, and then for only ten months. We really never learned to know each other.

Unfortunately for all concerned, I chose to run away on the very day he was being fired from his job at the Mine. This upset him terribly, especially when he found he was also to be a "banned" person because of his union activity. This meant he would be unable to get employment at all in the Transvaal and perhaps not even in any other place in South Africa.

Dad was a stockily-built man, only five feet four or five, with a short, thick neck that was often red. I am sure this was because of a too-tight collar. My uncles at Spring Valley Farm called him "roi-neck," a slang expression meaning a "red-necked Englishman." This made Dad unhappy, although he seldom heard the expression as he spent only a brief time on the farm.

His eyes were steel blue and appeared like gimlets boring into one when he was angry. His mouth was a straight line above a squared chin that showed determination, with a sort of defensive attitude as though he was daring anyone to refute, rebuke, or argue. He looked older than his years. Although he had a full head of hair until his death at age 76, he became very gray at an early age. He was proud of his appearance, always wearing tailor-made suits because of his stocky figure. This made him look "natty," as the British say.

It was, of course, Mother's hard work over the washboard that kept him looking natty: her hours of careful ironing of shirts and collars that were detached from the shirts. Woe to her if there was a crease in a collar. I've seen him toss one aside before accepting it as usable just because it had a tiny wrinkle in it. Yet he wore each collar only once. I'm sure he had no concept, nor consideration, of the hours it took to keep his supply of stiffly starched collars in perfect condition!

This whole episode was the beginning of a total change in our lives. Once again boxes were brought into our home but only the suitcases were packed with our personal things. All the household things were being sold. The boxes were for the convenience of the purchasers. It was very distressing to me to see strangers taking our furniture and other things. I asked, "Mommy, why are people taking our things?"

Mother lifted Jessie to her lap and held my hands as she said very quietly, "We are leaving this house. You girls and I are going on a long journey on the train to stay with your Grannie and Grandpa Green. We will see my three brothers and live on a farm. Daddy is going far away on a boat. We cannot take the household things with us." She squeezed my hands tightly as though afraid to let go. Softly she said, "I'll see Smiling Valley Farm again." Then she added sadly, "It's time for a 'brighter tomorrow.'" She seemed to brighten a bit and she gave a wee smile. "There is always a brighter tomorrow, you know."

Yes, a brighter tomorrow. I did not comprehend the need to leave this house, but I was glad because I felt too many unhappy things had happened here. Then I thought of the train ride.

We left Cullinan in late March of 1914, taking the train to Pretoria and then transferring to another going to East London. The train was a new experience for Jessie and me. I enjoyed the idea of going somewhere. It was especially nice to have Mother with us constantly and giving us undivided attention. We had a compartment, so could be very private. I thought Mother seemed happier, but how is a child to fathom the deep thoughts of a mother? I noticed she was in deep thought and sometimes I had to speak twice before she would answer. Years later she told me that returning to her parents home posed several questions. How would they feel having a daughter returning for a long period, when it was customary for a husband to provide for her? How so, especially, when there were two children and a third one expected in five months. A daughter was supposed to have married well, to have her own home. It would not be possible for her to expect any financial help, as the husband had taken the greater amount to pay for his travels and to provide for himself until he could find employment.

These and many other considerations went through her mind as she was journeying back to her parents' home. How could she support herself and family, should Sidney not keep his promise to send for his family later? How would she be received? English women simply did not return home once they were married. This inner apprehension must have been very wearing for her. Most assuredly she enjoyed the leisure of being waited upon, for the porter brought our meals and took away the dishes! I was not expecting our meals to be served and was delighted when the porter appeared the first time with food. I instantly wondered aloud about a table. Smiling, he touched the wall and pulled out a small table. I was enchanted. Jessie was only a little past three so was not as impressed as I. It was a respite for Mother from the almost constant toil of being a housewife, although only a brief respite from what was to be.

It was also wonderful to have Mother sit all through a meal instead of getting up to fetch some item from the kitchen, as she usually did. This was a fun time for us children and is one of my happier memories of that period.

On the third day of our journey, Mother began putting our things into the suitcase and dressed us with fresh clothing, saying, "We will soon leave the train and you will meet your uncles. I want you to be well behaved." She seemed excited. I was to learn there was a strong bond among her brothers and sisters. She had seven living brothers and four sisters, all married except the three brothers we were to meet.

The train began to slow down and the porter took our baggage to the end of the coach. We were standing in the aisle when Mother suddenly exclaimed, "Oh, there they are!" I did not know to whom she was referring, as many people stood on the platform, some to get aboard and others to greet arriving loved ones. The train finally stopped and the porter helped us down. Then a man with a mustache hugged and kissed Mother and two others greeted her.

"These are your uncles, girls," she said, finally turning to Jessie and me. "Sid, here are your nieces, Edna and Jessie. And this is your Uncle Clement and that's your Uncle Leonard, girls." Uncle Sid bent down to look each of us in the eye. He had smiling blue eyes, making me think of Uncle Billy Baker. He gave each of us a little hug. Uncle Clem did not seem to pay attention to us. He maintained his posture of six foot three, which meant I had to look up and up. He had flaming red hair and a small mustache. Uncle Len was about eighteen and was shy and a bit awkward, but he smiled and greeted us with handshakes. He had light brown hair and blue eyes. His brothers called him "Kid."

My first impression of Uncle Clem was that he did not feel so happy toward Mother as had the other two brothers. I had no time really to think about this, as Uncle Sid lifted me up. Mother was carrying Jessie, and the other two uncles had our baggage. I had mixed feelings about being lifted from the ground. I had never been carried so far as I could recall. I squirmed a bit and Uncle Sid's strong arms tightened as he said, "I know you are a big girl and can walk but there is much going on around here so this is the safest way to get you to the wagon." Finally he put me down. "Here we are."

As I had no conception of what this vehicle would be, I tried to notice it and all that was connected with it. It had a white covering and there were strange red animals in front of it; they had long things (horns) on their heads. I had just seen my first oxen.

At that moment a smiling black man approached Mother. He spoke to her but all I remember was his gleaming white teeth. Mother seemed to know him and I was astonished to hear her speak in a strange tongue. I did not realize she had known him for years. He was one of the oldest employees on Grandfather Green's farm and had known Mother since she was a child. They exchanged several remarks and he waved to two young blacks standing behind him, indicating these were his children. Pointing to me, he made some remark and Mother nodded. It was a time of mutual sharing between them.

This was my first time hearing this strange language, the Bantu. Little did I realize then that I too in time would learn to speak this.

By this time, the two younger uncles had climbed into the wagon, having already placed our baggage in it. Mother put Jessie on the wagon bed, while Uncle Sid lifted me up. He then helped Mother get in and hurriedly climbed aboard himself. We sat on some folded blankets, evidently provided for our comfort. I noticed the two others had sat upon a seat and Uncle Clem held the riems (reins) in one hand and a whip in the other. Much conversation flowed between Mother and Uncle Sid, while I, with my eyes, was surveying all the contents of the covered wagon.

Suddenly, with a loud clap Uncle Clem called out the names of the lead oxen. The noise startled me and I involuntarily grabbed hold of Uncle Sid. He laughed and explained that Uncle Clem had used the whip to alert the oxen to move. The latter called the names of each pair of oxen, beginning with the leaders.

"Why does the black man walk?" I could see him up front.

"He is our voorlopper, which means he leads the oxen. His boys walk beside the team, one on each side. This gives the oxen a sense of being cared for. They will not move until the voorlopper takes the riems from the leading ox's horns. He knows where to go and the oxen do not, so he leads them." I thought about this for a time, then said, "What do they wear on their heads?" Uncle Sid threw his head back and laughed. "You mean their horns?" He continued to chuckle. "The oxen don't 'wear them.' Those horns grow on their heads. You will see some with no horns, others with small ones, and then many like these with the large curved horns. This shows the animals are grown up. Everything is small to begin with. You are small but some day you girls will be grown like your mother."

"Oh!" I sat down to digest this information, while the adults continued to talk to each other, catching up on all the news. There was much to see as the wagon went through the city streets. I had never seen so many people, nor heard so many sounds. The "clop, clop" of animal hooves on the cobble stones, the funny two-wheeled carts sometimes pulled by an ox and some other animals with long ears; a donkey, as I learned later. Then the buggies would go by and the horse hooves beat with a faster rhythm. I liked the sound of these rhythms. Many of the city noises were meaningless to me, but I had no time to ask questions, for I hardly knew how to put the words together for these unknowns. I noticed people walking beside the road or streets. They laughed a lot but I did not know why. Many women carried sunshades or parasols; others wore strange head wear that shadowed their faces. I asked Mother about the latter.

"Those are sunbonnets called 'Kapjies' or 'Kappies.'" she said. I noticed they covered the whole head and were tied beneath the chin. The visor-shaped front was three or four inches wide. This protected their faces from the sun. I also noticed they were of different colors. Years later when I saw these "Kapjies" up close in a museum, I admired the intricate designs created by tiny stitches in the all white ones used for special church services such as weddings and "nagmaal" or communion services. Some had neat tucks and tiny laces inserted while others, for everyday use, were less intricate and elaborate and were often of colored fabrics. All were exquisitely sown. Those Boer women were experts in the art of creating their wearing apparel, all done by hand.

We soon came to a clearing but were still in the city. Sid pointed to it and Mother made some remark that I did not hear. Turning to me, she said, "That space is called the public market. We were there this morning." He pointed to the many empty boxes stacked behind us that I had been wondering about. "This morning those boxes had apples, oranges, tomatoes, and other foods in them." As he addressed his remarks directly to me, I felt I could ask him a question. Pointing to the sides and overhead, I said, What's that?"

He looked up. "This is a covered wagon and that is called a sail (canvas). It protects us from the sun and protects our load if it rains." He pointed to the arches that were evenly spaced the width of the wagon. "These are called the ribs. They hold the sail in place and we tie them to the wagon so they cannot blow away if it very windy." Squeezing me, he added, "You have ribs, too, you know, that hold your body together." I had never given a thought to my body and did not know what to make of his last remark. Then he changed the subject.

"Say, I'll bet your girls are getting hungry. Aren't little girls always hungry?" Uncle Sid chuckled "We are going to eat as soon as we cross the river." He pointed to his right into a vague distance. "Where's Jessie? Asleep?" He looked around. He spoke to Mother. "Ivy, it is another drought time and the river is dry as a bone. I hope it rains soon. Farmers here are always hoping for rain." Turning to me he said, "Yes, we will soon have food, little one. We have only a mile to go after we cross this river. We will outspan and spend the night there."

I was puzzled as I looked at the road we had crossed. I did not know what a river would be. There seemed to be only a trickle of water among all the stones we had driven over. Was a river important? "This is the Nahoon River," added Uncle Sid, "and sometimes it is really rushing." I could not comprehend all his words. Little did I know that three years hence I would be much aware of the Nahoon River and its rushing. I would then have one of the most outstanding experiences of my child life.[1]

Mother had been trying to get me to take a nap since Jessie was asleep but I did not want to miss anything. I was getting tired all right but was really too excited to give in. Soon the wagon began to make a turn off the road into a large space where many other wagons were already positioned. "This is the outspan," said Uncle Sid, "and soon we will eat." He leaped down from the wagon.

Uncle Clem was shouting, "Whoa" and flecking his whip. I noticed the animals were nearly alongside the wagon in front of us. The Xhosa boys were working with them and soon the oxen were separated from the wagon. One boy took them away, while the other one, with his dad and Uncle Len maneuvered the desselboom (tongue) of this wagon, beneath the one in front. Uncle Sid helped Mother to the ground and placed Jessie and me beside her. "Now I'll go see that the evening meal is begun," and away he went.

We three moved away from the wagon, Jessie holding tightly to Mother's hand. She never seemed secure in strange surroundings. I stood watching all the happenings. Other wagons were arriving, some going to the far side of the circle while others lined

---

[1] See Chapter 23.

up behind us. I looked up at Mother. "Why do some go over there and others stay here behind us?" I was pointing.

"Those wagons on the other side are loaded and will be leaving early to go to the market. Notice there is a road over there," pointing far ahead as she stepped to the right of our wagon. "That way it's easier for them to get onto the main road to cross the river to town. On this side the farmers have already been to market, as your uncles have done, and are now going home. The front wagon on this side will also go out that road but will make a turn and go the opposite direction." She turned me around so I could see that part of the road. "But, Mommy, why do they get so close to each other?" "This is what we call going into 'laager.' It was necessary long ago when people trekked long distances. They put many thorn trees in the open spaces and around the whole circle. This kept the fighting Xhosas from coming too close because those thorn trees have large thorns on them. That's where they get their name. I'll show you some when we get to the farm."

I looked around and saw many fires burning. Each wagon owner had his own cooking equipment. Uncle Sid was helping the lead man of our team prepare the evening meal on a grate placed over a small square made with bricks in which a small fire was burning brightly. Mother told me the little fireplaces were used over and over, as this place was frequently used when people were traveling. Finally Uncle Sid came over and spoke to Mother. "What can the children eat, Ivy?"

"Whatever is on the menu, Sid." They both laughed because they knew there was no choice.

Uncle arranged some logs and soon we were all sitting and eating. How strange to be eating from a tin plate while sitting on a log. It was almost more than I could handle but I managed. Mother had to feed Sister because she could not hold the plate with one hand and eat with the other. I have no recollection of what that meal consisted. I just know the food satisfied me and I was no longer hungry. I was intrigued by all the newness of this experience; seeing so many strangers, some of whom greeted Mother with much delight and enthusiasm, others with hugs and kisses. They would sit on their haunches and smilingly take my hand and talk to me and Jessie. These were uncles, cousins, and friends of Mother's.

I watched Mother particularly as she had not been much given to laughter, and this evening she laughed often. Len and Sid kept up a running conversation. Clem was more silent. I was to learn that he did not show his feelings very much and sometimes I wondered if he disapproved of Mother. I was to learn more about this later. Clem was never a favorite uncle.

Other wagons were still arriving and now the circle was almost complete. I was overwhelmed to see so many cattle, most of them red, some all black, while others were black and white, all very docile. They were all highly valued for their service in pulling the wagons and were kindly treated. I was interested in the activities of the blacks. Although these were Xhosas, they were not the fighting Xhosas spoken of earlier. Some stayed in the inner circle, tending the fires, cooking and doing dishes while others came and went. I wondered why the blacks kept coming and going so much, so I asked Uncle Sid.

He chuckled. "Well, they have to eat. They are the boys who walk beside the oxen. While one watches the animals, one comes to eat. Each wagon has three blacks, the voorlopper and two who care for the cattle; watering, feeding and herding them." He pointed ahead of the wagons. "A kraal where the animals are fed and watered is over there. The men watch over them all night. The oxen feel safe because the Xhosas they are used to, are close by. The oxen all get along well because their helpers are there."

I had to think about this. It was a new thought to me that animals had feelings and had to feel safe. I wondered what it was like not to be safe. I could not imagine that at all. My little mind was awhirl with thoughts that I did not know how to express. At last meal time was over and the head Xhosa was finishing washing the dishes. Some of the men began to smoke pipes, cigarettes, and an occasional cigar. I was astonished to see smoke rising from their mouths. "Mother! Look! What are they doing?" I was pointing to a man sitting in semi-darkness so his cigar was glowing. I had never seen anyone smoking, as my father was a non-smoker. At that time not even my uncles smoked. Mother laughed and explained that many men smoked. It was something I would get used to, even though I might not like the smell. At last my curiosity was satisfied.

Suddenly I heard music. This was different from the piano that Uncle Billy Baker played. Uncle Sid, who had been standing nearby talking to a man, turned to me and said, "Guess I'll get my come-to-me, go-from-me. Time for some music." I had no idea what he was talking about. Mother laughed. Seeing my puzzled look, she explained he meant his concertina. When I asked what the man in the wagons ahead of us was playing, she said it was an accordion. Soon it seemed that every man was playing something. Uncle Clem was playing his mouth harp, Uncle Len had a Jew's harp, some were playing violins. It all had a rollicking good sound.

Later when I wanted to try playing Uncle Len's Jew's harp, he warned me not to touch it. Uncle Clem had four different harmonicas and he at least permitted me to hold them. It seemed a musical evening was all part of a rendezvous. It was certainly an event for Jessie and me to witness for the first time. The most surprising thing to me, however, was seeing Mother get up and dance with one of the men. This gave me something new to think about. I'm sure it was not too comfortable to dance in the dirt, but before the evening was over she had danced with a number of the men.

Jessie and I huddled together and made comments. We had never seen anything like it and did not know what to make of it. Finally, the musicians put away their instruments and silence descended in the camp. I looked around for Mother and saw that she and Uncle Sid were looking up and pointing different places. I took Sister's hand and we walked over where I could tug at her skirt. "What are you looking at, Mommy?" Uncle Sid picked me up and Mother held Jessie. "Stars," said Uncle, as he pointed upward. "Do you see that very bright evening star?" I was silent because I did not know which one he meant. I learned later that these two were very knowledgeable about stars; they had need of this knowledge for the many times they were on transport to the Transkei. Dark nights made night travel impossible unless one had some star lore.

Mother gave a long sigh. "Oh, it's so beautiful. But, Sid, I think it is time I get these two to bed and I'm a bit tired myself. Morning comes quickly."

We all moved to the back of the wagon and Uncle Sid helped lift us children into the wagon bed, then helped Mother in. She helped us to lie down on the blankets provided, then covered us and tucked us in. We were asleep almost immediately.

The next thing I knew was feeling the wagon moving. We were already on the road leading to the farm and it was not quite dawn. Mother was already sitting up. She placed her finger on her lips so I would not awaken my sleeping sister. I was happy when she passed me a piece of fruit and a little later a buttered scone. I ate in silence, watching the sun begin to peek over the horizon. I had never seen a sunrise before and I caught my breath at its beauty. Jessie awakened at last and then I could talk. I wanted to know where we were going. Mother gave Jessie a piece of fruit, saying, "We will soon be at the farm where you will meet Grannie and Grandpa Green. See, the voorlopper is turning the oxen now to that road which will take us past the schoolhouse. Oh!" She pointed toward a square, red roofed building to our right. "There's the school where you girls will go when you are seven." It would be another year and a half before I could go. I eyed this building with interest and wondered what a school was and what would happen when I did go.

The wagon went about a mile straight ahead, turned, and went down hill, past a ravine, then up the hill for another half mile. Smiling Valley Farm at last! Soon we saw some little black children appear to open wide the big gate. Mother was straining to see if her parents were outdoors. They were, standing quietly, waiting for the wagon to stop. Again Uncle Sid assisted Mother to the ground, lifted Jessie down, then me. As the wagon moved away, Uncle said, "The boys are taking it down to the garden so it will be in place for our next loading."

Mother kissed and hugged her parents, then turned to us girls. "Jessie, Edna, this is your Grannie and Grandpa." I was surprised when Grandpa picked me up to hug and kiss me. I felt shy and awkward. I was not used to this type of response from my elders. Feeling the need of his smiling assurance, I looked around for Uncle Sid but he had disappeared. Grannie then greeted me as

Grandpa did while I was still in his arms. Finally we went in, entering the space between the kitchen and the dining room.

This was a broad area where large flat stones had been laid and cemented in between to make an even floor. This paved area extended outward about eight feet beyond the out walls of the rooms, all under one roof. It could be called a patio. It was referred to, however, as a stoep, sometimes as a verandah. When the weather was hot, evenings were often spent sitting out here, I learned.

A Xhosa woman had picked up our suitcases and carried them through the dining room into the living room. As I sat on Grandpa's lap, I could see her pass the window that was behind Grannie, the table in front of the window. Many books and papers were on this. Two rocking chairs, one on either side of the table, were always occupied in the afternoons by both grandparents. Grannie loved to read aloud to Grandpa. I was to learn later that he could neither read nor write.

The maid returned and went into the kitchen. Soon she came out to set teacups and other things on the table. At this time I was happy to see Uncle Sid return. He had freshened up. Grandpa set me down as Uncle brought in three or four chairs from the dining room. "I cannot drink my tea and hold you, child," said Grandpa. It was the only time he ever held me on his lap. Always, in the future, he would push me away, saying, "You are a big girl now."

Uncles Len and Clem arrived and we all had tea and cakes. Much conversation flowed among the adults, none of which I really understood. Jessie was nodding and Mother finally suggested that she should put her to bed for her nap. Excusing herself and taking us girls each by one hand, we left the family circle. It was then we passed through the dining room, turned right into the living room, which I eyed with great interest. Another turn to our left, down a long hall and Mother led us into a very large bedroom with two beds. "Well, girls, this is to be our home for a long time. Across the hall is the bedroom of Grannie and Grandpa. You are never to go into their room. I want that understood! We will respect their privacy. Unless Grannie asks you to go in when she does, you are never to enter there. Do you understand?" We both nodded.

She lay Jessie down on one bed and suggested I lie down also. I really was tired and did as she suggested. I do believe I was asleep before she covered me.

Thus began a totally new life for Mother and us girls. I was to learn much in the next five years. Mother was to experience much sorrow in that time, but we were unaware of these things that day. Her "brighter tomorrow" was not always so bright. These were to be my learning years, as they were Jessie's, and much would be embedded in my consciousness, never to be forgotten. Grannie and Uncle Sid were to be my main teachers in that home. This period of time was to be the only really happy time of my entire life and those years spent on the Smiling Valley Farm, situated between the Bulugha and Kwelegha Rivers left an indelible imprint on me.

It was to be a very tiring and trying episode in Mother's life and would result in some bitter feelings within the family circle but, at the moment, all was peaceful, loving, and happy. The greatest gift that life ever gave me was the opportunity to know and learn from the petite and elegant lady I called Grannie Green. I also got to know Grandpa Green, a man of great inner strength, integrity, honesty, who met life's struggles with much fortitude.

Chapter 7

Memories of Grannie Louisa Jane

Later in the afternoon of our arrival, Grannie invited Jessie and me to walk with her, as she wanted to see how her garden was doing. The walk was just around the house because her three gardens were planted on each side and in the rear. It took a longer time to make the rounds, because she was instructing as well as showing.

Her garden of herbs was on the west side, to our left as we left the stoep. Grannie explained each herb, giving its name as she pinched a leaf, then crushed it between her fingers so we could get the full benefit of its aroma. Just behind this bed of herbs was a plot of colorful, sweet-smelling, low-growing flowers. The riot of colors was breathtaking, and I learned about mignonettes with their delightful, delicate fragrance and small greenish-white and tiny yellow blossoms, the variegated verbenas, vivid blue bachelor buttons, of all colors and a variety of other flowers that grew a little taller. In the background were still taller plants, the hollyhocks and hibiscus, all fronted by vivid yellow marigolds of low and medium heights. Grannie had laid out this lovely garden herself and designed it as an artist would, arranging the flowers according to color and height. It was like a charming picture.

We followed the path that led to the rear of the house and saw other flowers of white and yellow, two lone rows flanking a hard dirt path that once had been intended for carriages entering through the wide gate in the distance. That distant gate was now padlocked because visitors approached the house from the other side. Rows of sweet-smelling honeysuckle had spread out in a riot of shrubbery and blossoms, but we did not get close to them because the bees were very busy. Grannie explained they were gathering honey. We could hear their steady hum and see them darting in and out. Grannie pointed to the grassy place to her left, saying it had been a paddock for visitors to keep their horses in bygone days. She promised to show it to us as soon as the honeysuckle flowers and bees were gone. She said she did not want us to get stung.

As we walked on she explained about the many wild flowers and how the plants of some were medicinal. She knew how to utilize their ability to aid in some ailments. Doctors were too far away and most of the early pioneers knew how to use herbal remedies. For instance, we girls were to get our early spring tonic of sulfur and molasses, along with all the adults. Not one of the family was exempt from this routine. Her rose garden, her pride and joy, was on the east side of the house. Grannie experimented in grafting these, as did her husband with his fruit trees. All the family shared her pride when a rose grafting proved successful and a different type of rose bloomed. No one else was permitted to prune and care for these.

Just beyond this was her latest experiment: dahlias in quite a large area. She raised flowers to be sold on the market. When her sons took produce to the city, along with her donations of butter and eggs were large bunches of bright flowers. All these added to the family income.

Walking among these flowers around the house became a daily ritual for us girls, but it was a routine habit for Grannie. Sometimes the dew would still be on the plants when the morning round was done after she finished breakfast, then repeated at sunset.

Sometimes Jessie did not want to go along (she was only three)[1], but I enjoyed every minute because I enjoyed Grannie. I think the enjoyment was partly because she paid attention to me. Mother was always too busy and, while I did not know it at the time, she was expecting her third child.

As we walked, I told Grannie about our garden in Cullinan. I felt important as she gave me undivided attention. She probably

---

[1] This, then, is 1914, as we learned in Chapter 6.

was amused at my giving her information I am sure she already knew, but perhaps she too enjoyed this companionship. She must have had some lonely moments before we came, especially because her younger sons were busy in the gardens with Grandpa. Most of her children lived too far away to visit, and those closer were involved in their own farms. Visiting was a rare treat because of transportation difficulties.

Gradually, I came to realize it was because of Grannie that Mother knew so much about flowers. Her working for years, as a growing girl and young woman on the farm, resulted in her knowledge of the vegetable and plant kingdom.

Living with the grandparents became a learning experience in several areas. There was something different to see and learn almost every day, especially in the days right after our arrival. Grannie often told me to watch and to look, the same advice she must have given my mother, who so often told me the same thing. This was excellent training that helped me all my life. Grannie patiently answered my questions when we were outdoors. She showed me how to feed the chickens and gather the eggs, how to put the mealies (corn) into the grinder and then grind it, how to adjust the grinder so the corn used for our corn meal mush each morning would be fine enough. She showed me how to gather chips and how to stack them in a box near the stove. These were bark that fell from the gum and wattle trees in the yard, and were used to start the morning fire to cook by. I had to gather the kindling that was chopped by one of the uncles, if he felt so inclined, but usually chopped by a native who kept the larger pieces stacked on the stoep near the kitchen.

Set up on a permanent structure near the grinder was a large bell that I was forbidden to touch unless especially told to do so. Grannie explained that it was for emergency only. When it was rung the men in the garden or fields would hurry to the house. It would be wrong for me to ring it otherwise, because that would take the men from their labors.

I heeded this advice, although I eyed that bell almost every evening when grinding seeds and corn, and at times was tempted, especially when I knew the uncles and Grandpa were home. If it had rung then, nobody would be brought home needlessly, so I believed, never giving thought to the neighbors a mile or so away. They, too, would hurry to this farm, as I was to find out before another year went by. It was then I would learn that ringing the bell was not a joyous occasion.

Grannie was petite and slim. She had borne fourteen children and worked hard for years. Women in those days had to work hard even though they might have servants, because there were always a few tasks the servants could not do. Her head was crowned with a wealth of dark hair among the graying curls that formed a soft halo around her face. She wore spectacles when reading, but otherwise her clear blue-gray eyes were not obstructed at all. I do not recall her in any other attire than the white, long-sleeved blouses, fashioned with tiny tucks and lace, her black alpaca skirt, and dark hose and shoes.

Sometimes, however, she would wear a blouse that she fastened at the throat with a jabot, though usually a small, lace trimmed collar was her favorite. Her jewelry consisted of a black, sometimes blue velvet bit of ribbon with a cameo pinned to it. This was used as a neck band. Upon her blouse was pinned a brooch-like ornament of gold that housed a long gold chain. At the end was her double-cased enclosed, round gold watch, beautifully engraved back and front. The watch was put in her skirt waistband to protect it; never was it left dangling loosely. At the end of the day this watch chain was drawn into the housing. She wore a plain gold band as a wedding ring. No other jewelry did I ever see her wear.

She apparently was a person of method, certain things being done at a definite time. I recall watching her as she brushed her long hair morning and night. She would bend over so the hair fell in front, and then brushed very methodically, counting until she reached fifty. When I inquired about this, she said the hair must be brushed long and well, if one wanted pretty hair. I later thought this was only part of her reasoning; another would be the scarcity of water, that it would be lacking for shampoo, especially during long drought that would last for months.

When I was invited I enjoyed being in her bedroom, a large room with a big double bed. I wondered why it was so high. She explained it was because of the two mattresses being fluffed up; the underneath one was of corn husks and the top was a feather mattress. This made a nice cozy bed in cold weather. She asked me not to be in her bedroom unless she invited me, as this was her private domain. Whenever I was invited, I noticed she picked up a small bottle from her dresser and tipped it against a finger, touching her ears and neck. This was her very special "4711 cologne" and one of her two extravagances. I understood neither term. I had detected a nice fragrance around her but somehow did not connect it with the contents of that bottle for a long time. When I finally became aware of why she had this delightful aroma around her, I imitated her way of applying it, never giving a thought that everyone would detect I had been in her room uninvited! I'm sure Grannie knew, though why she never scolded, I have no idea.

Occasionally I'd yield to the temptation of opening a low, wide jar on her dresser and removing one of the contents. This was a double strength peppermint. She must have had a throat problem, as this was her second extravagance and something she always kept in this container. When I first saw her take one, I asked if I could have one too. She said they cost too much to pass around, so it was sheer naughtiness on my part to have taken one. They were strongly flavored so I did not enjoy them and thus was not guilty too often of pilfering her peppermints.

I suppose I was trying to imitate her in every way possible.

She was so gracious and from her I learned much. I have been very thankful for the fate that brought me into her home and under her influence for those five years of my life. She was sixty-one when we went to live there,[2] but I was unconscious of age. She was so delightful I'm sure no one thought of age in connection with her. She had an interesting life, so much so, that when she was in her seventieth year, a gentleman who was writing a book about the early settlers visited her on the Bulugha farm to get her life's story. He was from Port Elizabeth, the place of her birth.

Her great grandparents[3] had been among the many who

---

[2] Born 18th February 1853, she was in 1914 61 years old, had been married 44 years, and had been at Smiling Valley 24 years. Her youngest child was 19 years old.

[3] Thomas Glass and his wife Anne Foricker Glass.

landed in Algoa Bay. These came to be referred to as the Settlers of 1820. I would liked to have known the feelings of this ancestor as she was rowed ashore from the sailing ship. Mingled feelings of relief and shock must have been hers; relief that the journey was over, and shock to see what conditions confronted them. How similar my own Grannie's feelings must have been when arriving at the wilderness from which a home, a farm, and a living had to be wrested!

Sir Rufane Donkin was then Acting Governor of the area known as The Cape. He was replacing the real Governor, Sir Charles Somerset, who had returned to England on a leave of absence due to illness of a daughter. This was a fortunate circumstance for these new settlers, as Sir Donkin had a quality of compassion and caring. He made it a point to leave Cape Town in time to greet these new arrivals at Algoa Bay. He also had been responsible for the accumulation of various foods and farm supplies that the emigrants would need in the new, to them, venture of becoming farmers. He had tents erected for their use as temporary shelters until their homes could be built.

Donkin was a visionary in that he saw the need for a good harbor and the creation of a city in this place where so many new arrivals had come. The first stone foundation for a house was laid on June 6, 1820 and ". . .so rapid was the advance of the port that within less than three decades it became—what it has ever since remained—the second most important town in the whole Colony, surpassing the other urban centres in population and commercial activity except Cape Town, founded more than a century and a half earlier."[4]

Sir Donkin had been on duty in India before being called to duty in the Cape. His dearly beloved wife, Elizabeth, dying just before he was to leave, was buried in India. He asked that her heart be removed first from her body. His intention was to have this buried in England. It was, however, buried at the site of the

---

[4] H. E. Hockly, *The Story Of British Settlers of 1820 in South Africa*, p 63.

new city, under the obelisk erected in her memory. This can still be seen in the city he named in her honor: Port Elizabeth.

It seemed an act of Providence that Sir Donkin was in a position to help these emigrants, because he had patience and compassion. Not only did he make their settlement easier by having the provisions for making a new life, but he was interested enough to check on their progress. When their first harvest of wheat turned out to be a total loss due to a disease called rust, he realized they would need food—for they could not make the necessary payments to the government on the advances they had received to emigrate. Many became greatly discouraged because they had these set-backs. Sir Donkin, realizing their plight, went to the Commissions of Cape Town to ask for special help to lessen their distress.

Loss of wheat crops occurred three years in a row, so many of these settlers were in dire straits. Some died because of starvation and many were in rags. Others gave up their allotments and moved closer to Port Elizabeth or Grahamstown. Sir Donkin was the only official who seemed to care about the circumstances the settlers found themselves in. Unfortunately for them, Sir Somerset returned to assume the responsibility of being Governor, though he had neither caring nor compassion for these discouraged emigrants. They bid a sad farewell to Sir Donkin who made an effort to see them for one last time after having been a true friend for only eighteen months.

Because of crop failures, the author's maternal great-great-great grandparents, Thomas and Ann Glass, did not remain at the farm allotted to them. They moved closer to Port Elizabeth to be near their married daughter, Elizabeth (Glass) Brown. In 1825, when she was twenty years of age, Elizabeth died in childbirth and the bereaved Mr. Brown named his new daughter Elizabeth Ann. Eventually this girl married a Mr. Nash and their first child, a girl, named Louisa Jane, became the Grannie of whom I write.

As often happened in those early days, these settlers suffered harassment by the Zulus who also were arriving this far south in the dark continent looking for grazing land for their cattle. Clashes were frequent, not because of color, but because both races fought to maintain their hold on the land. The blacks had a strong desire to own many cattle, for this represented wealth, even as it did to the white man. The blacks robbed the farmers of cattle and any goats or sheep they could find. Contrary to public opinion, the English settlers of 1820 did not usurp this land from the blacks, but actually were in this Zuurveld area first. The Zulus had been in an area called Zululand beyond the Great Fish River, east of the white settlement.

It was inevitable that many young men and husbands were killed in these forays. Consequently, a young widow would soon remarry. It was expedient that a man be the head of any household because life was difficult and dangerous. These pioneers had to work hard, always with a gun in one hand, as they labored in the fields. Woman had to defend their homes when husbands were away. It was a strain always to be alert, daily expecting attacks. They had a special brand of courage!

Great grandmother Nash was no exception to these experiences. After Louisa Jane was born, a brother came into the family, but before the third child could arrive, Mr. Nash was killed in a Zulu skirmish. She soon married a Mr. Saunders, and they had two sons. He too became a victim of a Zulu's spear. Soon after this widowhood she married a Mr. McMullin.

By this time Louisa Jane was ten years old. Apparently she did not like her second step-father, who had decided to move to Durban with his family. Many were at the dock-landing to get aboard the ship, talking and laughing as people do. This activity gave Louisa Jane the opportunity to wander away from the family group and then she ran to hide behind a sand dune farther down on the beach. It seems strange that none of the family missed her. Perhaps they thought she had boarded ahead of them. In the meantime the ship pulled away from the dock and by the time they had searched for the missing child, the ship was far out to sea.

As the evening shadows descended, Louisa Jane began to wonder what to do. She finally had courage to walk to the parsonage and told the minister all about her situation. Of course he and his wife could not turn her away, especially as it was now dark. They permitted her to stay, with the stipulation that she work for her room and board until they could hear from her mother.

A letter in those days took a long time to reach its destination, so Grannie continued to live with the minister and his family. Apparently her parents consented to this arrangement and eventually she was apprenticed to a seamstress where she learned the fine art of needlework. As Grannie later laughingly stated, "That is when I learned to make yards and yards of tucks."

Her mother's third marriage was of short duration, as her husband had a sudden heart attack. She then returned to Port Elizabeth where she met the man who was intended to be her fourth husband. He too had a heart attack and died before they were married! That man, William Robert Green, was the father of Louisa Jane's husband, Robert Frederick. Her father-in-law almost became her third stepfather.

I always felt a kinship with this great-grandmother, whom I never met, because I was pleased to know she had these multiple marriages. I had felt some embarrassment, later in life, for having this same experience. Losing husbands through death, however, seems less demeaning than losing them through the divorce courts!

Regretfully, I do not have knowledge of all the circumstances of the lives of these ancestors. They, like us, were prone to live each day without thinking life's experiences worthwhile writing down for posterity, so no recordings were made. I know this great-grandmother lived to ". . .be a very old lady of ninety-seven and always wore a little black bonnet, a white shawl around her shoulders, and black gloves that covered her hands but left the fingers naked. She invariably wore a black dress with much lace and many tucks; a very dainty, fragile looking little old woman," wrote my Aunt Lulu, an older sister of my mother's.[5] It is amazing that one who endured so many hardships could live to such an age. A photo of her, and as many of the 1820 settlers as is possible to collect, are on display at the Settler's Museum in Grahamstown.

---

[5] See Chapter 20.

Chapter 8

Grandpa Robert Frederick Green

My maternal Grandfather, Robert Frederick Green, was born at Bottisham, Cambridgeshire, England 23rd March 1846. His parents emigrated to South Africa with their four sons when Grandpa was six years of age. His mother had brothers already living near Port Elizabeth. This was a more fortunate situation for this family, than it had been for the families of 1820, because of having someone to greet and help them in their new environment. They settled nearby in area called Kragga Kama, west of Port Elizabeth.

His mother had been Susannah Clark. Her brothers had a farm called "Buffelsfontein" and grew produce for the Port Elizabeth settlement. The history of this farm is interesting in that it dates from 1776 when it was allotted to one Theunis Botha d'Oude, Botha being one of the insurgents arrested with Van Jaarsvald during the troubles at the town of Graff-Reinert. They led the few farmers left after the 1793 massacre by the Xhosas in a protest demonstration against the Drosty (governing body). The government had persistently avoided giving these people military protection. The farms were few and far apart so the blacks became bolder, at this particular time ruining 116 farms out of 120 and stealing all the animals and killing most of the people. The government was slow to act and there was some desultory fighting. An ignominious peace was patched up near Assegai Bush. Those who were active in this insurrection were taken to Cape Town by the soldiers who arrived late.

Botha died in "The Castle," a prison that had been established as a fort in 1652 when Johan van Riebeck was in charge. A section of it was used to incarcerate sundry prisoners. Once a captive, a prisoner could expect to remain incarcerated until the "angel of death became his savior." This is now a museum and visitors can see the rings imbedded in the wall and leg bands in the floor where prisoners were fastened against the wall, to remain in an upright position all the time. A guide will relate how, on bright sunny days, as an extra punishment in some cases, the prisoner would be led outdoors. Because he had been in total darkness, the bright sunshine would cause the eyes to pain so excruciatingly, he would scream and sometimes go totally blind.

Van Jaarsvald was hanged and the others released when the Batavian Government took over again in 1803. The noted historian, Theale, writing of this identifies Botha with Buffelsfontein.[1]

The farm eventually became the property of a family named Wood who rented it to an uncle of my Grandpa Green. This man had been brought to Port Elizabeth by his mother who became a widow when her husband died of smallpox in Cambridgeshire, England. Young Clark was eighteen at that time, but worked for another farmer for sometime before coming to Buffelsfontein. The Clark family had an important role in this area, as almost all of their produce went to the markets in Port Elizabeth.

The Buffelsfontein home had three-foot thick walls; the floors and beams were of yellowwood, a very strong, long lasting wood. A low loft had many features of a bygone age architecture. It is still sound and well kept. In the living room, old-fashioned candle brackets are still screwed into the door frames. The younger generations of the Clark family still occupy the home.

The farm teemed with snakes when the Clark family first began living there and the children were constantly being told to "watch out where you walk." One of the young children, Charles, found much more than snakes as he watched out. He found many coins from foreign lands, especially St. Helena and Mauritius; a Spade Guinea, circa 1790, a small 1 1/2 d piece of 1843, half the size of a tickey. (A tickey was 3d, half, size of an American dime.) He found coins from George IV to Queen Victoria's reign. His most important find was a "Strandlooper," a clay bowl with a coni-

---

[1] *East London Daily Dispatch*, 9th April 1966.

cal bottom. Apparently its purpose was to be set down into the sand, rather than to sit upon any hard surface. All these findings were given to the museum.

One of the daughters of the former owner, related that Buffelsfontein had been a recuperation center for sailors sick with scurvy, who were put ashore from sailing ships calling in the bay. These sailors probably dropped the coins. The "Strandlooper" was a relic of a bygone race of Bushmen called Strandloopers because they lived along the strand of the Indian Ocean, in caves or outdoors. They were a fish-eating people and methodical in putting their garbage in piles. These mounds were plentiful along the shores but the bowl, termed a Strandlooper was the only one found in its perfection of shape.

Grandpa Green's parents and siblings were members of the Presbyterian Church, which Grannie had attended since she was born, 18th February 1853. It is quite likely that Robert Frederick Green had been in the congregation for her christening ceremony in 1853. If this was so, it probably meant little to the then nine-year-old boy. On 18th November of 1870, when Louisa Jane was seventeen and Robert Frederick was twenty-four, they were married at the Baptist Chapel in Port Elizabeth by the Baptist minister with whom Grannie had boarded, since she hid from her mother when she was ten years old.

It was then Robert resigned from the police force as a patrolman and they rented the Buffelsfontein farm. They lived there for seventeen years and their first eleven children were born there. They provided farm produce for the markets in the nearby city of Port Elizabeth.

There is only one known incident of any tragedy in their lives during those years. Their third child, Robert Thomas, born 13th July 1875, was not a strong child. One May day in 1876, when wandering around the yard, he ventured into the area where an ox was being slaughtered for food. He witnessed the slashing of the animal's throat and at almost that same moment someone pulled the rope that had been thrown over a beam, the other end being tied to the rear hooves. Of course, the nerves in the body, still quivering, caused the animal's body to shake. This apparently was something quite horrifying to this three year old child. He became hysterical and died of shock or heart failure.[2]

In March of 1886 Grandpa Green decided to accept the offer, made by the Agriculture Department of a 300-acre farm as an experimental fruit growing project. This would mean a move about 200 miles farther east, to a place named East London, thence another 25 miles to the farm land between the Kwelegha and Bulugha rivers. No one had ever lived there and it was a sight unseen venture. It must have been a difficult decision to leave the home and security of their farm business, to trek those long miles to a part of the country unknown to them. The future was uncertain, there would be no returning, and no one would be there to greet them.

Grandpa, with help of sons and servants, got the wagon ready, placing as much of the furniture and other belongings in as they could, leaving space for the small children. Two sons, William and Robert,[3] were old enough to help herd the cattle en route. The twelve year old daughter Violet[4] cared for the five small children and the infant Ivy, who was then six months old.[5] Grannie drove most of the time, while Grandpa on horseback was the scout. He saw to it that all was well in front, then would go behind to encourage the few servants who had agreed to help with the cattle, sheep and goats. He tied his horse to the rear of the wagon, upon occasions that he took the riems when the going was rough or when Grannie needed a rest.

This would be a time consuming trip, as the oxen could not be driven beyond their ability to draw such a heavy load. A good farmer was very careful not to overwork his animals. Beneath the wagon were cages of chickens, a few small pigs, and some tools that could be anchored there. These pigs and chickens never reached their destination, because unseasonable rains flooded the

---

[2] This story must remain a puzzle as family records place the death at ten months old.

[3] William Robert Green was the eldest child of Robert Frederick Green and Louisa Jane Nash Green. He was born 5th October 1871 at Bufflesfontein.

[4] Violet Green was the first daughter, the second child, born 24th June, 1873, at Bufflesfontein.

[5] These ages confirm this part of the story to March or April of 1886.

creeks and rivers and at one crossing the depth of the water was such that the animals drowned. This was a real tragedy for the family, as they needed the few eggs the hens laid and the food they represented.

So many misfortunes occurred that it was a miracle the travelers persevered. The servants did not like walking in the rain. The journey was much farther than anticipated, and so some deserted during the night, taking a few cattle with them! The coloureds, however, remained with Grandpa. It was the blacks who deserted.

To add to the unpleasantness was the crying baby. Ivy seemed to cry all the time, so much so that one of the boys suggested leaving her behind a bush and going on without her. The crying child was the author's mother-to-be.

East London had been in existence since 1837 and there still was not a good road between it and port Elizabeth. Washouts from heavy rains caused the road to be especially rugged. So when the family finally arrived in East London to get food supplies and to inquire as to the location of the new farm, it was discouraging to learn they had another twenty-five miles to drive.

East London, situated on the Buffalo River, is the only river port in South Africa. This was surveyed by a Royal Navy Lieutenant, John Bailie, in 1835. If it had not been for the river, it is safe to say there would be no East London. In 1836 the first stores brought into this new city were for the troops who were to be stationed on the frontier. The town itself was fairly well established fifty years later when the grandparents stopped for supplies and directions. It was, further, an important port for the province of Natal to the east.

Five miles out of town the family crossed the Nahoon River for the first of many, many times in the next 45 years of their lives. They outspanned that night in the area which would later be known as "The Outspan," or often "The Rendezvous." Next morning early the weary travelers and weary animals made their first trek over a less identifiable road. After passing the Kwelegha River, eighteen miles farther, they began to feel elated, realizing their new home was near. They went down a long hill, crossed a ravine, then up another half mile or so, and finally Grandpa insisted this was the place. He would not go one step farther.

It can only be imagined how they all felt as they took the first view of this wilderness. There was not a soul within miles. They had passed no homes and there was no home for them except what they would build themselves. Their journey had ended, in a sense, but the hard work was yet to be done. It meant camping and sleeping in the wagon until a house could be erected.

A few faithful servants were adept at creating homes from mud, wattle boughs, and thatch. Under the direction of both adults they gathered the material and put up a sod house, large enough to cover the few pieces of furniture that had been brought from Port Elizabeth. At least the family had a roof over its head, although the house was not quite large enough to bed down all the members.

The next thing to be built was an outdoor oven, called by the natives in the Xhosa language, "The Ond." It was built of bricks and mud, but not plastered, with a chimney so the smoke could go out. Before breakfast the natives brought dry branches to the ond, making a large pile, plus a few long, thick pieces. As the bread would be ready to go into the ond by ten or eleven o'clock, after breakfast the fire was lighted to burn until the ond was very hot. When the fire was out, the ashes were pushed to the sides and back, leaving the center clear and open. The loaves of bread, well rubbed with dripping, or bacon grease, were placed three in a pan. The dripping helped the loaves to break apart easily after baking. After the bread was place with a long-handled spade-like object, in the hot center of the ond, a heavy iron was laid flat against the opening to keep the heat in. The bread would then bake for an hour.

Grannie used this oven for many years. It was not until 1902 that a larger and more permanent home was ready for the family to use and then there was a large stove in the spacious kitchen. Many of the Afrikaans people, living away from the cities, still use these onds to bake their bread.

After the temporary thatch-roofed house and the outdoor ond was completed, Grandpa turned his efforts to surveying the areas where the orchards would be. The Bulugha River formed a natural boundary line to the east of his property and it was along this long strip of land that the work began. All the brush and trees had to be uprooted and cleared away before the garden area was ready for planting. While nature was working with the newly planted trees, Grandpa turned his efforts to fencing the other three sides of the property. He hired a black man with several children, among them three teenage sons. Together with Grandpa's own two older sons, William and Robert, they began fencing the three hundred acres of land, taking weeks of hard labor.

Then the area for the homestead site itself was fenced in so grazing animals could not get into the vegetable and flower gardens Grannie was making. Fences also were, hopefully, a deterrent to any of the Bantu tribes that would come that way. These fences were still in place as late as 1979, showing that the work was well done. Whatever Grandpa Green undertook to do, he did well.

He was a big man, broad shouldered and strong. His deep blue eyes were stern at times but most often had a twinkle. Although he was a strict disciplinarian, he had a sense of fun and humor. He had a full gray beard that matched his slightly receding graying hair, all kept neatly trimmed by Grannie. He was a laughing, happy man and there was evidence of a deep love toward Grandmother.

If anything of his unusual ability was discussed, it was never in my hearing. The story was told by my mother and aunties who in letters to me wrote snatches but never the total story. One aunt sent me a clipping that relates more details; a newspaper item in the East London Daily Dispatch, dated 9th September 1909, that states:

"Mr. Green removed with his family from the Port Elizabeth District, where he had been farming, and took up an allotment between the Kwelegha and Bulugha rivers, and a few miles below where the Petersen Bridge now crosses the Kwelegha. This was about 1886, and a less inviting prospect for a man, with a large family, to face than some of the wind-swept coast lands, with their yellow sails (the wind-laden seashore sands) it is difficult to conceive. For the arable or agricultural land is in most cases conspicuous by its absence, the only redeemable feature in many instances being the pockets of alluvial soil to be found along the banks of the numerous streams intersecting the division. Mr. Green soon realized that if he had to depend upon the ordinary field crops it would be a blue look-out for him to pay rent and support his family, but finding himself stuck with the land he resolved to make the best of what he considered a bad business.

"At that time transport-riding was still remunerative and he could employ his wagons and oxen on the road, but the introduction shortly afterwards of red-water fever (a cattle disease) brought straight into the district by the transport used in connection with the useless Cape Infantry Regiment, swept off his oxen and entailed severe losses upon him, as in fact on every farmer in the district.

(The Cape Infantry Regiment was the instrument through which the government supplied material and supplies of food to the few forts that had been erected in the District of East London and those farther North and East. The disease was brought in on the wagon wheels and the hoofs of the oxen. It was a disease of the urinary tract and fatal to all these animals.)

"Fortunately for him, he had some land lying on the Bulugha adapted for fruit growing, and as soon as he took up his allotment he started to plant fruit trees of such varieties as were to be found in his neighborhood, which happened to be principally apples, but he was shrewd enough to see that to make fruit growing pay, especially at a distance of twenty-five miles from the nearest market, only the best varieties were worth growing. He thereupon cut his original trees back and used them as stocks to graft scions of choice varieties upon, and herein probably lies the secret of his success, for he has proved beyond a shadow of a doubt that to succeed with grafts the stocks must first be thoroughly acclimatized and adapted to local conditions of soil and climate. In fact, choice trees which he had obtained from first class nurserymen have failed to make any headway, whereas scions from the same trees grafted on his own stock are flourishing.

"Mr. Green's friends call him the 'Apple King' but, although apples are the main crop, they also run close by the superior orange, naartjes (tangerines), peaches, guavas, and bananas The orchard is irrigated from a small daw (dam) across the Bulugha, the water being held back by a concrete weir, of Mr. Green's own construction, and from this dam the water is pumped into a service reservoir where it is distributed by gravitation. The pump is . . . worked by a windmill . . . but Mr. Green contemplates displacing it by . . . an oil engine . . . .

"The homestead consists of a comfortable bungalow (completed in 1902) with wide verandah, on a ridge between the Bulugha and the Kwelegha rivers, from which a wide panorama of the surrounding country and sea is visible. Around the house are a number of ornamental trees, but not least, a bright flower garden the special province of Mrs. Green . . . .

"The farm buildings, consisting of a stable, cow sheds, dairy, workshop, etc., all display care in erection, combined with neatness, whilst convenient paddocks are also in evidence."

This is only a portion of a very long narrative from the Daily Newspaper of East London. It portrays a man of courage and daring. And of course, his wife, my grandmother, had an equal amount of these qualities.

That was all virgin land. No one had ever tilled that soil and probably no one, except roving Xhosas, had ever walked through those acres. My grandparents, then, were the very first tenants. It was overgrown with trees, the most predominant being what I would call squatty, wide spreading thorn trees four to five feet tall. They had vicious thorns, making them hard to root up and clear away, along with the grasses and shrubs. The clearing was necessary in order to have space for housing; at first temporary and later permanent houses and other structures. The land also had to be cleared for growing wheat and barley. It was a Herculean task and only individuals of much stamina and fortitude could have survived and succeeded. The family had severed all connections with Port Elizabeth, which fact gave them added incentive to work hard and achieve success. Snakes were abundant, as were wild animals, and crocodiles were in the river.

Grannie often related her stark unbelief to see, in one day, two very long black snakes, with bodies as round as a man's thigh. She was the only one able to handle the big gun and had nerve enough to shoot. She said, "It was a terrifying experience but I had to do it. No one else was round. After I shot the second one, I was completely unnerved. Fortunately we never saw any more. Grandpa measured them and found they were sixteen and twenty feet long."

Those giant serpents may have been the last of the African pythons, quite common in Natal in those days but an infrequent sight in this particular area. Perhaps the two were mates and had wandered from their natural habitat, seeking an area less peopled.

Wild game was plentiful at first, but men killed many and others went farther north into the forests. There is evidence that elephants, lions, rhinoceros, besides several species of springbok, had been prevalent in the Eastern Province. The only creature I saw as a child was the "legavon"—an alligator that came to the yard, probably to seek food or water. The rivers were drying up because of a drought at that time.

Once the farm fowls made such a noise that Grannie, with me following, went to see what was the cause. She never thought of taking her gun. When I saw this awful creature, I began asking questions. All she said was, "Child, run into the house! Quickly! This is no time to ask questions. If that creature hits your legs with its tail, you won't have any leg! Fortunately, Uncle Sid was in the workshop and quickly realized the situation and, as I was running to the house, I saw him aim the gun. Grannie was right behind me and would not permit me to see what happened after he shot. Within a week or two, a similar situation occurred and, after that shooting, we never had any other alligators come to the farm.

It has always been my joy to have had good memories of a close relationship with both my grandparents. Although Grannie and I spent more time together than did Grandpa and I, the latter and I sort of understood each other. He knew I was given to doing things forbidden, and he sometimes reprimanded me in a most unexpected way. He would say little—it was the way he acted and looked, with perhaps a shake of the head as though he could not believe Edna would do such a thing. Now, I think it was suppressed amusement; perhaps he was proud to have such a smart grandchild!

I used to make daily visits to the peach orchard near the house. Grandpa had seen me try to climb the trees once or twice and had forbidden me to do this. After that I always looked around before attempting to climb one. One day I noticed a branch extending parallel to the ground and the bark seemed to be shiny. I felt it and found it smooth. I put my hand upon it to shinny up and got the idea of swinging by placing my legs over the branch, with head hanging down. I was in this position when I heard Grandpa exclaim, "Child, you damn little devil!" I could not scramble down fast enough. "I've told you *not* to climb my peach trees! What an unladylike position to get into. I can see your brookies (panties). You should be ashamed. I'll let you off this time but next time I'll switch your bottom!" I saw his lips twitch into a tiny smile as he suddenly turned his back. The words "switch your bottom," however, brought to mind my dad's doing just that, so thereafter I was careful to leave his peach trees alone.

I admired Grandpa Green when I was a child, and I admire the memory today of this giant of a man. He had a strength of character that had been an inspiration to me. He had so many of the qualities, not only necessary of a true pioneer, but as a person. He was a man of honor, integrity and total devotion to wife, family and purpose.

It was not known for a certainty that the soil on his property, so close to the ocean, would be productive. The challenge was given to Grandpa. He was like a diamond in the rough, wresting from that soil a living for self and a large family and earning, in the process, a name that became a byword throughout the fruit industry for high quality of everything that was marketed under the name of "R. F. Green, Esq., Smiling Valley Farm." The coming of the railroads made it possible for his fruits to be sold over a very large area and his name became known throughout the Cape Province and to some cities in the Transvaal.

Grannie was responsible for the name, "Smiling Valley." She said she had a mental vision of the beauty of the place when she first saw it. "I told Grandpa then," she said, "that it would take time to build but I could see this as a smiling valley, a fruitful place to make our living and rear our family." She smiled. "He agreed."

Chapter 9

First Days with the Grandparents

We had been with the grandparents about three weeks when one day Mother said, "Girls, I'm taking you for a walk to the big garden after lunch so don't play too far away. I'll call you when we are ready." I wondered what a "big garden" would be and also what flowers would grow there. I thought Grannie's gardens at the house were big when I compared them to what we had in Cullinan.

It was with great anticipation that Jessie and I walked along with Mother holding our hands. She told us we could not run ahead, because we should watch out for snakes. The path to the garden was not very wide and on each side was brush and tall, spindly trees, some of which were entwined with vines. Occasionally we saw wild flowers and I wanted to know what they were. "We will look at those another time," said Mother. "It is a hot afternoon and we must watch for snakes. Keep your eyes on the path." As I had never seen a snake, I began to wonder why all the caution and asked, "Will a snake bite?"

Mother's answer was bewildering to me. "That is why we must look where we are going. If we see it first, it won't bite, because I will know how to avoid it." By the time I digested all those words and was on the verge of asking another question, Mother said, "Here we are!" Dropping our hands, she gestured with both of hers.

"Oh, a house," I said.

"No," she shook her head. "A packing shed." Stepping closer. Jessie ran into the shed, probably expecting to see something to eat. She sounded disappointed as she said, "Only empty boxes."

"Yes, but those boxes hold the fruit when it is ready to go to market," Mother explained. "Come, I'll show you the reservoir." Again she held our hands firmly, as we walked a few more steps to stop at an opening where grew a large circular stand of trees. These trees were entwined with creepers, a kind of flaring vine having bell-shaped flowers in red, orange and pink. "What flowers, Mommie?" I pointed with my free hand. "Trumpet vines," was her brief reply. "See the water," she pointed to the gloomy opening. As my eyes became accustomed to the darkness within, I could see there was water.

"Why is it so dark?" I asked. She looked upward, saying, "See how the trees meet overhead?" Indeed, no sun could come through. "These are very old trees and the vines have twisted among them so they form a thick canopy overhead. This is a very deep reservoir and you must never come here alone. If you fell in we could never find you."

Although I was intrigued with the quietness, I felt the brooding atmosphere. An occasional bird call was the only sound. I wondered what snakes or other strange things would be lurking in that gloom. At the same time I felt a bit frightened and awed but did not understand the reason. Afterwards, I recalled the incident when my father had frightened me so terribly in the dark, and I think it was the gloomy darkness that made me so fearful. "Come," said Mother, "let's see if we can find Uncle Sid. He is working in the apple orchard today. Oh, look, there are some calla lilies blooming!" She stopped walking and looked all around. "This is Grannie's special garden for the callas and Easter lilies. When it is the right time for blooming, I will bring you to see them. There are hundreds and such a lovely sight. It is a bit late for the callas so we are fortunate to see these." We turned to leave and she added, "They have such a lovely fragrance one can smell long before actually entering the garden. City dwellers like to buy them. Oh, there's Sid."

She pulled us along to meet her favorite brother. "Hello, what are you doing today, Sid?" Uncle Sid stopped his work and smiled at us. "Hello, girls. So you're taking your mother for a walk. I'm glad you're here." He looked at Mother and asked, "Are you feeling all right, Ivy?" I thought Mother always felt all right, so I thought this was an odd question. She just nodded. He continued, "Well, I'm just checking my new grafts and I find that pesky woolly aphis is on some of my apple trees. They are hard pests to get rid of but I'm trying a new spray that should help."

At that moment a Xhosa came to speak to Uncle and they had a brief conversation in Bantu. Then the black man smiled, said "Baas," tipped his hat to Mother, whom he seemed to know, smiled at us girls, and walked away.

"What did he say, Mommy?" I touched her hand. "'Yes, Boss.' They understand some English, but they usually talk in Bantu." Then I saw something. "What is that he is carrying?" "A hoe," said Uncle Sid, chuckling. "Didn't you ever see a hoe? Watch him as he changes the water with it."

The black man began digging, and I watched, wondering how he could change water with such a thing. I had noticed that some dirt was piled a bit higher in some places. Soon he smiled broadly and waved his hand. We walked closer and sure enough, there was the water running along a new little ditch where he had been digging. Uncle Sid seemed to comprehend my amazement so he carefully explained that the garden was irrigated by these diggings called furrows. When water was needed by different trees, the man used the hoe to make it go another way by digging a new furrow. I found this quite interesting.

Jessie put the toe of her shoe into the little stream and was rather surprised when her sock got wet. We both were wearing black shoes with straps over the instep and white socks. Mother always dressed us alike—I was small for my age—and because of our attire, those who did not know us, would ask if we were twins.

"Trees need a drink, too," said Uncle. I was often to discover that he answered a question not yet voiced by myself. We were kindred spirits, I believe, but this was never discussed. It was only in later years this realization dawned upon my consciousness.

"Come! Let us go see the oranges." He turned. Walking beside Mother, Uncle and she spoke of things incomprehensible to Jessie and me, but we were too busily engaged in looking here and there to care. We saw many black men with hoes working the garden, making furrows. Then we came to the orange grove.

I stood in awe at the beautiful sight. Rows and rows of gorgeous trees with dark green, shiny leaves, with tiny white sweet-smelling blossoms, and not a blade of grass or a weed anywhere. It was like a park. I took a deep breath to drink in the fragrance. Mother picked a blossom to show us how creamy-white and dainty it was. She said, "The blossoms will eventually become oranges. Here is a blossom nearly dead. See the little green bulb, big as a pimple? That will grow big like this," touching a larger green one. "Soon it will get like this. Girls, I want you to notice how the oranges change color. This is just going from green to orange and this one is all golden, but this one is ready to pick and eat." Taking it from the tree she peeled it and shared the orange sections with us. Oh, it was good! So juicy!

"Put your heads over like this," she demonstrated. "The juice won't run down your chins then." This was my very first experience of eating a tree-ripened orange! I never heard Sister say how she felt about her first orange picked from the tree, but I never forgot it.

She and I were to have several "very firsts" when it came to eating the various fruits as they ripened; loquots, cherry guavas, and naartjes. We would see and taste a great variety of other fruits later. "You are going to have a good crop this year, Sid," Mother glanced up at him.

"It looks that way, Ivy, and I only hope the price is better than it was last year. It is difficult to make a living when people, buying at the market, think that a shilling a box is too much for a flat of oranges. Some even feel we should be able to give them free produce, especially when it comes to carrots and peas." He shook his head before going on. "It amazes me that city folk have no concept of how these things grow and how much work it takes. They have no idea of the processes involved in preparation for market. All they know is that the fruit comes in boxes. Of course, 'Smiling Valley' fruits are always in demand, so we never return with leftovers. The boys put on a good face and are pleasant to all, even the ones we discuss later with a lot of laughter."

He turned as though to go. "You know, Dad has an 'A-One' reputation in this fruit business and his sons are expected to maintain that image." Both laughed. I could see no reason for laughter, but I suspected it was a private joke. I had already concluded that the adults around me laughed a lot when nothing was funny. I had also observed that my mother was happier looking when she was alone with Sid.

Leaving the orange grove, we came to a section of the apple orchard where some varieties were forming into fruits. The first section contained younger trees, more in the experimental state of his grafting. Apparently Uncle Sid had a natural ability for this work, started earlier by his dad. He had been taught by him but I never knew who taught Grandpa. I suppose Grandpa was just gifted in the art of being a fruit grower. He was many things, I was to discover. Among his talents was raising cattle, "prize beef" I heard one of the uncles call them. He was a splendid horseman, no doubt from his many years of being a police patrolman. His sons had a good reputation to uphold!

As we passed different apple trees, I noticed Uncle Sid would stop for a moment and examine the flowers and young fruit forming among the leaves. "Why do you do that, Uncle?" I asked. "I'm looking for the pests that plague the trees when they are in flower. We can't let them grow to kill the trees." He lifted another small branch. "See here. This is what I look for, pointing to some white stuff near a flower. "This is called 'wooly-aphis' and if it grows this whole tree would begin to die."

At that, he removed the gadget attached to his belt, which he called his "spray can," and pressed on top and a liquid spray enveloped the area where the aphis were clustered. Putting the can back in its place, he said, "We could lose a whole orchard with these bugs."

I wrinkled my nose at the smell and we went on to the rest of the orchard. As time passed, and with my numerous visits to the garden with Mother or an older cousin or an uncle, I became knowledgeable about these procedures. Occasionally I became bolder and went to the garden by myself, but never felt really comfortable as I knew this was forbidden.

The garden did not seem so friendly without an adult beside me. I recall one time when I had an impulse to go inside the gloomy reservoir. I seemed drawn to it and I wondered about this. The very idea of such a thought frightened me. The eerie feeling of being dragged in was the main reason I refrained from going alone to the garden again. No adult ever knew this; I did, however, tell my cousin Ivy who was older than I when we went together.

Soon after the visit and while chatting in the garden with Uncle Sid, my mother seemed not very well. One September evening she did not put Jessie and me to bed as usual but Grannie did, in her spare bedroom. When I awakened I could not accept my new surroundings. Grannie came in to help us dress. Jessie was three and a half and I was two years older. I felt rather apprehensive because Grannie seemed not quite herself and would not answer my questions. Finally, taking Jessie and me each by the hand she led us into the big bedroom which we shared with Mother. She was still in bed!

Grannie then announced, "You have a little brother!" She lifted Jessie up to see the new child. Jessie reacted immediately. She screamed and kicked and made quite a scene. As I was staring at her and wondering why she was acting that way, Grannie lifted me and my reactions were the exact opposite. I fell in love with him right away and wanted to hold him.

After Grannie put me back on the floor, I asked where the baby came from and received two answers. Mother said he came from under a cabbage leaf (there was a large field of cabbages a short distance from her window), and Grannie said the doctor brought him in his satchel. I ran to the window in time to see a tall, slim man, dressed in a dark coat and carrying a large satchel, standing by Grandpa's carriage, with Uncle Sid in the driver's seat. I said, "How can one baby come from two places?" No one answered me.

That afternoon Jessie and I were walking up and down the rows of cabbages, bending over at any large one and lifting a leaf. Uncle Sid had returned from taking the doctor back to the city and he watched us for a few minutes. "What are you two doing?" he finally asked. I stood tall and looked right at him. "We are looking for another baby brother."

Without any apparent reason he went into spasms of laughter. I could not understand his reaction and somehow I felt ashamed. This feeling bothered me and his laughter puzzled me. I experienced a new feeling, humiliation. I resented the adults in my life not telling the truth. It took a long time to become the trusting child I had been, especially after I overheard Uncle Sid tell his brothers about the incident. Their laughter again created many negative feelings within me. Somehow I pinned my resentment on my mother, for I had always accepted her statements as true.

My brother Leonard Sidney Walker, was born 4th September 1914, just after midnight, although there was some question as to whether it had been 3rd September when it was discovered the clock was four minutes fast. He became the darling of the grandparents. He was the first grandchild born in their home and my uncles adored him, especially when he began to talk and walk. Although he became a very spoiled child, I always loved him. Jessie also finally accepted him and we had some good times together.

I often wondered what Mother's feeling were about that event. I'm sure she herself wondered if her son would ever see his father. She told me years later that she was apprehensive as to whether Dad would ever send her any money for our passage to travel to the United States, as he had promised, because he was not sending her money then. What would her lot in life be if she were tied to the farm with no way to support her children? Who would take care of the children if anything happened to her? I personally am sure, if something had happened, her parents would have kept us three children. But who knows?

For once she could get no comfort from the thought of a "brighter tomorrow" for her. It had been months since she had heard from my father. Sometime during that period I was sure that he never really wanted any of us and that we would never see him again.

I began to do much strange thinking when I would see Grannie rocking Jessie and Grandpa having the new manny cosily propped on his lap. Sometimes I would approach the grandparents, asking to be held. The response was always the same, "You are a big girl now, you don't need to be held." I felt completely unloved. My father did not want us, my grandparents would not hold me. Mother would not hold me either, because she had no time, so I began to feel like an outcast. One day I realized that the only adult in my life who had held me lovingly and rocked me was my Aunt Agnes,[1] but that was a long time ago. She had been one person who did love me! I continued to hug that thought to me as I watched life go on around me.

The grandparents shared every afternoon in their respective rocking chairs having afternoon tea. A table between them, on the stoep, always held books and farm journals or magazines and Grannie would often read to Grandpa. Even if they were holding the children Grannie would read, but I never remember seeing Grandpa pick up newspaper or a book. I did not know then that he could not read. Years later a cousin wrote me, saying, "Of course Grandpa never did learn to read. He never went to school, so Grannie did all the reading and all the business accounts."

He had a good memory, so undoubtedly, with the help of Grannie, he memorized many of the Bible passages, because I heard him quote the Lord's Prayer and the 23rd Psalm, more than once. He could even speak some of the religious passages in Bantu.

I witnessed one phase of their togetherness of which I'm sure no other family member was aware. My persistent desire to be where Grannie was led me to observe their ceremony. I wanted to relate something to her and entered the door from the stoep into the parlor. They entered from the far end at the same time from the long hallway which I knew led to their bedroom. The fact that they were dressed in their best clothing caused me to be silent as I watched. With some ceremony Grandpa led her to the old-fashioned, tapestry covered, stationary rocker. He then brought up an easy chair and sat down facing her. Neither had seen me as they were so intent with each other. I did not hear, nor did I try to eavesdrop; I just wondered about all this unusual happening. They talked quietly for some time and he held her hands. They seemed to be in agreement about something decided—or remembered.

Finally Grandpa arose, put his chair where it belonged, then gallantly extended his hand which she took. He then helped her

---

[1] See Chapter 3.

out of the chair, putting her arm through his. They walked toward the end of the parlor where I had been observing them. (When they began to move, I backed away from the door but could still see them.) He went to the sideboard, which was kept locked, removed a key from his vest pocket, and opened the door. He then reached in and put a small silver plate or tray on top of the sideboard, placed two glasses upon this and poured some wine into one glass. He put this bottle away and removed another to partly fill the second glass, then returned that to the shelf. (Perhaps this was brandy or whisky.) They lifted their glasses, clinked them together and he said something. They had their little drink and smiled at each other. He put away the glasses and tray and locked the sideboard, returning the key to his pocket, and held out his arms. She embraced him and laughed, leaning against him.

I was still the silent observer. There was some inner feeling that caused me to respect this little ceremony. I cannot say how often this was repeated, but somehow I realized they were honoring each other in the remembrance of some special occasion to them; something that kept their romance alive. They had been married forty-four years when we came into their home. Quietly, I turned and went out but I could never forget that little scene.

Chapter 10

The Peach Tree, A Gramophone, and A Fire

One day I took a walk in Grannie's dahlia garden, or what had been her dahlia garden. The plants had been uprooted and the soil prepared for a special planting of peach trees that finally became a small orchard. Grandpa wanted to watch over these himself and it was much easier for him to have the planting close to the house rather than to go over to the naval garden which was a long walk. I'm sure this had been with Grannie's consent, as they never entered into any major endeavor without talking it over and coming to a mutual agreement. This must have been one secret of their long and happy marriage.

The trees were still small, but they were beginning to flower and fruits to appear. As the days passed, a tree planted near the water tank also bore fruit. It was larger and must have been a special grafting experiment since it grew apart from the others.

Most evenings the family would gather near that tree while the men discussed its progress and the results expected. It bore several very large peaches and this seemed to please both Grandpa and Uncle Sid. They were kindred spirits when it came to the art of grafting, and no doubt this had been a mutual venture. As the fruit matured and began to ripen, I remembered one evening ceremony when everyone was gathered around looking at the tree and discussing it. Grandpa suddenly turned to me and said, "Now you damn little devil, don't you take any of these peaches!" I suppose he said this because I had taken some fruit from the garden earlier. Until that moment the idea of taking one of those special peaches had never entered my mind. I was not one, however, to let such a challenge pass; if Grandpa thought I could take a peach from that tree, I'd have to find a way to do it.

Now I stood looking up at the tree. It would not be easy, I could see that. If I took a peach from a lower branch, the adults would be sure to blame me. It would have to be the very topmost peach but how? One was even with the roof, but the tree was not strong enough to hold my skinny self, although I could shinny up most trees quickly. I walked slowly around the house and finally decided that I could climb up one of the supporting standards and reach the edge of the roof. I proceeded to do so. I was dismayed when I saw the roof was not smooth. It was of corrugated, galvanized tin and I certainly could not walk over that without being heard if anyone was in the patio underneath.

Finally, I removed my shoes, lay on my stomach, and crawled slowly and quietly over the roof. I managed to reach the edge where I thought the peach would be easy to pick. I was dismayed when I discovered more space between roof and tree than I had expected. I kept stretching and at one point almost lost my balance. Hanging grimly onto the gutter, which must have been well anchored, I gave one last desperate reach and got hold of that peach! The branch almost broke as I tugged. At last the peach was mine! I lay still for a moment and caught my breath, then I took a big bite. Victory was not sweet! The peach was not ripe! I almost spit it out, then I looked at it. What should I do with it? I could not throw it away as it might be found. I could not climb down the roof safely while holding it, so I continued to lie on my stomach and ate as much as I could. Then I thought of the gutter. I left the balance of that peach in the gutter.

Now I had to get down. I turned around to crawl to the rear of the house roof. I put my shoes back on and had fearful moments as I tried to get my footing and slid down the post upon which I had climbed. I could not go down any other way except backwards. It was truly dreadful! At last I made it to the ground, then looked down at my dirty dress. I had not expected to find the roof so dirty nor had I expected to crawl. I brushed off as much dirt as I could but knew I would have to change or someone would notice.

That evening when we gathered around the tree again, I learned that the peaches had been counted! Now one was missing! Who could have taken it? All the adults looked at me. I tried to look innocent. (I've often wondered what I really did look like.) Grannie finally said, "It could not have been the child. There are no marks of a ladder and she certainly could not have reached it!" Grandpa just looked at me! Did I see a gleam of amusement in those twinkling blue eyes? Nothing more was said then by anyone.

This achievement did not bring me any sense of joy; instead, I felt guilty and shamefaced, and was glad when it was time for bed. Several months later, Grandpa said to me, "You damn little devil, I know you took that peach. I was angry at first because a prized peach was stolen, but I did have some admiration for you to think you outsmarted all of us grownups." He shook his head.

"But Grandpa, why do you think I did it?"

He grinned. "Well, when the first rains came, we could not understand why the water overflowed the gutter so I got a ladder to clear it. Half a peach was there causing the overflow. It had to be you, but I still don't know how you did it." I did not tell him, but I cannot express how I felt at being found out. I should have been spanked but no one ever even scolded.

I cannot recall Grandpa ever calling me by name. It was always, "You damn little devil, you." which sounds awful, but I felt it was his way of expressing some caring about me. I did earn the name because I was so often doing something which had been forbidden.

One time later after I started going to school, Cousin Ivy,[1] five years older than I, came to stay overnight. We had gone to the garden, climbed a loquat tree and sat there eating that delicious fruit, spitting out the rich shiny brown seeds, large as date seeds. We saw Grandpa approaching and kept quiet as mice. We watched him stop and look down at the pile of seeds and fully expected him to look up, but he did not. The gardens were always free from from weeds or any undergrowth, so we should have known he would notice the seeds. He must also have seen our footprints. We felt rather triumphant that he had not seen us.

When we left the garden, each of us had an apron full of different fruits which we decided to take to school and share the

---

[1] This must be Ivy Sonnenberger.

next morning. En route home we found a place with long grass and proceeded to build a nest to keep the fruit safer until time to go to school. The next morning we could not find the fruit. Both of us knew where the nest was, but where was the fruit? As we hunted and talked to each other about it we heard a chuckle. There was Grandpa!

Of course he was suspicious. He knew very well we had been in that loquat tree and quite possibly had even seen us carrying the fruit in our aprons. Perhaps he even noticed that morning that we did not take the regular path toward the school, but had gone in the opposite direction. We had intended to walk through the adjoining Bauer farm, and thus get to school without having to pass our house. At any rate, there was Grandpa, quietly surveying us with an amused smile. "Well, girls, I took the fruit. I saw you making this nest, and I examined it to see what you were putting in it. Had you asked me for this fruit, I would have given permission to take it, but because you took it without asking I had to remove it. You must understand that taking things like that is stealing and I will not tolerate stealing."

While Grandpa and I did not have the togetherness shared by Grannie and me, we sort of understood each other in a very different manner. I learned that lesson very well.

There were occasions when Grandpa had to confer with other farmers. There were no telephones, so he would mount his beautiful gray stallion with the shining white mane and tail. They had been master and horse for many years and there was a bond of affection between them. This was evident when the big horse would run toward him and nuzzle him. He would pat and talk to the animal. When saddled, sometimes Silver Prince would paw the dirt in his impatience to get moving. Both man and animal had an affinity for each other and looked like one unit as they sped over the road.

I would watch until they passed the schoolhouse a mile away to see which farm he might be going to. When he turned left, I knew he was going to the Bauer farm and when right, it would be the Schultz farm. There seemed to be a special rivalry going on between Mr. Schultz and Grandpa, but the nature of it I was never able to discern. Each had composed words to be sung to the tune of *Battle Hymn of the Republic*, a sort of fun thing, and each would try to outdo the other in singing this loudly. The song was a sort of mockery, I presume, because the last words of both were, "And I'll see you in your grave." I used to wonder what that meant. Both men were in good voice and both would end up by slapping each other on the back and laughing with abandon. I felt the whole thing was a private joke between them, as Grandpa would say, "You old Boer, you," and Mr. Schultz would come back with, "You old roineck," as the English were called.

One Sunday morning, soon after breakfast, a covered wagon was seen turning from the road passing the shoolhouse. As I watched it, I became excited because it took the right turn to pass over the ravine. I hurried into the patio area to tell those seated, "A wagon is coming here! Come and see!"

Grandparents, two uncles, and Mother followed me into the yard and soon the occupants of the weagon were climbing down. It was Aunt Florrie[2] and Uncle Adolph with my six cousins.[3] It was unusual for them to arrive so early but the grandparents were happy to see them. It was my first time of beginning to know these cousins who would play a larger part in my life than any other cousins. I was to become very fond of this family.

It was a bigger surprise when other wagons began to arrive, neighbors and relatives. Of course, the grandparents became a bit curious. Finally Uncle Sid called us children and said, "Go to the verandah there," pointing to the one leading into the parlor. Aunt Florrie asked us to be quiet, as we then gathered in our excitement. Uncles Leonard and Clem brought into the parlor a large box, placing it in front of their parents. Uncle Sid proceeded with his little speech, telling his parents that "we are all gathered today to give you honor and a gift; to let you know that we are proud to be children of such wonderful parents. We also wanted you to

---

[2] Florence Ethel Green, the third daughter, the sixth child, was born 10th October 1880 at Bufflesfontein. She married Adolph Sonnenberger, a native of Budapest, on 9th September 1901.

[3] The cousins are Mabel, Ivy, Harry, Sydney, Bessie, and Ivan. Three others were born later: Myrtle, Victoria, and Victor.

have something special as a token of your devotion to each other and to us on this ocasion of your golden wedding anniversary."[4]

The younger uncles helped uncrate the package and Grannie put her hand to her bosom in great surprise, for the treasure unwrapped proved to be a gramophone. The uncles set it upon a small table Uncle Clem had made. When they got it assembled, it was a thing of beauty. The base was square and white, the horn was like a full blown morning glory of a purplish hue. Most intriguing was the replica of a small black and white dog sitting on the floor in a listening pose, presumably "listening to his Master's voice."

Then suddenly all became quiet as Uncle Sid placed a black disc on the machine. Soon beautiful sounds of lovely music flooded the room. We were awed at the sound of this wonderful music. That was the first gramophone in the whole family, certainly the first one I had ever seen, and what a momentous occasion it was. This was especially so for Grannie, because the last record played was *Over the Waves*, at which she dabbed at her eyes with her dainty handkerchief. This tune seemed to touch her deeply and I often wished I knew why; it must have had a special meaning. This lovely gift of the gramophone was given by all her children.

Later I decided that perhaps she had always wanted to go "over the waves" to visit England, the home of her forbears. This idea, however, was purely imagination on my part. I never found out.

Soon a feast appeared as the aunts and Mother began to place food on the table, with the very best tea service being used. Seven sons and two daughters, with twenty-two grandchildren, added to this great occasion. It was a happy day and a good time was had by all.

One afternoon when Grannie, Jessie and I were listening to the gramophone, she shut it off. Unlocking a door of her glass-

---

[4] Robert Frederick Green and Louisa Jane Nash were married 18th November 1870. Their golden anniversary, presuming that to mean their 50th, would then have been November 1920. Ivy Green Walker with her three children had emigrated from South Africa earlier that year and Edna May would not have been present. Further, from Edna May's story it would appear that brother Leonard Sidney Walker, born 1914, was at best a toddler. Perhaps, then, this was a 45th anniversary, 1915.

fronted, tall china cabinet, which contained her treasures, she removed from the bottom shelf a beautifully made box that had a tiny gold clasp. She opened it to show us *her* "music box." From another less ornate box, she removed a cylinder and placed it over the arm in the other box. Soon we heard the tinkling sounds of *Over the Waves* as the cylinder rotated and the needle moved along. Again this piece indicated, to me, something of significance.

We were never permitted to touch *her* music box and through the years I longed to own that small instrument, as I began to realize its value, sentimentally as well as otherwise. I've never seen another such treasure. It was with profound sorrow that Mother, on a return trip to that home in 1952, discovered the box in pieces in the youngster's sand box. Such a loss! I would have treasured it and had it placed in a museum.

While having breakfast one morning, we heard the fowls set up a loud cackling, indicating something they feared. We all rushed from the table, Grandpa grabbing his gun. Perhaps the chickens thought another legavon was in the yard, but they were looking up. We all looked up and saw a bird flying in a circular manner, coming down. Thinking it was a chicken hawk, Grandpa aimed and shot. Uncle Len picked it up and he and Grandpa examined the legs. Then I heard the latter, in a surprised voice, say, "Yes, it is banded. We will have to report this."

Soon the carriage was ready and he, with Uncle Sid driving, left for town, while the remaining four adults discussed what would happen now. Somewhat subdued they all finally went about their tasks. I wondered what it was all about, but did not learn until the travellers returned in late afternoon and later we all were gathered around the table for an earlier evening meal. The bird had been a carrier pigeon, banded by the government. This was during World War I and it seems the birds were used to convey messages; to whom and about what, I never learned.

During that period, after evening chores were done, it was the family custom to sit around the dining room table to listen to Grannie read the daily paper, with emphasis on the casualty list. No one had taken the time, naturally, to tell me that a war was going on, therefore the reading of his list never made an impression, except one evening the name read caused a gasp throughout the adults. It was one of Grandpa's relatives. It was through this reading that Grannie had also read that if anyone found a banded bird it should be returned to a certain place; that is how it happened Uncle Sid and Grandpa took the trip, most unexpectedly, to the city.

Another unexpected incident happened soon after, which shattered us all. A drought had been continuing for a long time, with hot winds at times wilting plants and people. This one day, however, was calm and Grandpa decided to burn the tall grasses of the pasture area west of the acreage. He walked down the hill, past the ravine and set the grass afire, which was supposed to burn all the way to the Kwelegha River and thus burn itself out. He turned to come home and half way up the hill, the wind turned and Grandpa looked back to see flames coming toward him.

Grannie, holding Leonard who had become a sickly infant by that time, and I were inspecting her herbal garden. When she saw Grandpa running and shouting, she realized instantly what was happening. Turning to me she commanded, "Run! Ring the bell a long time!" Obeying instantly, I at last had the opportunity to ring that bell as I had longed to do for months. It was not such a joyous experience, after all. As I pulled the rope I began to shake with fear, and trembling with effort I almost stopped, when an uncle hurrying into the area told me to stop, that everyone was there.

I ran toward the house to see what was happening. I was astonished to see so much activity. Mother was shoving a plow while Uncle Sid was doing similarly, each plow being pulled by a pair of oxen. They were making furrows around the hay barn. Others with wetted gunnysacks were slapping the grass and trees. Still others were chopping the lower branches of trees. Blacks and whites were all working frantically together to prevent the fire from crossing the nearest line of trees, for the house would be next.

I was frightened to see all the activity and so much fire. The smoke was so thick it was an eerie sight. Grannie finally thrust baby brother (he was about eight months old[5]) into my arms, saying, "I'm going to help. You girls stay in the house."

After awhile my alarm caused me to feel I should take Leonard out of the house, but where? Strangely, I did not think of Jessie in this time of stress. I managed to bundle Brother up. We crossed the yard and went into the barn where the carriage was. How I managed to climb into the seat with the bundle, I don't know, but there I sat, fearful of the dark and desiring to return to the house and not knowing how to descend from the buggy and get the bundled brother down too. I just sat there a long time. Finally I heard my name being called and answered in a trembling voice. It was Grannie, with Jessie holding her hand. It was the only time I ever remember seeing Grannie distressed, the only time she ever spoke sharply to me. I realized somehow that her sharpness was caused by her sense of relief.

"Of all the places to come!" she said. "The barn is full of straw and had the fire come this far, you would have been burned up. Why didn't you stay in the house as I told you?"

Jessie told me later that Grandpa had taken her back to the house because he did not want her to be in the smoke. Grannie then wanted to know where the baby was. Jessie told her I had taken him outside. Poor Grannie—she had enough to worry about that evening without my adding to her problems.

The fire burned throughout the night, as we had many gum wattle and eucalyptus trees and these, being highly inflammable, continued to burn. They were very old trees, thick of trunk and towered into the air. This was the reason lower branches had been cut when the fire approached, so at least some were saved, but many were deeply scarred.

At last, at Grannie's command, we children tumbled into bed, so I do not know how late into the night the struggle continued. The house and hay barn were saved and that seemed to be the most important to all concerned. The precious water had been used, but how thankful everyone was to have had that water. I learned that the farmers from four and five miles distant had hurried on horseback to help in this emergency.

It was really the most alarming and exciting episode in my life with Grandpa and Grannie Green—perhaps in my entire life.

---

[5] This would make the events to be about May 1915.

Chapter 11

Uncle Sidney Victor Green

Of the three uncles, Sid, Clem, and Len, I felt the most comfortable with Uncle Sid.[1] He never was impatient with us children. He always called me by name, never "Bully" as did Uncle Len, nor "Hey, Pest" by Uncle Clem. Being an aggressive child, I was a pest, always wanting to know and often being underfoot as they worked in the tool shed. When out of the house, I felt free to talk and to question, because I had to remain silent at meal times.

Sidney Victor Green was the tenth child, the first, however, to be born at the Smiling Valley Farm. Uncle Sid had an abundance of dark hair, but his pride was the mustache that he kept waxed and trimmed to a fine point at each end. It was wider in the center than at the ends and he referred to it as his handlebar mustache. He was charming and never seemed morose or out of sorts. In the time we were together I felt much warmth toward this uncle who seemed also to enjoy me. Perhaps it was not so much me as it was that I was the daughter of his favorite sister, Ivy. At any rate, we had a good relationship all the years I lived in that home.

My empathy with Uncle Sid was such that the pain of Uncle Billy Baker's departure from my life finally left me. Uncle Sid, so different from Daddy, had much to do with the healing of this too-serious child, and I was always able to be my real self with him. Never was I roughly told to not ask questions. I know that Uncle Sid had a tender feeling for Mother, and her situation of having to live with her parents again was of considerable concern to him.

---

[1] Sidney Victor Green, the sixth son, tenth child, of Robert Frederick Green and Louisa Jane Nash Green, was born 17th September 1887, the first at Smiling Valley Farm.

When they were young, he had been her teacher. The boys in that family were required to get an education but the girls were not. There was always homework and as Sid studied in the evenings he would read his lessons aloud and explain to this older sister what he had learned at school. She had a great thirst for knowledge and studied many subjects at home after we came to America. Uncle Sid had been Mother's moral support at the time she learned her fiancé Johnny had drowned.[2] He and Sid had known each other for many years, so he too lost a friend. I do not think that Mother ever really recovered from Johnny's untimely death, although having her brother Sid to lean on helped.

Once he got permission to take Ivy on a trip to the Transkei at a time when transporting fruits and farm produce to market. Today it would be called "therapy," but then it was just plain, good understanding listening by one who cared. The oxen being plodders resulted in the journey's being a six-day round trip, because there was no traveling at night. Oxen had to rest and it was a time of communication with other travelers, a little social event while they were in laager. Uncle Sid taught Mother everything he knew about stars, because farmers knew this knowledge would help when traveling in unfamiliar areas. There were no maps to refer to. Both could have been good meteorologists had they been born in a different place, with a chance of learning.

Several days away from the home environment, talking, studying the stars, and visiting with friends helped Mother more than anyone realized. The bond between brother and sister was forever strengthened.

Now Uncle Sid became busy, in the early evenings and at other times when the garden did not demand his attention, building a house about half a mile from the main farm house. We could have seen it as we sat on the stoep, except the hay barn lay halfway between Grandpa's home and the new one in progress. I was very emphatically forbidden to go there. With all my eavesdropping I could not learn what this new building was to be.

I often saw Uncle Sid washing his feet in a basin on the side stoep, near his bedroom, which had been built on part of the east

---

[2] See Chapter 5.

wall of the house some years after it had been completed. It could be entered only from the outside of the house. One of the three water tanks was situated on this side too. I always asked the same question, "Why are you washing your feet?" He always replied, "I'm going to see my flower, so of course I want to be clean." As soon as he was clean, he would mount his bicycle and ride away.

When I asked Mother what he meant and where he went, she said, "Sid is courting a young lady. He calls her his flower because she is pretty." Now I had a new word to think about. Mother had not explained what "courting" meant.

One evening when I went around to his room, I found Mother there. He was showing her a pretty white dress and white shoes. I heard him say, "I bought this wedding dress for Minnie. She is never permitted to go to town for any shopping. I've already arranged with the pastor to do the marriage ceremony when I can get her to the parsonage."

Another evening after his feet-washing ritual, he dressed up in his best suit. I was surprised to see him get into Grandpa's carriage so, of course, my curiosity abounded. The next morning he came to the house with his new wife, Bertha Kirchoff Green, known as "Minnie." She was the sister of Edith Kirchoff, who was the wife of another brother, Uncle Robert Frederick Green, Jr., called "Rob" for short. He operated a trading post at a place called "Lillyfontein," about three miles away. It was there where many farmers went to pick up the mail that Uncle Sid met his future wife.

As usual I did some eavesdropping and learned that the two had eloped because her parents objected to her marrying. Uncle Sid was saying, "I parked the carriage not too close to the house, and during the day she had placed a ladder at the back of the house. This was all prearranged in case I was not permitted to enter the house. It was her custom to retire to her bedroom early after the evening meal and dishes were done, so it was no problem for her this particular evening. She came down the ladder and we quietly got into the carriage and went on to the parsonage."[3]

Mother laughed. "My word! What would you have done had you been discovered?"

---

[3] Available family records do not include the date of this marriage.

He laughed also. "Well, that never entered my mind. Anyway, the minister's wife helped her get into her new dress and we were married. We drove home in the dark but the horses knew their way.

I had my answer at last as to what he had been building. Later I asked Mother about this situation and she said the objections were not only a matter of religious prejudice, but also the fact her parents did not want her to marry because she was expected to take care of them in their old age.

A year passed, during which I did not see much of Uncle Sid except when he worked in the tool shed. One morning he showed up while we were at breakfast, excited and asking if he could use the carriage. "This is the day!" he said. "I need to drive to the Hill farm to get Mrs. Hill." I perked up my ears and without thinking, blurted out, "May I go with you?"

The adults looked at me, at him, at each other. There seemed to be a silent conversation going on. Expecting a reprimand for asking such a question, I was pleasantly surprised to recognize a mutual consent. Someone said, "It might be best to have her go." Soon the carriage was out and Uncle Sid and I on the seat. He gave a brisk "giddap" and the horses went into action. Down the hill, over the ravine, up the other side, and when we reached the main road leading to the schoolhouse, the pace became swifter. I kept up a chatter, sometimes expressing my happiness at being with him to go on a visit and sometimes asking questions.

I could not understand his silence! He had always given me prompt answers. Had I done something to make him unhappy? Because he was special to me, I finally lapsed into a brooding silence. My joy in the trip began to fade away. Under the circumstances I did not enjoy the lovely sunny morning. The horses turned into the road leading to the Hill Farm. Our arrival was apparently expected because a boy stood at the wide open gate, so Uncle Sid did not need to get down. Mr. Hill had the front door open, saying, "Come in, come in!"

We entered and found Mrs. Hill with her bonnet on, a small portmanteau (suitcase) on the table, into which she was placing baby things, much to my interest. Then we hurried back to the carriage, Uncle telling me to climb into the back while he helped

Mrs. Hill to the front seat where I had been unhappily seated. I felt very much left out and wanted to sit in front too, mainly to overhear anything that was said. In the position I found myself in back, I could not hear their lowered voices.

Again the gate was opened wide for our departure. It did seem that Uncle Sid was urging the horses to go much faster than usual. It was uncomfortable, being jostled as I sat upon the floor boards in this box like section, usually used to carry packages and not little girls.

We arrived at the home farm and, stopping only a moment, Uncle told me to get out and go to the house. The tone of his voice made me realize this was no time for any arguments or questions. Nonetheless, I ran after the vehicle and caught hold of the back board, jumping to place my feet onto the axle and was at his home the same moment he was. My triumph was short lived. He was so busy helping Mrs. Hill down that he did not see Aunt Minnie come onto the stoep but suddenly did see me. Then he whirled around as she moaned and sat down on the step.

Never before or after did he ever speak so sharply to me. "Go home at once!" Turning to Auntie, he said, "Darling, shouldn't you be in bed?" I walked home slowly and sadly, pondering his strange behavior and wondering why he thought Auntie should be in bed when it was not even lunch time yet.

After lunch he came onto the stoep where we were sitting, very happy, smiling and saying over and over, "It's a boy! It's a boy!"[4] Even Grandpa smiled and I learned then that boys were very important to a farmer who needed sons to help and to carry on the farm later.

While the adults were all talking, I quietly escaped and ran as fast as I could to Uncle's house and, without knocking, walked into the bedroom. Mrs. Hill was just putting a little shirt on Harry and also a bandage on his tummy. She had not seen me and was startled when I asked, "Oh, how did he hurt his tummy?"

Silence. I looked at Aunt Minnie and asked, "Where did the baby come from?" Silence again. Then I happened to notice that

---

[4] This may be Harry Green whose birth date is not in available family records.

she had her hands folded over her bedspread at her middle. "Oh, Auntie, are you sick? You had such a big tummy and now you are flat." That observation from a nine-year-old[5] was more than Mrs. Hill could cope with. She said very sternly, "You are a cheeky little girl! Go home right now!" I knew she meant it and left.

Again I walked slowly, pondering about adults and why they acted so strangely. I remembered how I had received two different answers when I asked about where baby brother had come from, nearly three years before. In those days, matters of intimacy were never discussed and children were not informed.

Uncle Sid committed his whole life to his family, to the garden with its requirements of pruning, grafting, spraying, and the tender care of his fruit trees. His dream was to graft until an apple tree produced two, three, or even four varieties of fruit. He achieved that dream far more than expected, for his experiments were very successful. It was a source of family pride when he proudly showed us one tree with four varieties of apples.

Grandpa was very proud of this son's accomplishments. They were of the same mind when it came to fruit growing. They had the same daring and willingness for hard, tedious work, meeting disappointment agreeably and going forward with hope for "better luck next time." The other two uncles did their work well, but were not totally dedicated to fruit culture.

Sid was my favorite uncle simply because he treated me almost as an equal, not as a child. He often took me to the garden with him and many a free lesson in horticulture was expounded. Unfortunately this did not influence my way of life, and the instruction was not assimilated. Perhaps, if fate had not caused Mother and us children to leave for the United States, life would have found me even more influenced by this uncle.

Near the house was a large workshop wherein all the farm tools were kept when not in use. Here the sickles and scythes were hanging on the wall till harvest time, all clean and sharpened and shining. Other tools were in their right places. All repairs were

---

[5] That would place the date of the story in 1918.

done in this space; harness, ox yokes, wagon wheels, and anything else that needed to be repaired. A large work bench had an anvil, a vise, a large emery wheel, all of which I became acquainted with and knew their reason for being in the shop, simply by watching the way they were used. All three uncles were adept at any of the tasks that had to be done here. Off the main room, large enough to become a dance hall for special occasions, was a large bedroom where the two younger uncles slept and kept their personal belongings.

I liked to go there, especially evenings when they all would play their musical instruments. Clem usually had one of his four harmonicas, or mouth harp, Len had his Jew's harp and Uncle Sid his concertina. Occasionally Mother would play the accordion or she would dance with one of her brothers. They had good times together and all seemed to be very harmonious with one another.

One day Uncle Sid, holding a small board in a vise, was sharpening long nails that he had driven through it. The board, about five inches wide and six to eight inches long, was filled with the nails he was filing to a fine point. "Why are you doing that?" I asked. "I'm making a trap to put in the navel garden by the banana plants. Bananas will soon be ready to harvest and the blacks often steal them. This is to teach them a lesson not to steal."

Wide-eyed, I looked at him. "How do you do that?" He glanced down at me, then said, "Ask your mother if you can go with me to the navel garden and I'll show you." Consent was given and I happily walked beside him, wondering what a navel garden was and what a banana plant looked like. We walked down hall toward the river, then about a mile alongside the river before going up an incline about half a mile. Soon the fragrance of orange blossoms wafted toward us.

"Are we going to see oranges again?" I took a big breath. I loved the smell of the blossoms. "Yes," said Uncle Sid. "Navels are large oranges and very sweet. They do much better on a hillside with more sun, just as the bananas do. They too like sunshine. Navels are a special orange and this is Grandpa's prize garden." He reached up to pick an orange, then peeled it to show me the navel, and handed me a portion of the fruit which I promptly began to eat.

"Good, isn't it?"

Remembering how Mother showed us how to eat oranges, I leaned over so the juice would not drip down my chin. "Um–" was all I could say, nodding vigorously. Uncle Sid went on, "These are sweeter than the other oranges. Here are the banana plants." He was standing beside a plant that was not a tree nor a bush. I walked over and stood beside him.

I pointed to an odd looking flower, purple and green in color. "What is that?"

"That is the banana flower." Gently he touched it. "See how this little finger pushes upward? When the flower begins to fade, the little bananas, called fingers, begin to grow. Here is a big bunch that will soon be ready for cutting. See how the fruit grows upward?" He pointed to a big, heavy looking bunch, quite long. Then he indicated a section of this bunch and said, "This is what we call a 'hand' when it is cut off the main stem. We cut the bunches off at the top and put them in that shed over there. He pointed to a small building nearby. "They begin to ripen, but before they are too ripe, we get them ready to market. We have special knives to cut them down. We use long gloves to protect our hands and arms because sometimes a big, hairy spider, a tarantula, might be in the bunch. If we disturb him he can bite and this is very painful."

He turned. "Come along with me to the river." He pointed to slender tree. "See that broken bush next to that tree?" I nodded. "That tells me the blacks are already watching the bananas, so we will fix them." Using the heavy rake he took from the little shed, he began to rake the soil from the river edge to the closest banana plant. He seemed to measure the distance before placing the trap. He dug a long shallow trench, then placed the board with the sharpened nails upward, lightly covering it with soil.

"Now watch closely." He then proceeded to rake an area where no banana plants were and covered an area along the river bank for some distance. He looked at me and smiled. I said nothing. "I raked all that area because I want the blacks to think I have just been working. I do not want them to be suspicious. We will move to the next tree and repeat all this. Come along."

I followed silently to observe him set another trap and carefully cover it, raking the surrounding area. I watched in silent wonder as these sharpened nail traps were placed at other trees close to likely crossing places at the river edge. When he had completed his task, Uncle Sid exclaimed with some satisfaction, "Well that's done and when the black comes looking for free bananas, he is apt to keep his eye on the plant, perhaps looking around to see if any white man is in the area, and not look where he steps.

"But Uncle! That will hurt his feet!" I exclaimed.

"Exactly! That is the purpose of the trap. He must learn not to steal or he will have to pay the price. I'm sure you will never come here alone, but if you should, remember to look where you walk."

I thought this extremely cruel. Later I wondered if the black would be smart enough to use his big stick or his "knobkerrie," which a Xhosa usually carried, and press it in the ground ahead of him. I never knew, but because I, a child, could think of that precaution, surely an adult would.

Only once in those five years on the farm did I ever overhear a discussion about one of the "black devils" putting his foot in the wrong place. I still cringe just thinking about it.

All the years of using sprays to keep his fruit trees in good shape finally took its toll on Uncle Sid's skin. Toward the last of his useful life, skin cancers appeared on his face, hands, and forearms. He took his first plane ride to Cape Town in the company of a hospital nurse to enter him at Groot Schuur Hospital for treatment, when nothing could be done for him locally. He had several operations and skin grafts that were successful. He died 24th May 1974 and thus once again joined his "flower" who had preceded him[6] in this final journey we all can and do expect. Most of his eighty-seven years of life was spent on the Smiling Valley Farm to which he devoted his total energies.

---

[6] Bertha Wilhelmina "Minnie" Kraemer Green died 25th November 1962.

Chapter 12

To Market

One morning the adults were discussing the day's work and getting ready for market. As usual children were to be seen and not heard, but it was difficult for me to keep silent. As soon as I could get away from the table I asked Mother if I could go to the garden and watch. She said she would take both Jessie and me after lunch. It seemed a long time to wait, but at the appointed time we went hand in hand and en route Mother pointed out some poisonous plants that we were never to touch. She also showed us some edible roots we could eat raw. Mother had learned these things in her girlhood and also on her trek to the Transkei when she went on transport with her brothers. During the drought season, one could survive in the veld if one had the knowledge of the edible roots. Jessie and I eventually became quite adept at finding these, but when one does not use the knowledge, it is soon forgotten.

We began to hear voices long before we arrived at the garden. I was surprised to see many more blacks than usual and learned these were extra helpers during the harvesting time. It happened to be an especially good harvest and the uncles were eager to take a large load to the city market. Some of the black men were picking apples and others were working in the orange groves. Steady streams of women were going to the packing shed with baskets of fruit on their heads, then returning to the pickup point, still carrying these baskets the same way. It was the custom never to carry things in the hands. Trained from childhood, the women were able to walk for miles with large loads in this manner. In addition, they carried heavy sticks for protection against any animal that might charge, for killing snakes, or for protection from some strange man they might meet en route. When their hands were free, the women were more in command of any situation than would be the case if they carried the loads in their hands.

Uncle Len was packing the citrus fruits, while Uncle Sid was placing apples in the boxes. These were one-layer boxes, used repeatedly after being emptied from the wagon at market time. Boxes for rail transportation were larger, held more and were covered. Both uncles were adept at their appointed tasks, and between them they kept a young black man working at top speed to remove filled boxes and place them on the dolly, a low, flat wheeled frame which, when loaded, was moved out to where the wagon was. The latter would then take another dolly into the shed to be loaded while two other blacks loaded the wagon. These men had worked at these tasks for so long they knew what to do without being repeatedly instructed. In fact, they had grown up with the uncles!

Oranges were stacked on one side of the wagon, while apples were placed on the other. In the front center, boxes of other fruits were stacked. The center rear half of the wagon bed was left for farm produce which would be loaded last. All boxes were then roped into place so that the loads would not shift in transit. This method expedited the unloading at the market and saved time in arrangements. The routine of picking, carrying, packing, and loading went on and on, with no time to chat or pass the time of day. We watched for a short time, then Mother suggested that we go for a walk to see what else was happening and especially see if the cherry-guavas were ripe. These had red colored skins covering the white flesh, with tiny seeds in the center. They were delicious! Grandpa had planted a few trees some years earlier, especially for the grandchildren. The trees were not tall, so it was easy for children to reach the fruits, which were the size of cherries, (hence the name) but they tasted like guavas.

For a time we watched the black women walking back and forth. Smiling, many spoke to Mother, who returned their smiles, but with none did she have lengthy conversations. Finally Mother said, "I think we had better leave while it is so busy. Let's go see what Uncle Clem is doing in the vegetable garden."

We turned homeward. The vegetable garden was near the house. Again we heard voices but here was more laughter. Only the black women worked in this area. Some picked peas and beans while others uprooted the carrots, beets and turnips. The root vegetables were then taken to two women who washed them carefully and grouped them in bunches of a dozen or two, tying them with special reeds that were soaking in water so they would be pliable. The workers all seemed to know what to do. Mother said these women, too, had been working for Grandpa many years. Uncle Clem was busy going from one place to another since he was in charge. He liked to handle the produce better than he did the orchard fruits.

Whenever there was such a gathering, there was a jovial attitude with some singing intersprersed with the chatter. As the women walked back and forth, their feet kept time to their singing. This was a natural part of their life-style. Their red-blanket skirts were wrapped securely around their waists. The young women were bare breasted, but the older women usually had their collars of bead-work large enough to cover the bosom. All the women wore these bead necklaces, anklets, and bracelets, which they were so adept at creating, some of which were quite intricate in design.

Older women often had infants strapped onto their backs. These babies were used to spending days close to the mother's body. They were all handsome women with flawless skins, shining black eyes and gleaming white teeth. As they had bean trained to carry loads on their heads, they had graceful bodies and a rhythm to their walking. They also were taught from childhood how to wash their mouths and carefully' brush their gums with a finger after eating. I've seen many a man and woman doing this. They ate simply and never needed contact with a dentist in those days; simple people, living simple lives, not as yet contaminated by white man's way of eating. Most of all, they never hurried! This style of carefree living has changed. Living in cities, partaking of different foods and drinking soft drinks and, at times, more potent liquids, has brought need for dentists.

I noticed one young woman kept pointing at Uncle Clem, then touching her head as she spoke to one of the workers. I asked Mother why, and she said she was a new worker, having recently married into that family, and probably had never seen a person over six feet tall, especially one with red hair. Uncle Clement George Green[1] was six feet four, very thin, and his well-trimmed mustache matched the hair. He also had a pronounced limp from a birth defect.

Toward evening we could hear the singing women as they came toward the house, bringing the vegetables, the wash tubs and their other containers. These were set down in the area from whence they would be loaded onto the wagon which arrived soon. The men lifted the vegetable containers into place and then they all stood around, chatting and laughing.

After conferring with Sid and Clem, Grandpa came out of the house and paid each one his or her wage. The men were given some tobacco, in addition to the money, and the women were given sugar. Both these items were expected and were considered part of the wages. While they were good, dependable, and loyal workers, they were uneducated and could not accept anything other than a daily wage. Soon all went to their kraals, about a mile from the house, to the area allotted them just below the main road. We watched them singing and laughing as they went. Their obvious joy in living made an impression on me and often the mental picture returns.

Grannie had been busy in her dairy, forming butter during the week into the shapes of her choosing. The dairy building, rather small, had thick walls made of mud and a thatched roof, so it was cool at all times. The eggs were kept there and they were in special containers to be loaded also. Grannie would cut her flowers for market early in the morning so they could be as fresh as possible. Her contributions to the family project were the last items loaded, usually when the oxen were being yoked and the uncles were about ready to take their places on the seat for driving.

Because it had been a long day after an early rising, it was early to bed for everyone. I was excited to be a part of all this, my first time of seeing how getting ready for market progressed. I

---

[1] Clement George Green was the 13th child, the eighth son, of Robert Frederick Green and Louisa Jane Nash Green and the fourth to be born at Smiling Valley Farm.

thought it would be impossible to sleep but the next thing I knew Mother was gently calling my name. It was time to get up and dress. Family members were all at the breakfast table and the black men who were to go with the wagon were outdoors eating the food Grannie gave them. It was her custom to provide food for these men when they went to the city on days like this. By the time the uncles were finished with breakfast, the young black men had the oxen ready and were at their places.

The two younger uncles, Clem and Len, were going this time. They rotated usually but always two went on these trips. They sat on the seat which also served as a tool box and contained other things that might be needed on a trek. Standing outdoors in the cool of the morning just at daybreak, the family watched Uncle Clem crack the whip and call the names of the lead oxen, followed by names of the others, as the lead black man took the riems from the horns of the front oxen. Although the lead oxen were the most intelligent and thus were chosen for this trait, the pair of oxen closest to the wagon were chosen for their strength, because this strength would be needed nearest the load. This time twelve pairs were pulling. It was a thrilling sight to see these almost perfectly matched red animals with the large curved horns take the white-sailed covered wagon down the hill, over the ravine, up the other side, and along to the schoolhouse, where they turned right and out of sight.

Uncle Sid told me the reason for careful selection of these draft oxen was because they, like people, got along better with one than they did with another. He added, "Some oxen can be hitched to another, like a marriage, and others must remain apart. They each have a personality."

Grandpa was very proud of his "Africander" breed of cattle, one of several different breeds. I was fearful of these as the horns were sharply pointed, yet they were docile animals if they were well treated and cared for.

Grannie and Mother both told me later that my Aunt Florence was very fond of these cattle and often, after playing out in the veld, would come home sometimes riding on the back of one. She often sent part of her clothing home, one bloomer leg over one horn and the other leg on the second horn. She did not like to

be confined with clothing! No matter how often scolded, she continued this method of sending her bloomers home. Mother said it
was amusing at first but Grannie became very unhappy with her
young daughter for being so immodest.

Many of the farmers lost large numbers of their herds, if not
all, from a cattle disease called "rinderpest."[2] It started in the far
north of Africa in Somaliland in 1889, then progressed slowly
southward, reaching Rhodesia in 1896. At this point, South Africa, especially through the government of Cape Colony, took re-
strictions to prevent the disease from spreading into this area. All
railroad travellers and their baggage had to be rigorously disinfected when arriving at the frontier. All baggage, regardless of
contents, had to be placed in airtight corrugated containers, sealed
and fumigated for thirty minutes. Passengers had to lie back and
extend their legs while an individual with a bucket of chloride of
lime and water swabbed the soles of their boots. Each passenger
received a ticket indicating "disinfected" that had to be shown on
demand.

Many a farmer, including Grandpa Green, lost much in the
way of finances when his cattle died from this, meaning thereby
no meat and no transport animals. It also created great hardship in
replacing stock, which had to be shipped in from other countries.
The veterinarians were finally able to formulate an inoculation
that stemmed the tide. The hardship on the black people was greater
as they had no means to have their cattle replaced. They, too, depended on these animals for food. Most of all, they lost their sta-
tus symbol, because the cattle represented their wealth.

---

[2] *South Africa Yearbook*, 1938, pgs 503-4: "In spite of these and other
more serious precautions, this rinderpest succeeded in sweeping through
Cape Colony and inflicted a loss of nearly 40% of the total number of
cattle there, besides putting the Cape Government into a heavy financial
loss. Rinderpest may be described as an eruptive fever of a most
destructive type, somewhat resembling in appearance smallpox in human
beings. The actual cause is described as an organism of a globular shape,
gradually lengthening into a bacillus and communicable in a variety of
ways, but not by means of the atmosphere."

Chapter 13

My Education

Mother was my first teacher. My sixth birthday found me the proud possessor of a slate, pencils, ABC Book, and a counting board called an abacus. These were all new ideas to me. Mother explained that, as I would attend school when I was seven, I must learn my ABC's and she would teach me to read. She also explained that the use of the abacus was to teach me how to count and do sums. Because there were no kindergartens, it was customary for parents to teach their children the basics: how to print and letters of the alphabet, how to spell simple words and how to add and subtract.

I knew where the schoolhouse, a mile and a half away, was because we could see the building from the stoep and, of course, we had passed it from time to time as we went some place. I did not know what we would learn or who would be there. Mother tried to explain that it was a place where children learned many things. Then she named several cousins I had already met who would be going. I liked these cousins, so I was satisfied. If I thought about school at all after that, my feelings were that it would be fun, a play time. How different that first day in the real school would be.

Now we sat down at the dining room table for an hour each afternoon. The ABC Book was first and Mother went through this, showing me pictures and pointing out the letters. She explained how those letters were formed and how words were made from them. Patiently, she taught me to print both the letters and the numbers.

---

[1] 4th January, 1915.

My greatest enjoyment was the use of the abacus. It was fun to put the little beads in place and to do sums, as Mother termed it. There were six wires, representing lines; the wooden colored beads were moved to do the adding. I was pleased when she would praise me. I learned quickly. I am sure that part of my enjoyment was the fact that Mother was giving me her undivided attention, something she had not done in two years. By the time my seventh birthday arrived,[2] I was well versed in the basic fundamentals; I could read simple sentences and I could spell.

At last that first big day arrived. I was proud of my pretty white dress and I carried the sack that held my lunch and the school bag that held pencils, slate, and books. As I had never walked any distance unattended, for the first fifteen months I would have an escort going to and coming from school. Twombie, a tall, slim, fourteen year-old very black girl would be with me each morning and late afternoon. She lived at the end of the road that led into the Schultz Farm. Grandpa Green had allotted Twombie's parents a small portion in this area where they had their five rondevals to house their large family, with space to raise a small vegetable garden. Many younger children herded the assorted cattle and goats and cared for the dogs, cats and fowls. Twombie, when younger, had herded her parents' cattle and she also knew how to kill snakes with the big stick she always carried. Because there were no bulls grazing in the area where we walked, we had no fear of any cattle attacking us.

She and I had good times during those walks and we laughed a lot. We tried to teach each other our respective language by pointing to a tree, a flower, a stone, or whatever, and then speaking the proper words. We would go into gales of laughter because I could not make the correct clicking sounds so much a part of the Bantu language.

In March of 1917 Twombie told Mother she was to be married and could not be with me any more. After fifteen months I was no longer afraid of the cattle and we had had no problem with snakes. Also, Rover, our black dog, had begun to go with me and always seemed to know when it was time to be at school for my

---

[2] 4th January, 1916.

return. I enjoyed Rover and was very sad when he died of poisoned meat put out by a neighboring farmer to kill jackals that had been eating his sheep.

But now it was my first day of school. Twombie was very much a part of my life. I was sorry to see her leave me that day and would have been even more sorry had I known that first day would be such a disaster! It was not at all the play time I had anticipated. My cousins would not speak to me during the school hours, because this was forbidden. I was ignored when I spoke, until Mr. Rankillor, the teacher, finally scolded me. I was terribly embarrassed to have him reprimand me in front of the thirteen other pupils, many of them my cousins.

I had observed that, when these fellow pupils were called to the teacher's desk for their recitation period, they stood in front of him. He asked questions and they answered. My name was called in mid-afternoon. As I was the youngest and the only new pupil, I faced him all alone. He explained that this was a spelling and reading session during which I would spell a word and then read it. He began turning pages on the easel, showing me pictures of farm scenes such as animals, garden produce, and others. Finally, he turned the pages back and asked me to spell the words to which he pointed. I was getting tired by this time and wanted to go home. When he turned to a page on which a little girl was sitting on a bench looking at a cat in front of her, I saw only a rat peeking out from a home in the corner.

"Spell this," pointing to the cat. With my eyes on the rat, I spelled, "R-a-t."

"No! Spell 'cat'"

Again I spelled "r-a-t," this time with more emphasis. He began getting annoyed and I, more perverse. I was impudent in my manner and persistent in spelling "r-a-t."

"Go stand in that corner!" He pointed to the end of the room. I promptly went to my desk and sat down. By this time he was angry. He followed me, bodily lifted me, and placed me in the corner. "Now stand there until I tell you to sit down!"

I did not know what to think of this very unexpected development. Many new feelings were surging through me. What would Mother think of my misbehaving on my first day? Should I tell her? If I did not, she would learn either from the teacher or a cousin. I knew she would be very unhappy with me. I was in a dilemma. I decided I would tell her myself.

I was so ashamed! How could I turn around and face the pupils? I had never before been punished like this. Slowly tears began to flow. I do not know how long I stood there until at last the teacher came and took me by the hand. As he led me back to my seat, neither of us said a word. I glanced around but no one seemed to be noticing so I felt better.

Mother had told me that I would be sitting at a long bench attached to an equally long, low desk. "All new pupils sit at that desk," she had said. "I did for the two weeks I went to school. Then my father found out and forbade me to go. He insisted that education for girls was not necessary, as they would learn all household duties from their mothers. According to him, it was a waste of money sending girls to school." As I sat at this desk, which had spaces for eight children, I kept wondering in which place Mother had sat. I looked to my right and saw all those empty places. I knew that the other pupils all had separate desks. I felt very lonely.

My back was to the rest of the room and all I could see was the blank wall in front of me and the teacher at his desk to the left. That desk stood at an angle to the corner, with a window just behind him. Farther along the wall was one other window. Both windows looked out upon the school playground. In the corner to my right was a space filled with hanging coats or jackets and even lunch pails. Opposite that was the supply cabinet and between these was the door, the only entrance to the room. Just inside of the door was a crude bench holding a water pail with a long-handled dipper and a wash basin. I wanted to turn around and look at the far wall behind me, but I dared not move. On that wall, I had already learned, were maps that interested me greatly because I had never seen any before. And in the corner nearby was my disgrace where I had just stood.

At last the day was over and Twombie saw me home. I burst into tears in Mother's arms while blurting out my awful first day. She held me tightly as she soothed me, saying, "Oh, my dear little Edna, don't cry. Tomorrow will be a brighter day. I just know it will!" Her arms and voice were comforting and I soon stopped crying. Tomorrow was a brighter day, but I never forgot that terrible first day.

After that everything went along pretty well until three months later when we had another new pupil whom I tried to make welcome. Albert (last name forgotten) was very thin and an extremely shy boy. When I tried to show him the lesson, he became red-faced, especially after the teacher told me to sit down and behave. His mother and mine were good friends, both born on the same day in the same year. I never recalled seeing Albert before, even though we had visited in his home. I presume that he, being so shy, just made himself busy elsewhere when visitors arrived.

The teacher had placed Albert three spaces below me. As the day progressed I liked the idea of his being there and decided to sit closer. As I slid over he kept moving down. Finally, there was nowhere for him to move, unless he sat on the floor. He became fidgety and his face turned so red that the teacher became aware of Albert's problems. Mr. Rankillor told me to move back to my own space, but I did not obey him instantly. He became angry and left his desk in a hurry. He lifted me bodily and moved me back to where I belonged, setting me down roughly. Because he had put me down on my dress, which I always lifted to hang over the seat, I became rebellious and began squirming. I did not want that dress wrinkled! Our battle of wills ended at last when he realized why I was being naughty. He let me straighten out my dress and I never again crowded Albert. During recess Cousin Ivy[2] told me quietly that it was not ladylike to behave like that. One must always try to be a lady. I think this bit of advice did me more good than the teacher's reprimands.

Albert was the fifteenth pupil in the class. Later, four more of his cousins attended. They were not related to me, but at that time I did have seven cousins in school, making this sort of a family affair school. The fathers of all had attended the same school, all except for my own father.

After my eighth month, we had another beginning pupil. Herbert, Albert's cousin, was fair-haired and a bit on the chubby side, as well as being very out-going. I did not crowd him off the seat as I had Albert. I quickly became aware of him as a person,

---

[3] Ivy Sonnenberger.

not just another boy. He was the first love of my life, and it seemed to be a mutual feeling. As we went in the same general direction homeward, our friendship grew. After Twombie left to be married, I used to walk that extra half mile to the gate where Herbert's father's farm was separated from that of my grandpa's.

This amused my uncles greatly. I did not know that they sometimes watched us through their binoculars, especially on the few rainy days when it was too muddy to work in the garden. On one particular day, when it was raining extra hard, Mother decided it was too wet for me to attend school. She thought the ravine might flood and I could not get across to come home. I had other ideas. I always insisted on wearing my nice white dress, so Mother provided an umbrella. As was to be expected, all the other children, who had twice the distance to walk compared to me, failed to show up, all except Herbert! The teacher sent us home. As we left school, hand in hand, I discovered the road was very slippery. Herbert tried to hold me up but suddenly down I went. Oh, my beautiful white dress, now all wet and muddy! I tried not to cry in my distress and shame. Herbert struggled to get me to my feet.

He was barefooted and used to walking on the wet earth. I was wearing my shoes. Finally he suggested that I take them off and carry them, then I could walk on the grass down my usual route and not walk to the end of that road. I followed his advice, feeling relieved to escape the situation. When I arrived home I found a sympathetic mother and a gleeful group of uncles! They teased me unmercifully as they related all they had witnessed via the field glasses. I had so many mixed feelings I could not even cry. Fickle female that I was, this episode sort of cooled my ardor for Herbert. I was embarrassed for a long time by the whole situation.

Our daily school procedure began when the teacher rang the bell at 8:30 a.m. and we pupils all went to our seats. When he came into the classroom, our greeting was always, "Good morning, Mr. Rankillor." His living quarters were under the same roof that covered the school section. He would greet us then begin reading a few words of scripture and elucidating upon this. We all then sang *Praise God From Whom All Blessings Flow*. Our school day had begun.

Class divisions were called "standards," not "grades," as is the African custom. When a child completed the sixth standard, the education received was equivalent to most American high schools and one was then ready for college work.

Beginning with the first standard pupils, the several classes would take their turns at the teacher's desk, turning in their homework. The teacher would glance at this quickly to see that the work was neat and clean. Untidy homework he refused. He would then record this in a notebook that became a permanent record. Our assignments for the next evening's work would be noted at the end of each section of homework and the notebook returned to us before the school day ended. All work assigned after receiving the notebooks was done on our slates and would be presented at recitation time. Everyone in the six standards did this.

Each day began at 8:30 a.m. in the summer and spring months, with a 3:30 p.m. dismissal. In the winter months we started half an hour earlier and left for home at 3 p.m. Some children had from three to five miles to walk each way, meaning it was dark when they left for school and again when they arrived home. The four cousins of Albert and Herbert, who had to walk five miles, came on horseback in the winter months. Our lunch times were almost an hour long, too long as we had nothing special to do. We all brought our lunches and sometimes we would exchange food.

Often Cousin Cyril[3] and I quite innocently would start teasing one another. This eventually would end in a quarrel, sometimes in a knockdown fight. Although it was usually in fun, occasionally one or the other of us would become really angry. Then it became a fight in earnest. We actually were very good friends and often got into much mischief together, but at school we had this battle almost every lunch hour.

One lunch time Mr. Rankillor came out early and saw Cyril and me rolling on the ground. He grabbed hold of each of us and marched us into his living room. His lecture about our being ruffians made us both ashamed and thereafter we behaved as we were supposed to. I do not recall all that he said, but I do remember his comments made me feel very small. This was a good lesson for both of us.

During one recitation period, standing where I could look

[4] Cyril Sonnenberger.

out of the window and see some of the children playing, I noticed Cyril suddenly stand on his left foot, with a snake dangling from the uplifted right foot. I gasped and interrupted the teacher, telling him what was happened. I started to say more but he didn't wait. He grabbed the heavy stick used for this purpose and rushed out, killing the snake and taking Cyril to his private quarters. He then came to the schoolroom door and asked our cousin Sam[5] to take Cyril to the Smiling Valley Farm.

As the two boys left the schoolyard, Mr. Rankillor took from his pocket a small mirror and began signalling toward home. Because there were no telephones in that area then, mirror signals were the only means of quick communication. We soon saw signals being returned. Finally the teacher put the mirror in his pocket and turned, a signal for us who were watching through the door to rush back to our seats. When he came in he must have been surprised to see us all so busily engaged with our books.

When I reached home after school, Cyril was still with Mother, his foot in a permanganate solution to prevent infection. The crystals had turned the water a deep purple. Mother had cut the area between his big toe and the next, sucking out the poison and then spitting it out. She was always the person to do the emergency treatments. Cyril had been bitten by a small puff adder, a venomous snake that puffs up when irritated. They usually flip backward when attacking. The young ones are as venomous as the mature puff adders and all are a "vaal" color, the color of the dry sands in that area.

Later he said, "Aunt Ivy had everything ready when I got there. Teacher had given me a good drink of whiskey, so by the time I arrived and Aunt Ivy cut my toe. I didn't feel a thing." He seemed to be very proud of the fact that he did not cry, but he did not feel very good afterwards for quite a while.

Once, after an overnight stay with the Hill children and en route to school, I was nearly bitten by a puff adder. Fortunately, the older boy John knew the tricks of these snakes and always walked behind his three siblings. I happened to be behind the three when suddenly I felt the sharp edge of a ruler against my leg. Wrathfully, I turned and demanded to know why he hit me. He just

---

[5] Sydney Samuel Sonnenberger.

pointed to a mature puff adder writhing on the ground. "Oh!" I cried, clapping my hands over my mouth and backed away. I felt creepy all over. I don't ever remember that I even thanked him. This was my only personal encounter with one of those deadly creatures.

One afternoon the teacher said he was going to show us how to play a new American game called baseball. He showed us the bat and ball and then explained how the game was played around a "diamond." All the children, myself included, entered into this with enthusiasm. Unfortunately, it was the only time we ever played that game. Apparently, enthusiastic children told some parents who objected to paying for education that was wasted on foreign games. I have often wondered how Mr. Rankillor felt, considering that none of the cost of this equipment came from family pockets! The playground was certainly not adapted to the English game of rickets or bowls.

The only event, thereafter, that was fun was a school picnic on Saturday. We ran races for prizes; gunnysack races, three-legged races, and one event in which each racer held an egg on a table-spoon, running to a goal while trying to keep the egg from tumbling off the spoon. I won one prize, a sewing basket that was labelled "made in Japan." I wondered what "Japan" meant and did not value the basket as I was never domestically inclined.

We attended school eleven months of the year, having ten days' holiday at Easter and ten days again at Christmas, with an extra free day in commemoration of Queen Victoria's Day, 24th May and upon the occasion of Guy Fawkes Day, 5th November.

One morning Mr. Rankillor told us there was to be an eclipse of the sun that day. He then gave us a short lecture about eclipses and how they occurred and he promised we could have time out to look at it. He then gave us some exposed film and a few pieces of smoked glass and cautioned us to look at the sun only through one of these or we might go blind. This all sounded very mysterious and exciting. We were surprised, though very pleased, when Mother and Aunt Libby arrived. They too were going to watch this phenomena. Actually, it was not all that exciting, but we all enjoyed the few minutes free from the usual curriculum. Having visitors added to our enjoyment. It was indeed a rare treat when any mother came to the school.

The winds often blew hot, and one day an east wind from the Indian Ocean was blowing harder than usual, bringing in "yellow sails," or yellow sands from the beaches. The teacher evidently thought this was a good time to talk about trees and how they could break the wind near a building. He explained about trees that grew fast and about those that grew slowly, showing us pictures of trees unfamiliar to our area. He then showed us some packets of seeds, explaining that trees called Lombardy poplars could grow from these particular seeds and make a good windbreak. "Because we have no trees around the school, what do you think of planting some?" asked Mr. Rankillor. "The seeds will grow fast and trees from them will be tall and slim so we can plant them quite close together." We all looked at each other. We were not used to being asked an opinion. Adults in our lives usually made the decisions. Freddie Bauer, being the oldest boy in the school, finally said he thought it was a good idea. Then there was much discussion.

When the teacher asked the bigger boys to go with him, the rest of us did not know what to make this. Some of us watched out of the door and we soon saw the boys reappear with rakes, hoes and shovels. I was surprised, because I did not know there was such a thing in the shed in back, a shed that was always kept locked. We were further astonished when Mr. Rankillor asked us all, even the small children, to go out into the yard. There he handed us each a small packet of seeds and explained his plan. We listened with more and more interest.

He evidently had planned everything carefully the previous evening, because he had marked off a long row, divided into sections, with string near the fence. We listened to his instructions and drew numbered lots, which meant that number one was to choose space first, and so on, until all the spaces had been allotted. We each had about six feet of space in which to till the soil and plant the seeds. The larger children knew how to do this, of course, as all were farm children, but I had never done anything like it. We had to take turns using the shovels and rakes before planting the seeds. The teacher had placed nearby watering cans that the big boys kept filled from the big water tank and we used those to sprinkle our seeds once they were planted.

My dress did not stay white long. We were dirty but happy

after we finished this very unexpected project. After all this was completed, we went back into the schoolroom where it was hard to get back to studying again. Before we settled down Mr. Rankillor said, "This is an adventure for all of you in actual production. Each of you is to be responsible for your own little trees; you are to keep the seeds watered and then the plants. They will eventually have to be thinned so that the trees will have space in which to develop."

We all avidly watched for the first tiny plants to appear. It was a great thrill when the actual trees began to take form. After a few weeks we began to thin them out to make room for those left, and every tiny seedling pulled up was planted along the fence. I attended that school long enough to see those trees become all of six feet tall. It was a joy to all of us.

En route home one afternoon, I decided to step off the beaten path and investigate a nice shadowy area I had noticed earlier. I was alone, as Twombie had left and our dog Rover had died, but the family thought I was responsible enough to go back and forth without needing an escort. Jessie had not reached age seven[6] so was not attending school. I was pleasantly surprised to find a pool of water in this shadowy area. There was a scooped out indentation in a reddish rock formation. It was filled with shallow water, probably from the recent rain. I was always interested to look deep into any water so I sat down to see what might be swimming around. It was so pleasantly quiet that I sat there a long time. I felt a soothing atmosphere and became dreamy and seemed to be in another dimension of thought. I thought I was listening to someone or something. Suddenly I was very thirsty. Without even thinking about results, I cupped my hands and caught up enough water to drink. Then I became aware of a shadow and looked up into the staring eyes of a red-faced cow. She had been drinking also because water was dripping from her mouth. We seemed to look at each other at the same time, I began moving slowly away just as she began to urinate into the pool.

I don't remember whether I ever told Mother I had been drinking from this pool, but it was not long before I became ill with typhoid fever. Since I had periodic attacks of malaria, Mother

---

[6] This dates the story to the end of 1917 or early 1918.

marked the days of illness and recuperation on a calendar. It would usually take two to three weeks for me to run through a cycle.

After a long stay at home, it was good to get back to school again. My favorite recitations were in mental arithmetic and in poetry. I enjoyed the verbal work. It was important to me to be quicker with replies than the three boys in this class with me. We four would stand before the teacher, doing sums mentally as he verbally gave us addition, subtraction, multiplication, and division. We all had to be alert, because we could give answers only when his pointer was toward us. This was excellent training to think on our feet. We also learned much poetry, and again recitations were given as he pointed to us. We all enjoyed the poetry and felt equally important when none of us missed a word.

This same procedure was the norm for all classes in all the standards. Beginning with the third standard, we had more subjects. Grammar is an example; we were drilled and drilled in grammar. We were also drilled well in spelling. The fourth standard brought us our next major subject, geography. What agony it was for the three boys to draw a full map of Africa, especially when all the several countries had to be placed properly. I was guilty of helping them cheat in this because they floundered so much. I would trade slates quickly with the boy next to me, draw his map, a bit more carelessly than mine, and return it to him. In time the boys got the idea that "she will do it" and I ended up trading slates until all four maps actually were my drawing. This was not wise nor good policy. I often wondered how they managed after I left that school. Map drawing would be one of the things they would have to present to the Inspector!

Because it was expected and accepted, no one ever complained about homework. As we advanced in the standards we had more subjects to study so we had more to write at home. Most of the pupils automatically did this homework right after supper, using the family table, Not I! I did mine in a tree.

Working in the tree, however, proved to be disastrous after I began using pen and ink. My first dilemma was in holding onto the bottle of ink as I climbed the tree. Then keeping my balance while opening the bottle was hard, and closing it without spilling any and thus ruining my writing was impossible. Spots appeared.

The page was so messy I rewrote the lesson twice but it was still untidy work. I had to present it as it was, I dared not remove more pages as Mother had to pay for all things used and she would notice a too-thin notebook.

When we entered his domain, Mr. Rankillor had total authority, even to spanking us if necessary. Cyril got the cane over his bottom at least three times a week. Poor Cyril would receive two, three, and sometimes five whacks of the quince stick, depending upon what rule he had broken. He was very brave and never once cried while in front of us, though sometimes I noticed he hid his face behind his slate or a book. Because Mr. Rankillor was such a stern disciplinarian, it was with fear and trembling I presented my notebook. He looked at it in great surprise.

"What is the meaning of this untidy work? Do you expect me to accept this?" He lifted the notebook gingerly by one corner. "You had better sit down and do it over." He handed me the book. As the other pupils were looking at me and I was embarrassed, I took the book and turned with a flippant attitude. Suddenly I heard his stern, "Come back here!" I returned and just looked at him, my head held high. His eyes were snapping. "Now you go back to your desk as a lady should." I turned on my heel and walked with swaying hips. Someone snickered, I felt my face become hot when he called my name again.

"Return to my desk." He rose from his seat and picked up the quince stick. "Hold out your hands." A quince stick is very pliable and used right it can wrap itself around a hand. I bit my lip as he gave me a whack on one hand, then the other. Cyril didn't cry and neither would I, but now I felt more sympathy for him. "Now go back to your seat."

I walked to my desk, head held high, still determined not to cry. I was a very quiet girl, however, the rest of the day and never again did I do my homework in the tree. Later that day, as was his custom, Mr. Rankillor walked around the room to check our work. Recitations were done for the day and assigned work was to be presented on our slates for his perusal.He paused at my desk and looked down at my empty slate. "Why are you not doing your sums?" I spread out my hands for an answer. Both were swollen from the whacks. I looked up at him with much resentment. He did not say anything but silently went on his way. I looked over to see Cyril watching me. At that moment I wondered if his bottom became as swollen as my hands when he had those whacks. I never had the courage to ask because personal questions were not ladylike.

One afternoon a week was devoted to music. A couple of the larger boys brought in from his private living room the teacher's organ. He would then choose the music, explain something about it and about the composer, and would begin to play. Sometimes we would sing from copies of the song and sometime he would have us sing roundelays. Often he printed the words on the blackboard. Roundelays were fun. The pupils would be divided into three or four groups, depending upon the tune. The first group would sing the first line, the second group would begin the same, then the third and fourth groups, until all the groups were singing different lines at the same time. At a signal, when the first group had come to the end of a song, the children would stop singing, until finally the last group would finish. We always enjoyed the songfests.

Another class that I enjoyed was art, or drawing classes, every two weeks. As a third standard pupil, I was given still life assignments in which I used crayons and later colored pencils. The next year, however, I was ill so often that I missed much school and thus missed the art work. Mr. Rankillor was an artist when it came to calligraphy. He taught this to the fifth and sixth standard pupils. He brought an ostrich egg to show them how the lettering and designs could be applied to this surface. I wanted so much to learn that but never had a chance.

I sometimes listened when the older pupils recited history and longed for the day when I could read about the English kings and queens. It so happened that I did not get this detailed history of England at that school. What I did learn later in the American schools was a modified form in the study of European History and some Ancient History. While Mr. Rankillor gave us good groundwork in all the subjects for each standard, he had nothing to do with or to say about our being promoted to the next standard. It was the policy of the school board to send an Inspector to the school around the middle of June, and he would do the assignments for that day. He would also conduct the recitations and the questions in all our subjects. It was a traumatic time for many of us, because he was a total stranger. Some of the pupils would be so nervous they could hardly speak. The oldest girl, Maria, was particularly distraught by his presence and would suffer sick headaches. She would have to stay later to finish her examination. He based his decision on our being promoted solely on our performance of that one day. This is one of the reasons Mr. Rankillor was so strict with us during the school year. He was patient also, although we did not realize it at the time. Our responses to the Inspector also was a determining factor as to Mr. Rankillor's being reassigned to that school. When the pupils did well, this indicated he was a good teacher.

We were especially proud of him on the day the Inspector came. He was immaculate about his appearance, a tall slender man, with a tiny, well trimmed black mustache and always neat in his grooming. He was a real British school teacher, with excellent manners. The Inspector was rotund and, as the day progressed, he became disheveled, running his hands through his sandy colored hair, untying his tie, opening a button at the top of his shirt. By the end of the day he looked absolutely worn out, whereas our Mr, Rankillor was cool and collected. It was hard not to make comparisons between these two men as they played such important roles in my life.

Unfortunately for Jessie and me, we left the school on 9th June 1920. The Inspector was expected the following week, so that time we could not have our examinations. This posed a problem in assigning us to our proper grades after we arrived at the Omaha, Nebraska schools that year in the United States. We had a good basic education at that South African school and, as Jessie often remarked, "We learned more there in three years than we did in the schools in Omaha." Those were happy school days. In later years I have appreciated them so much and have often mentally saluted Mr. Rankillor. He was a progressive teacher, considering that he was a staid Britisher and a bachelor. It must have been a lonely life without family and living all alone. He seemed to enjoy teaching and was at that school for twenty years, respected by all who knew him. His only companion was his organ and he apparently was a good musician. He certainly was a good teacher, and, although a stern disciplinarian, he made the work interesting.

Chapter 14

At the Ocean

We seldom went to the ocean, although it was only five miles away and could be seen from some vantage points on the farm. Mode of travel was one hindrance, but the demands of the farm and orchard were the main reason. During the five years we were at Smiling Valley, we went at Christmas of 1915 and Easter of 1917, both memorable times for me, though for different reasons. These became big gatherings, almost a community affair, with covered wagons filled with happy, shouting people coming from various farms. As this was before the days of telephone, friends and relatives would greet each other after months of no communication. Casual visits were not made easily. One or two people could go on horseback or by carriage, but one family never visited another by ox-drawn wagon. If a dance were held at a home, then whole families would attend, dancing until dawn and, after the dance, they would sleep in the wagons. It was wonderful to be with relatives and friends again after those long months of no communication.

Now many things had to be considered for any trip: men getting equipment ready, greasing wagon wheels, checking wheel rims and spokes, getting deep-sea fishing gear ready, and so forth. The women had the larger share of work: getting bedding and clothing ready as well as cooking utensils, working out menus, and baking, baking, baking for the first few days of encampment. We might be away only a week but we had to eat. Besides bread, biscuits, and cakes, we had luscious, deluxe plum puddings. After being in camp a short time, the women would begin to sample and compare those puddings and discuss the merits of each.

"Lucky pieces" such as a silver coin, a silver thimble, a ring, or even a safety pin, were baked into the puddings and there would be much laughter and joking when these symbols were found. Each had a meaning to the adults. Now it was the Christmas season, so the puddings were important.

At last it was time to load the wagon with a trunk of clothing, one with tableware, then the bedding and the prepared foods. Containers of live chickens hung beneath the wagon, for fresh eggs to go with the bacon. I would learn later that fresh fish would be caught for breakfast part of the time. Mother had been so busy she barely had time for us children. Grannie, as usual, was very helpful. The grandparents were not going with us now, but would join the merrymaking later. Finally, we children were bursting with excitement as Mother told us to get into the covered wagon and she climbed in to sit beside us. The uncles settled themselves, the lead boy took the riems from the oxen, Uncle Clem flecked the whip and called the animals by name and black children ran to open wide the gate. We were off! I could barely breathe. What would happen next?

Before long our wagon became one of many as other families began to join us. There were many loud hellos and shouted comments and I recognized some of the cousins I had met. I was glad I would know someone.

As we neared the ocean, we could smell the distinctive sea breezes, and the terrain began to look different because of the winds blowing sand inland. Also, plant life in the vicinity of the ocean was different from that on the veld. Nearing the beach, the larger children jumped from the wagons and raced ahead, wanting to be first to put their bare feet into the salt water. Adults were also showing signs of excitement, not because of the appearance of the sea but because they were looking for friends and relatives.

As wagons were maneuvered into their spaces, the blacks of each wagon began to unspan the oxen and remove them to an area where a kraal had been arranged by some long-ago encampment. These animals would remain there, attended by their respective blacks who were also enjoying the different routine of their daily lives. A few cows among the animals would supply fresh milk for the duration of the holiday. The servants did not have to remain constantly on duty. Some were free to roam about, while others watched the animals; they arranged this time among themselves. All were fed by their particular "baas."

With the wagons now in place, the men set up a center pole or two in the space between each wagon. They then placed the canvas sails as a protection from wind or rain over this area, tying a sail to the wagon on each side. Fires were kindled and soon the women's part of the work began, the feeding of their families. They heated water for coffee and tea, and began unpacking the food they had been so busy preparing for so long. Finally each woman called her children and her husband to say that all was ready.

We children ate as though we were famished, even Brother Len, who now at fifteen months was somewhat of a finicky eater. Jessie and I were so busy eating we had no time to look around or to pay attention to anyone else. Soon, however, I became aware of the constant chatter and then much laughter as adults began to circulate, visiting one neighbor, then another. A woman would stop to coo over a baby and compliment the older children. Sometimes I heard the words, "Mooi meisie," pretty girl, which of course was pleasing to child and mother. At other times I heard, "My! but you have grown a lot since I last saw you," this usually spoken to a young boy.

One thing was very noticeable to me: everybody was happy! I particularly observed Mother. I had never seen her so relaxed and smiling. She had not seen some of these people, many of whom had known her from her childhood, for nearly nine years.

Upon finishing eating, the men began smoking pipes and an occasional cigar as they sat and talked about crops and their prices, the animals and breeding of stock. Sometimes an amusing remark would cause loud laughter. Jessie, Brother, and I had fun with other children running to the beach to see what we could find, then returning with some new treasure to show our mother. After her inspection we rushed back to the beach. It was a fun time for all.

During this Christmas time of 1915 the sea shells lay so thick upon the sand that we walked upon them. Their variety of shapes, colors, and sizes made us imagine all kinds of things: donkeys, cows, dogs, and more. We spent hours picking up both shells and pretty pebbles, discarding and picking up again. It was hard to decide what to keep. Occasionally shouts of delight were heard as someone found a "purse." This was a type of seaweed that was pretty when wet, brown and velvety soft, with a fringe at the bottom. Our joy faded, however, when the "purse" became dry and no longer opened. We each had a small container for our favorite findings of shells or stones that we wanted to take home. Some way or other they seemed to lose their charm on the farm.

Near the camp site were sand dunes formed with years of winds blowing sand up against the tree-strewn hills, some of which had been on a high bank. Some of the older and more venturesome children began to climb these, and as the sand loosened, began to slide back to ground level. Some of us had persistence, and we learned that stepping sideways, or climbing at an angle rather than straight up, enabled us to arrive at the top. We then lay down and began to roll over and over so that watchers could not distinguish a child from a ball of sand. It was great fun for us, but our mothers had a trying time getting the sand out of our hair. This took many shampooings and tedious brushing. Washing the sand from our garments was a nuisance, as the grains of sand seemed to penetrate the seams and hems.

Evenings were enjoyable while camp fires glowed and the men played their various instruments. Murmurings of adults and their soft laughter added to the enjoyment. As I looked out and saw the dusk coming into the trees and in the distance hidden untold "terrors and dangers," I always felt safe, knowing so many adults were present. The tranquility and harmony that came from so many happy individuals was reassuring.

We children usually had "mealies" (corn) roasting on the coals after the evening meal had been cooked. Embers would be low, just right for roasting, not only the corn but the mussels and periwinkles we had pried from the rocks at low tide. This was a new tasting experience for most of us living on farms and not used to sea food.

Suddenly, I heard a different kind of singing and looked toward the darkened area to see a camp fire had been kindled. The blacks were dancing to the music in their particular style, stomping their feet and, at times, yelling and throwing their arms around in what I felt was an alarming manner. My older cousins, however, seemed unconcerned so I relaxed. After all, the blacks, too, were on a holiday and this was their way of playing.

The Bulugha River mouth became the swimming pool for all of us children. This was an area where the river flowed into the ocean, although I could see no visible channel. Cousin Sam, fourteen years of age then, was responsible for us most of the time. We spent an hour or two mornings and afternoons playing in this pool. One morning, from the rock upon which he sat, he would not allow us to jump into the pool. He thought an octopus was lurking at the edge of the rock, so he sent some of the boys to camp to ask someone to come. Soon two men arrived with a spear and a net and began to prod around the rock. Sure enough, the water became inky. This blue liquid is spurted out as a defense or protective tactic. The creature, a small one, was finally netted; yet even such a small one would have given a child a harrowing experience by wrapping its tentacles around a leg. It was fortunate that Sam had noticed this before allowing us to jump in.

During lunch time I heard the adults discussing the incident. No one had ever seen or heard of an octopus in that bathing area, and most of those adults had played in the same pool as children. They decided the tide must have been higher than usual during the night. We continued to play in this mouth of the river but we were watchful for the rest of the time we were there.

I was the only child who wore shoes. Mother thought this was a precaution against my having colds, as I was a sickly child. The octopus had been spread out near the tents with the tentacles upward since early morning. After the evening meal some of us were looking down at it when some of the children dared me to put my foot on one of the arms. At first I refused but finally I cautiously did. Much to my horror, there was enough life in that one tentacle to cause a strong suction. I could not withdraw my foot. I was terrified and began to scream. When the adults saw my dilemma, Uncle Len came running over as one of the men was trying to force my foot loose by pulling me upward. It did not work! It seemed that whatever life force was still in that poor thing, which had lain in the hot sun all day, had all rushed to that one arm. Finally Uncle Len decided to sever the arm where it joined the head, but even this did not free my shoe. He offered some sage advice, "Well, Bully, let this be a lesson to you. You'll have to stand there until the suction cups die. Perhaps you will not be so quick to take a dare next time and won't always do what others tell you." Mother finally unbuttoned the shoe and I was free, though the shoe was still held by the suction cups of that arm. (An octopus has eight of these arms and on a full grown one, they can be long!) In the morning I found the shoe beside the other and the octopus gone.

It seemed to me that breakfast at the seashore was the best meal of all. I enjoyed being awakened by the fragrance of coffee and bacon and lost no time in making my appearance. One morning Aunt Florence said, "We will have fish for breakfast this morning if you want to wait. Your mother is out there fishing. I looked toward where she was pointing and was amazed to see Mother throwing out her line attached to a long bamboo fishing pole. I became apprehensive because I knew the tide was coming in, having overheard the men talking about it, and now I saw they had moved to rocks closer to the shore while Mother was still absorbed in her fishing. I learned later she loved this sport, especially with the ocean waves splashing around her. I was relieved when finally I saw Uncle Sid go out to her, helping her to safety. They were almost waist deep in water as the waves swished by them.

Aunt Florence had apparently discerned my anxiety because she said, "Your mother was always a good fisherwoman so don't worry." I liked this aunt very much. I had seen her twice before when she visited the grandparents and felt close to her. She was five years Mother's senior and they had a close relationship. Both had been the last girls at home for a long time and both had to work in the fields hoeing or whatever needed to be done during their younger years.

We all enjoyed the fish because it was delicious; nevertheless I hoped that Mother would never go out again. She did, however, as that was her morning enjoyment and she had not fished for years. I finally learned to accept the situation. In retrospect I realized that those days at the beach were one of the few periods I was ever to see Mother really happy.

Shortly before we had to leave for the farm, one morning we were all delightfully surprised to see a carriage approach. There were Grannie and Grandpa! We children all loved her so much we had been sorry that they had not come with us. "Just in time for morning tea, Mother and Dad," said Aunt Florence. "Do come in and sit down." What a happy family gathering! We all crowded into the same space until finally Mother told us to run and play until lunch time. I obeyed rather reluctantly because I did not want to miss anything.

After lunch, while still at the table, Grannie said, "I want all of you children to follow me, because I have something to show you." Excitedly, we followed her to where the carriage was standing. She took from the carriage a small chair and a bulging pillow case. Finding a suitable place to put the chair, she sat down and said to all her grandchildren pressing in around her, "This is Christmas Day, you know, so I have a little gift for each of you. When I call your name, put your hand into this pillow case and take the first package your hand touches."

When my turn came, I touched a fat package and pulled it out. Mine had a purple strip of paper covering it, while the others had packages of different colors. Grannie smiled. "These are called 'lucky packets,' because each one has a toy inside, besides some sweets. If you take off the pretty paper carefully and hold it in your hand, it will curl up." Of course we all did this, and it was almost more enjoyable than the sweets; at least, it lasted longer!

I opened my packet. "Oh, a doll!" I exclaimed. "No," Grannie shook her head. "No, child, that is a Buddha, a symbol of a pagan god. See his fat tummy and the way he is sitting? A doll would not be made like that." I had no idea what she was talking about, but I was happy with this little fat Buddha and liked its light green color. It was my first real toy. I had this treasure until it was taken from me by my Aunt Libby four years later when we lived with her. She thought it would look nice on her buffet. I cried when I told Mother and wanted her to retrieve it for me but she said to let her have it. When we left Libby's house, the beginning step toward our departure for America, again I asked her for it and she promptly said, "It is mine!"

Mother and I discussed this situation much later. She said, "Libby was that kind of a person. I had a few choice things I valued, but she demanded that I give them to her, saying that it was to pay for our room and board." (I am sure her husband, my mother's brother, my Uncle Bert, never knew this.) Mother continued, "I didn't want to be the cause of any quarrel between her and Bert and we did get along without the item. One should not be attached too much to things." This was Mother's philosophy and eventually became part of mine.

We children had to keep our early-to-bed routine even during this holiday time. One night I awakened with a bright light shining in my face. It was the full moon. I was a bit bewildered by this great ball of light in the sky. The path of light went from the moon across the water right into the wagon. My eyes followed this golden path and it looked so inviting and solid I was tempted to get out of bed and try to walk on it. I wondered what would happen if I did. Little did I know then that eventually people would actually walk on the moon.

It was a momentous occasion in my life, that first trip to the ocean, and I have many fond memories of that first holiday. I made the acquaintance of five families of relatives besides several of the parents of those who would become my school friends. It was confusing at first to have to keep in mind which uncle and aunt belonged together and also where several cousins belonged.

All too soon the women began packing, and the men started to dismantle the poles that held up the sails. Blacks were bringing the oxen to the individual wagons, yoking and placing them in the position to which they were accustomed. Our holiday was over. Regretfully, with Jessie and brother Leonard, I took my place in the wagon with Mother and the uncles and kept my eyes on the ocean as long as I could see it. Would I ever return?

Although I had been quite well during this holiday time, I was often inclined to be rather sickly. When I was six years old, something happened that was to affect me the rest of my life. I was bitten by a mosquito while Mother and I were visiting Aunt

Martha and Uncle Steve and their children Cyril and Amy. We had made the trip on foot to their place, just before their second daughter, May, was born on 15th July 1915. I remember seeing tall anthills on that walk, with Mother's explaining about the way anteaters broke them open to eat the ants. For some reason Grandpa's farm had none, so I found this interesting.

The day May was born was unusual only because Aunt Libby stopped by with her two children, Gladys and Arthur, to pick up Cyril, Amy, and me. Her asking us to take a walk with her to the school should have alerted me that something unusual was going to happen, but I was happy to be with the other children and thought nothing of it. When we arrived, she sat down to read a book and told us to play. The "flay" (pond) surrounded by bulrushes were new to me, and I could see that the pond was full of stagnant water. Cyril spent some time catching tadpoles but I was not interested in those slimy things. So when he wandered off to be with Amy, I was suddenly interested in the odd looking mosquito that landed on my hand.

The mosquito bite seemed such a little thing when it happened, because from the time I could walk, I had watched bugs and found them interesting. This particular gray, fragile looking bug caught my interest, because it seemed different somehow. It was transparent and I could see right through it. The bite was sharp, and its needle was longer than any I had seen on other mosquitoes. When I shook my hand it did not fly away, so I had to brush it off with my other hand. I was surprised to see a dot of blood. When we arrived back at Uncle Steven's we were shown the new baby, which I did not think much of because she was too little to do anything. Later, when I told Mother about the bite, she seemed concerned though not overly so. She knew that water in the flay was stagnant.

When I began having periodic severe chills and raging fevers, however, she knew that I had recurrent malaria. From November 1915 through December 1922 I experienced severe repetitions on a regular basis, so regular, in fact, that Mother kept her calendar marked and sometimes I had to be hospitalized. I was treated with great quantities of quinine.

For instance, later, in November, when Amy and Cyril came

to the farm to celebrate his birthday, we had gone to the ravine to see what was happening and, while peering into the pool to look for flowers, I suddenly felt too ill to move and was very cold.

"Cyril, I'm cold!" I exclaimed. He laughed. "It isn't cold. The sun is shining and there is no wind. It is a pretty spring day." I began to shiver and shake. "I'm going home." I discovered I could not walk well because I was shaking so hard. At first Cyril made fun of me, but soon realized that something really was wrong. He ran ahead, with the two girls following him, while I struggled to keep up.

He must have told Mother because soon she came running and scooped me up in her arms. I went into such a chill she could barely hold me. At the house Grannie met us anxiously. She told Grandpa to care for the children while Mother took me into Grannie's bedroom to put me to bed in the latter's feather mattress, and Grannie herself went out and soon came back with hot bricks to put at my feet. I began to relax from the warmth, then suddenly I became very hot with fever. I did not remember what happened for several days.

This was my first attack of malaria, while I was not yet seven years old. I was to experience these severe chills with raging fevers, followed by exhausting sweating periods for about six week, then be well for six weeks. This was a recurrent type of malaria. Mother would mark a calendar when the attacks occurred and in that way knew when the next attack would arrive.

Although my bouncing back to normal each time was quick, this malady was to interfere with my education after I started going to school. I was able to keep up with classes only by studying hard.

One other family member, Aunt Lulu, Grannie's fourth child and Mother's second elder sister, also had it, so Grannie knew what to do and how to help me. Years later Aunt Lulu Bryson wrote me that her attacks were the bane of her existence. She died at age 69 during her final attack.

Chapter 15

Of Mice and Snakes and a Horse

One evening in the fall of 1916, the men did not leave the dining area so quickly as usual. We girls had not been given permission to leave, so I listened to the conversation. They were talking about what was to be done the next day, speaking about haying, something I had not heard of previously.

Grandpa asked Uncle Clem if Yellow Face had told him how many helpers they would have and if they would be at the house by seven o'clock. Clem's "Yes" seemed to satisfy Grandpa. Yellow Face was related somehow to the oldest black helper, perhaps coming from Port Elizabeth to work with this old man. He was not a person I wanted to be around. I always had an uneasy feeling when near him. He was considered a good worker. He was probably a mulatto, as he was much lighter skinned than any of the others. I never could understand why he seemed always around the yard when most of the others were working. I never asked questions, however; perhaps he had duties of which I knew nothing.

Grandpa was speaking to Uncle Sid: "Are the scythes and sickles all sharpened?" "Yes, Dad. I've been working on them all week." "Good," Grandpa nodded in satisfaction. "Then we can get an early start and should have that whole field cut by the end of the day."

I began to feel excited as I realized something different was going to happen tomorrow. I wanted to ask questions but I had begun to learn that answers would be forthcoming if I were just patient. Although I thought I was too excited to sleep, I soon drifted into dreamland. Mother awakened us girls and said, "If you hurry and get dressed, you can have breakfast with us and then I want to show you something in the hay mow." We were soon at the break-fast table and had the rare treat of having Grandpa address us directly.

"Would you two like to earn a few pennies today?" Naturally, we did. He went on, "For every twelve mice tails you show me, I'll give you a half-penny. Your mother will show you what to do." As money was a strange commodity to me, I wondered what a half-penny could be. The only time I had handled any was when Mother would give me the needed amount when I went to get eggs while were living in Cullinan. I had seen none since then.

By the time breakfast was over, there were several blacks waiting in the yard, both men and women, all chatting or singing. Uncle Sid spoke to them and they followed him to the work shed. He gave the men scythes and the women sickles. All then followed him and Uncle Clem to the hay field beyond the building where the dried hay was stored. As soon as Mother finished the breakfast dishes, she picked up a broom and a rake and told us to follow her. I felt that an adventure was coming up as we walked the half mile to the hay mow. As we went in she said, "I will rake the floor to get the old hay together, then sweep because the new hay will be put here." By now she had the hay deep on the floor and was moving hay back and forth with her hands. Suddenly she stopped and pointed. "See! This is a nest of baby mice. We are to kill all we can find. I'll show you how."

Picking up a baby mouse she cradled it in one hand, showing us how transparent it was and how the veins and inner organs could be seen. "See the eyes are closed. Mice are born blind. They are so destructive that Grandpa wants you to kill all you can find and give him the tails. Each tail means a dead mouse." Suddenly she lifted the tiny mouse by the tail, gave it a flip of her wrist, and lo! the tail was in hand and the body on the floor.

"Mother! Why didn't the mouse run away?" I stared down at the dead mouse. "It is too little. This is a nest of new-born. Here, you try it. It won't hurt you." Gingerly I took one of those tiny mice by the tail and saw something pulsing away. Pointing to it I wanted to know what it was. "That is the heart beating. Everything in the animal world has a heart just as you and Jessie and I have."

Satisfied with this explanation, I tried to flip the mouse but its body did not separate from the tail. Mother showed me again. Again I tried and soon had the knack and was happy as the pile of tails grew bigger. Sister seemed to get the hang of flipping more quickly than I, and we spent a busy morning finding new nests and adding to our piles of tails!

Finally we found no more mice nests. I was beginning to be bored with this task, and anyway, I never felt really good about what I was doing. Killing those little creatures, even though they were considered pests, created some inner feeling I did not like. Mother finished sweeping the floor, and taking all the mice tails in a little box, I carried them as we trudged along to the house. By the time we had scrubbed our hands well for lunch, the blacks and the uncles had returned also, and Mother was beginning to pass out the food to everyone. Lunch was a fun time because there was much laughter, and smiling black faces in the yard and the men indoors were all in a happy mood.

After lunch back to the fields they all went while we girls were feeling very pleased with our few half-pennies. Grandpa was almost jovial as he presented Jessie with five and me with six. This great sum of money represented one hundred and thirty-two dead mice! I have no recollection what we did with the money, a total of five pence half-penny, or almost seven cents in American coin. This was my first experience of earning money.

Two hours later Mother said, "Come, girls, Grannie and I are taking afternoon tea to the field. You can help carry some biscuits (cookies). We will carry the cups and tea." We walked past the now clean hay mow which Grannie inspected and commented upon, then continued toward the grain field. I had no idea what was being done so was somewhat startled to see all the activity. The men with the scythes were swinging these and the grain stalks would fall to the ground. The women with their sickles walked behind and sort of raked the stalks together. Then, tying them into bundles, they would toss them to one side while other women picked these up and stacked them on the ends to form an upright mound. I watched all with wonder and many unvoiced questions.

As we appeared, work stopped and slowly the black workers all sat down nearby. Mother gave us the biscuits to pass to them, while she set a small tablecloth on the ground. The uncles and Grandpa squatted on the ground near the tablecloth while Grannie arranged the cups and cakes. In the meantime Mother was passing water or tea to the blacks. They enjoyed this special attention, as it was unusual for them to be waited upon. Grandpa was in a happy mood. I did not realize that this harvest of grain meant a good crop to him and, of course, it did augment the income besides being food for the horses later. He looked at Grannie as though deciding whether to say what he had on his mind.

"Louisa, do you remember the time you came to bring me tea at our first harvest?" Turning to the uncles, he said, "You were all just young sprouts then. Mother used to wear pantaloons and while she was standing pouring tea, she dropped the cup and grabbed at her knee, screaming as she did so. I could not imagine what could have happened. She kept saying, 'Get it out! Get it out!' while hanging onto her knee. Finally, I realized a mouse must have run up her pantaloons so I put my hand into the garment and sure enough, there was a mouse." He was smiling and the uncles laughed—even Grannie smiled, but I felt she did not really appreciate having the story told. Some years later, I saw a picture of a woman wearing pantaloons. It was only then that I could appreciate the predicament Grannie had experienced.

I loved my grandmother dearly and spent much time watching her expressive face. Her eyes, almost violet in color, had such a kindly, loving expression. I realized later that they also portrayed great patience and stamina. Life had been difficult, as she had lived through a time of Xhosa wars; a childhood as an apprentice to a seamstress, without the comfort of parents; then the difficult task of becoming a farmer's wife, homemaker, and mother of so many children. This life on a frontier farm required all the household needs of sewing, baking, caring, and cleaning for this family. Perhaps the experience of giving up the home she lived in for seventeen years and trekking to this new place, to wrest a living and a home out of the virgin soil, was difficult for her. Hard work and frugal living was the keynote of most pioneers of that day. It brought forth the stamina, strength, and courage of these grandparents.

But now she was enjoying the fruits of her labor. She had the pleasure of her many grandchildren and the visits of the five married children who lived closest, on their own farms, and she had the total devotion of a loving husband. She had everything that was of real value. I do not believe she ever gave thought to all the history of which she had been a part. Perhaps the early pioneers took everything in stride and gave no thought to anything as being "historical." It was simply a matter of hard work in order to survive.

There was work for all on the farm and I was not exempt. Grannie soon taught me how to look for the nests where the hens laid their eggs, mostly in the grasses that grew up around the fence that formed the kraal. This was a large enclosure where the milk cows would be brought for the morning and evening milking. It was a large semicircle made of stakes driven into the ground, with pliable young trees woven in and out of the stakes. A double row of stakes with weaving made it a sturdy fenced-in section. The wide gate was anchored at one end onto the outer wall of the carriage house, and the barns, forming the other half of the kraal, housed farm machinery such as plows, harrows and extra wagon wheels. The fenced-in kraal was a smaller part of the large paddock, to keep the horses and donkeys separate from the grazing area on the opposite side of the home property. This was a safe place to play when the animals were at the farther end of the paddock. A fence ran alongside the house garden, so the animals could not wander into the yard proper. It was here that later I would have my adventure with Jacob, Uncle Len's pet donkey. On the edge of this was a row of oak trees, one of which I would eventually climb to do my homework after school began.

On most Saturdays the shoes of family members would be lined up on the stoep. I was the official shoe polisher for the eight pairs, so it was a time-consuming task. Eventually I learned how to do this task without getting too much polish on myself. At first I was happy with this assignment, but when I saw Jessie playing I began to fuss with her to help me. She was a willing helper. One Saturday we became overly enthusiastic, as we had a new can of black polish. All the shoes were in a row, polished and shining. I wanted to polish something else so I polished Jessie's face and arms, then she did mine. I was so enthusiastic with my clever idea that I ran into the house to show Mother.

She was in the living room, taking the prisms that she intended to wash from the overhead lamp. I watched for a moment, then decided to say something cheeky in Xhosa. Because I was standing in the dining area door she saw only my black face. "Go away, little one. What are you doing in the house?" She barely glanced at me. Then I laughed to think she did not realize I was her child. Startled, she turned to stare at me and when she rushed at me, I ran out to my favorite tree in front of the stoep and climbed up.

Jessie, unfortunately, ran into the washroom, which was not to be used by us children. I could see into this room as I climbed higher and saw Mother catch her and smack her bottom, at which Sister began to cry. At that moment Grannie took over and began to clean the black off her face. Mother got a broom and came out to the tree, trying to reach me with that. I laughed and climbed higher until I saw she was beginning to cry. I came down quickly and, instead of spanking me as I deserved, she began hurriedly began to wipe off the polish. It was only then I realized that something was wrong.

It seems this polish contained something that was considered poisonous if left on the skin too long. I felt ashamed and very naughty indeed, which word I heard often during the cleaning process. I also began to realize that Mother had enough to do without spending time with our getting into mischief. This situation caused me to begin thinking about all that she did. It was she who kept the house immaculate, who did all the cooking and the laundry, besides sewing clothing for her children and whatever else was needed. It was only a short time after this episode that I was to hear her refer to herself as the "family slave." I also began to realize something in our lives was not quite right. She seldom had time to sit and chat with us. Only when she was helping us get ready for bed or helping us to dress each morning or seeing that we had our weekly bath, did she seem like our mother. Brother was still considered a baby and most of the time Grannie cared for him.

Our baths took a whole Saturday afternoon. It was also the

day of baking bread. Galvanized cans of water were put on the front of the stove and in the back would be a large pot of soup simmering for the evening meal. It took good planning to make use of the whole top of the stove. The kitchen would be cozy warm after the noon meal, when the round galvanized washtub would be brought in and the kitchen door closed for the next two or three hours. Sometimes Brother would be first, then Jessie, then me. Next time it would be the reverse, so each third time a different child would be first or last. We all bathed in the same water because we never knew when the rains would come and water was too precious.

The stove seemed very large to my child eyes. I used to stand before it and wonder what all was involved in its functioning. When I was first taught how to gather the chips and pieces of bark fallen or pulled from the eucalyptus trees, placing these in the box provided for them close to the stove, I was cautioned never to touch the stove. It was hot from early morning to late evening. When Grannie said that it would burn me, I wondered how it could do this, not realizing that touching it was the answer.

I recall one cold Saturday when I was first in the tub and was forbidden to open the kitchen door to go out because I might catch cold. I was standing near the table where the freshly baked loaves were placed and covered with a clean cloth. The bread smelled so good. Watching to see that Mother did not see me, I finally yielded to the temptation of breaking into a loaf and began to eat from the inside, tearing off small pieces at a time. It was delicious. After the other children were bathed and dressed, Mother began to put the loaves away. As she picked up the one closest to me, it collapsed. Unbelief spread across Mother's face.

"Oh, you naughty girl!" She burst into tears. "You have eaten the whole inside of this loaf. How could you do such a thing?" I could not understand why she cried. I no longer felt very smart and no matter how good it smelled, I never again helped myself to hot bread.

We spoke of this much later and Mother said, "Yes, I remember. It was a small thing to trigger tears, but I had so much stress in those days. I was unhappy when there was no mail from your father and of course he was not sending any money. I was constantly torn between wondering if he would send for us and what I would do if he did not. There were tensions in the family circle too." She sighed deeply. "One can never look back on what is past. I always felt it was darkest before dawn and there had to be a brighter tomorrow. I don't think I could have continued to live if I hadn't felt strongly that every cloud has a silver lining." We children grew up with these bits of her philosophy and they helped me so much later in my own life. Even Jessie remembered how she always tried to look on the bright side of things.

One day Grannie took Jessie and me behind the dairy barn to do a new task. There on a pile of sea sand were pots, pans, and silver. We had been to the seashore, but I was unaware that a sack of sand had been brought back. Grannie showed us how to dampen a small cloth, then dip it in the sand and apply it as a polish to these household articles. It was fun to rub and rub and make them shine and, because it did not happen frequently, we never tired of this task. We liked to hear the praise we received and this was probably part of our enjoyment.

I usually went alone to the kraal to gather the daily supply of eggs. One day Jessie went with me and we saw an unusual sight, a snake trying to eat a frog. It was the only time I ever saw a snake in that area. It was a long one with a large bulge behind its jaw. We could not figure out what the bulge was until we saw a frog's foot protruding from the mouth. "Jessie," I gasped. "Run and get Uncle Sid. I think he's in the tool shed." Away she went while I watched the snake go tail first down a hole. I had not noticed the hole before. It could not slide way down because of the bulging frog's body in its throat.

Finally Uncle Sid arrived, carrying a large stick and a spade. I just pointed to where the snake had gone. Using the spade to dig the reptile out about a foot, he held its head down with the stick, then, just behind the bulge, chopped it off with the spade. The frog jumped free. This was quite an experience for us girls and we talked about it for a long time. We also learned that some snakes live in ground.

On the opposite side of the house, by the gates that led into the grazing area, was a large clump of bushes. I had been attracted to this because orange colored flowers had begun to bloom and I thought they were pretty. I had discovered a flat surface among the bushes and decided this would be a nice play house. Soon we girls had our accumulation of wooden dolls and shells and other things we called toys gathered on this spot. For some reason, I made an opening toward the rear of the bushes. We could not be seen by anyone walking to or from the gate, so Jessie and I often played here. We could look out easily, but the thickest section of bushes faced toward the walk way, so no one could see us.

One particularly hot day, Uncle Len came from the guava orchard planted near the ravine, downward from the house. We saw him approaching so were very quiet. Suddenly he stood still, staring at the ground in front of him, yelling, "Ivy, where are the children?" Mother came to the east verandah, from the parlour where she had been working. "I don't know where they are, Len. Why?" Pointing downward, he said, "Snakes! And this is poisonous!" I heard Mother gasp as she grabbed the hoe from the corner of the verandah. This was always kept sharpened and replaced in that spot us for just such an emergency. As she handed it to Uncle she started yelling our names.

My first impulse was to remain quiet. Suddenly, however, I had that very strange inner feeling I often experienced and I grabbed Jessie's hand and we emerged from our hiding place. They were astonished to see us. "Good heavens!" said Uncle Len for no particular reason that I could see. "What are you girls doing there?" Not waiting for an answer he said, "Edna, run and ring the bell. Quick!" Not daring to take time to ask questions, away I went, with Jessie following, wondering why the bell should be rung when there was no fire. I did not realize what a fright the adults had on seeing such a poisonous snake. Neither did I know it was breeding time for them.

Alarmed at this turn of events, I rang the bell and soon the men from the garden came. I told them where to go and then Jessie and I ran after them. Leonard and Mother were dismantling our play house as they cleared the brush and she was trying to gather up our toys. As more help arrived, she moved away and put our things on the verandah. I was appalled at what they were doing to the shrubs, but was more appalled when, in lifting a large flat stone, they began slashing snakes. And to think, Jessie and I had been sitting so near them! It must have been the breeding place for at least two pairs of those deadly reptiles, because there were four big snakes and a lot of little ones!

Because a bite from even a small snake was considered deadly, the adults were being extremely cautious and quick acting when they saw another snake emerge. I never knew what species these were. I heard them referred to as a red-lipped snake. I was not permitted to come closer to see one. Jessie and I, along with the grandparents, watched all this activity from a safe distance.

Mother, quite shaken by this experience, took us both into her bedroom and talked much about how fortunate that our guardian angels had been watching over us. Had we been bitten, the adults would never have known where to look for us. I began to realize that we had been fortunate indeed and hoped we would never go through anything like that again. Actually, we did not see many of these creatures, although they had been plentiful when the grandparents had first arrived. Between the farm animals and the activity of the adults, no doubt, most of the snakes departed for other areas. Also, Grannie always killed those she saw, which might have been parents, thus eliminating many. For a long time Uncle Len did not let me forget how close Sister and I came to disaster, having our playhouse under those bushes.

One day Grannie and I were at the fence that separated the yard from the paddock where the carriage horses and Grandpa's riding horse usually roamed. Grannie kept calling, "Jacob, Jacob," and finally from the far end of the kraal came a gray-haired, black-eared, slow-walking animal. When he came up to the fence, Grannie patted his face, pulling gently on his ears as he tried to nuzzle her. "This is Jacob, our pet donkey." She held out a carrot. "He was born soon after Uncle Leonard so he is an old man now. Uncle Len used to ride him to school. We are going to keep him close to the house so we can watch him. The other donkeys have been moved to the lower part of this paddock." While she was talking, Jacob was munching the carrot.

"Why does he walk so slowly, Grannie? Can't he run?" I asked.

"No, child. He is a very old animal and a bit lame." I began to wonder about the size of this place, for the area I surveyed was very large from my point of view; to realize there was a "lower part" was incomprehensible to me.

Sometime later I decided that if Uncle Len could ride Jacob, I could too. Eventually I was able to take a carrot from the kitchen without being seen and ran to the paddock, loudly saying, "Jessie! Come with me, come with me." I often beguiled, and sometimes demanded, Jessie to take part in some of my escapades, especially when I needed help. I explained that I was going to ride Jacob.

"I will need you to hold the carrot, while I climb the fence. Don't give it to him right away; tease him until I can get on his back, then let him have the carrot."

Oh how fortunate to see Jacob was at the fence! I had been concerned that in my calling to him, Grannie might hear me.

Jessie eyed me solemnly, obediently holding the carrot so that Jacob could see it, but saying, "I don't think you should do this."

Jacob moved his body so that it was alongside the fence. I bravely threw one leg over his back, just as he had the carrot in his mouth. I did not realize the nature of the animal! Jacob's reaction was very unexpected! Before I could grasp his mane and get comfortable (my legs were not long enough to go around his broad back), Jacob forgot the carrot and proceeded to run, kicking up his heels. I went flying over his rump and landed hard on the ground only a few feet from where we had started!

It was Jessie's voice, anxiously calling my name, that made me open my eyes that would barely focus on her worried face as she bent over me. "I told you not to! I thought you were dead, because you lay so still." Poor Sister! In retrospect, I would often realize her quiet words for my welfare showed better judgment than my impulses, even years later when we both were older.

She tried to help me onto my feet and as I waited for my vision to adjust, I said, "Now! Don't you tell anyone about this!"

She was silent. Did I discern a bit of reproof? Did she wonder if she should tell? I know, however, that she never told Mother because I know that a scolding would have been a result. I did learn a lesson, however, as never again did I aspire to get on the back of any animal.

Consequently, the adults were astonished at my reaction a few evenings after the Jacob episode. We all were in the paddock, gathered around Grandpa who had ridden Silver Prince earlier in the day for a conference with some neighbors. This apparently was an important affair, as they stood for several minutes, listening to Grandpa, who was holding Prince's bridle. Suddenly, Uncle Leonard playfully lifted me from the ground, saying, "Hold Prince's mane and I'll give you a ride around the paddock." It was so very unlike Uncle Leonard to be playful! I screamed, howled, and held onto the mane in terror. No one could not understand my terror. Even Prince turned his head to look at me with some surprise, and that look alarmed me even more. I thought he was going to run and toss me over his rump! I was too terrified to realize that Grandpa was still holding his bridle and that Prince was different from Jacob.

"My goodness! Why does she react in such a manner! Take her down, Len." I reached for Mother as she had spoken, but it was Uncle who lifted me down. None of the adults ever asked why I was so frightened. I think Jessie was the only one who understood, but she remained her quiet, thoughtful, self.

Chapter 16

A Wedding, a Funeral, and a Fire

When I left for school one morning, I noticed the men of the family talking in the area halfway from the house toward the ra- vine. I wondered about this as they seemed to be measuring dis- tances. Two uncles had a long "string" between them, which I later learned was a tape measure. I thought about this during the day so hurried home faster than usual, then stood in amazement as I watched many blacks working together. Some had set up pieces of timber to form a large square shape on the ground, others had started to dig a shallow ditch.

As time went on, I noticed that within the outer square smaller elongated pieces of wood had been fashioned and set in. Some blacks were digging what seemed to be a deeper hole a short dis- tance away, others were bringing petrol cans full of water. I be- came curious.

That evening at the dinner table I listened carefully and learned that bricks were being made and were being dried by the hot sun. The uncles were elated at the success of this undertaking. New "mud" was poured into the brick molds and the process was repeated many times. As the bricks were finished and placed on a dolly, they were moved to the area south of the main house and a bit toward the east. This, I discovered, was to be the location of Uncle Clem's new home. He was going to be married!

Also, I learned much later that this had been the site of Grannie's first thatched roof home, the large rondeval, when they had arrived in this area. The rains and winds had finally caused that building to disintegrate because it was made of mud and thatch. Clem had been born in that house, and in his new home on the same general location he would die. His whole life would be lived in this one place.

The day came when this new home was finished and furniture was placed in it. With Mother's holding my hand to keep me from touching things we walked through this new home guided by the young woman who would be my new Aunt Sophia.[1] She was the one Uncle Clem had been visiting. When I learned their wedding was to be the very next day, I became very excited at all the activity. I vaguely remember Uncle Billy Baker's wedding— but that was so long ago and I was so young that this one became much more real.

Things were being moved out of the shop and covered with a tarpaulin. The parlor furniture was being rearranged, the far end being left open except for a pedestal to be used later. The table had already been moved, all its leaves added and placed close to the entrance that led to the verandah. This made it easier for people to come and go. It was now set with snowy-white linens, the best of silver, china, and glassware together with a colorful flower arrangement. Many bright flowers decorated the room.

Soon visitors were arriving in their ox-drawn wagons that were placed between the dairy and the haymow area, while the several blacks took their teams to the paddock. The activity of this day was becoming very exciting.

Mother finally called me into her bedroom and there was my aunt-to-be dressed in a lovely, long white dress. She was of medium height, slender and pretty, with her soft auburn hair framing her face.

Mother said, "Edna, Will you please tie the bow to her sash? You always tie such a pretty bow." She smiled at me. To Sophia she said, "Edna really can tie a pretty bow and I'm sure you will be pleased." This was the first public praise ever given me and I felt very important, yet a bit apprehensive as I had never tied such a wide, satiny ribbon into a bow. It was pink and four inches wide and everyone who saw it later was pleased.

We girls were wearing our prettiest white dresses and it was then I noticed that all present, men, women and children, were

[1] This is Sophia Pachonik.

also dressed in their best clothing. It began to dawn upon me that a wedding was an important occasion.

The phonograph began playing *The Wedding March* and everyone became quiet. A man with vestments went to the makeshift podium, then Uncle Clem with his best man, Uncle Sid, came to one side, and the bride came with her sister Alice as her attendant. The ceremony proceeded and soon the minister pronounced them man and wife.[2]

Uncle Clem lifted her veil and kissed her in front of everyone, which I thought was strange. A lot of conversation went on, hugging and kissing followed, and then a toast was given to the bride and groom. Some older cousins ushered all of us younger children out onto the verandah and soon served us food. It was a fun time for most of us and it was a treat to have so much different food from our usual fare.

As the afternoon drew to a close, the minister left for the parsonage some distance away. Then there was much going back and forth from the house to the work shed, and soon we learned that a dance was about to begin. I went to the shed and was astonished to see how prettily it had been decorated with flowers; bunting and streamers of white and pink were intertwined the length of the room just under the ceiling. In the center hung a large white paper ball.

It was so unexpected that I just stood and stared. This was my first time to see such decorations. Several men and a couple of women stood at one end of the room with their musical instruments. As they began to play their concertinas, accordions, and violins, Uncle Clem walked in holding Aunt Sophia by the arm. We all watched them dance the first waltz, after which other dancers joined them. Then the newlyweds left and went to their new home. They returned later but Aunt Sophia's bridal dress had been changed. I liked the way her hair was now twisted into a chignon. It was such a pretty auburn color and harmonized with Clem's red hair.

It was at this party I learned to dance. Some of my uncles and older cousins were kind enough to ask me and other children

---

[2] Clement George Green married Sophia Pachonik on 1st October, 1919.

to dance. I quickly caught onto the steps of the mazurka, the schottische, the polka, waltz, and some other pattern dances.

An intermission was called and then an announcement was made that there would be a demonstration of an American dance called a fox trot to be done by Violet and her friend. Violet was Aunt Lulu's daughter whom I was to visit the following year. These two young women were attending a finishing school and had learned different dances there. They consulted with the violinist and when the music began, it was entirely different from anything we were used to. The two girls began to dance and it seemed all they did was go backward and forward; a strange way to dance! I don't know if they finally stopped because so many of us were laughing, which in turn started them to laughing, or if they were embarrassed or angry. Anyway, it was an experience for all.

Some of us, myself included, danced into the wee hours of the morning—but it was finally over. Families went to their respective wagons to get some sleep. Many of the children had been asleep for hours. I had refused and Mother humored me. It really was the most exciting, enjoyable, and exhilarating event of my total child's life. I am positive it was not only the last and happiest event of Smiling Valley farm for many years, but also a fitting prelude to Mother's sad time of decision to leave her old home.

Quite unexpectedly I was to see Twombie again, for the last time. During lunch one day the adults were talking about a funeral and they decided the whole family would attend. As I had no concept of the meaning "funeral," and Mother had cautioned both Sister and me to be very quiet at this sad occasion, I was curious. I became even more so as we all walked, not only to the kraal where all the blacks lived, but also farther down toward the Kwelegha River. Here I saw Twombie. I was about to speak when Mother jerked my hand and mouthed, "No!" as she shook her head slightly. Then I noticed that most of the black women were crying.

The most surprising thing was to see Grandpa standing near a wooden box and, speaking in the Xhosa language, start "reading" from a small book. As I knew he could not read, he obviously had memorized this. He was giving "comfort to the family."

Twombie's younger sister had died. As the story was told to Grandpa when a member of the Twombie's family first went to him, this girl had crossed the river on the rocks, upon which they all had crossed many times. This time, however, the "water witch" pulled her into his home down under the water. By the time they did the ritual to make him let her come up, she was dead.

I do not know exactly what was said, as the conversations were all in the Bantu language. Only when I saw tears and heard mourning as the coffin was lowered and some of the male blacks began to cover it with dirt and Grannie laid flowers on top, did I begin to understand. I also learned that one of the first things they did when a drowning took place was to kill a cow at the water's edge. As the blood flowed into the river, this was supposed to appease the "water witch." Whether this was done in the case of Twombie's sister, I never learned.

I later often wondered how Grandpa happened to do that "reading." I suppose it was because this family had been with the grandparents for so many years and they depended upon the "Big Baas" in so many that it was natural for them to turn to him for a funeral service. On the other hand, their culture was based on so many superstitions it would have been natural for them to have had a witch doctor to do these rituals.

When I was almost ten an incident that could have been a disaster happened one evening as Jessie and I were getting ready for bed. Sharing brush and comb, we both had been taught to brush our long hair well. As Jessie was using the hair brush, I was using the comb. We always used a candle for light, as electricity was unknown and an oil lamp was not thought safe with children. I began to pass the comb through the candle flame. My idea was to see how close I could come to the wick and still not till the flame.

Jessie kept saying, "I don't think you should do that." This may have been the reason I kept doing just that. I could be quite perverse at times. We had been standing side by side, but Jessie began backing away from me.

Suddenly, with an odd swishing sound, the comb became a flaming torch. I threw it back of me, forgetting that Jessie might be behind me. I turned quickly, thinking I had thrown it into her face. Her guardian angle must have been on duty! She had jumped upon the bed the moment she heard the odd sound and had quickly drawn up the overhanging bed covers. The little rug was burning fiercely. Had the bed covers not been pulled up, they would have ignited. I do not recall which of us screamed for help, but Mother came rushing.

"Oh, my God, Sid! Bring water quick! Fire! Fire!"

By this time I was petrified at the result of my prank. The carpet was burning and the wooden floor was becoming charred. Mother picked up one end of the rug and turned it over the blaze, which sort of smothered the flames. But water was needed really to put them out and prevent the wooden floor from burning more.

While the adults were taking care of the fire, Jessie kept saying, "I told her not to, Mommy. I told her not to!" Not a word was said by anyone else. I looked beyond Mother and Uncle Sid to see Grannie and Grandpa standing silently together, arms around each other. I assumed then that when all the fuss and scare was over, Grandpa would give me a good spanking, but he never said so much as a word of reprimand. Mother never said anything either. The mess was cleaned up and I crawled meekly into bed.

The next morning the floor showed the results of the fire. As she examined it, Mother said, "I cannot buy another rug so from now on you girls will have to stand on the cold floor." Every time I saw that charred spot and felt the grittiness of it under my bare feet, I felt guilty. I was thankful that Jessie had the presence of mind to jump on the bed and pull the bedding up. It would have been a total disaster had the blankets caught fire.

Chapter 17

Uncle Leonard Cyril Green

Uncle Leonard was a person I admired and I was always hanging around him when he was in the shop. He was nearly twelve years my senior.[1] I watched him when he whistled and in time I, too, could whistle. He began to smoke cigarettes with obvious enjoyment, so I thought they must taste good and pestered him to give me one.

He finally lit one for me, saying. "Now Bully (his name for me), you smoke every bit of that because cigarettes cost lots of money." I took one drag, as I had seen him do, and began to sputter and choke; tears came to my eyes. I ran from his room, wondering how he could enjoy such an awful taste! I did not realize he had followed me, and as I discarded the cigarette, his hand held my shoulder and he commanded me, "Pick that up! You wanted it, so smoke it to the end!" He kept hold of me while I went through the motions of smoking and when I had smoked enough to his satisfaction, he said, "Now stamp it out well so that no spark can set the grass afire. Let this be a lesson to you and don't pester me again!"

I was ill most of the day and would not tell Mother what had happened. This was the kindest thing that Uncle Len could have done for me, as I never bad a desire to smoke again. He never told Mother about this.

---

[1] Leonard Cyril Green was born 21st August 1895 at Smiling Valley Farm, the fourteenth and last of the children of Robert Frederick Green and Louisa Jane Nash Green. He was thirteen years older than Edna May.

In thinking of our relationships in later years, I recalled how much impressed I was that my uncles never complained to Mother about my pestering them and being around them so often. Had this been discussed, Mother would have sat down, quietly held my hands and told me how to behave.

One evening I noticed Uncle Len get on his bicycle and ride away, after he and Mother had been talking. I went to her, asking, as I reached for her hand, "Where is he going?" Mother looked thoughtful as she watched his departure, and gravely said, "Uncle Len is courting now and I suppose he went to see his girl."

We discussed this years later, and I mentioned my feeling of her concern. She laughed, saying, "Well, I had a feeling brother Len was making a dreadful mistake. He loved the farm life and Alice lived in the city, although she was visiting at Lilyfontein then. Alice was what we called "A Townie," a city girl. I could never envision her as a domestic, as a farm woman. How sad that I was so totally correct!" She did not, however, relate what happened, but I learned through letters later that Alice divorced Uncle Len after their three daughters were born, seven years later.

A week later, Grannie and Grandpa were going to get the mail, which meant a carriage ride of about three miles. Their second son Robert Frederick, Jr., was the owner of a Trading Post and the mail was left there by a mail carrier from the city. Jessie and I were allowed to go along that day, Jessie sitting on the front seat between the grandparents and I uncomfortable in the back, sitting on the floor boards. At least, however, I was going somewhere even if I could not take part in the conversation.

After travelling about a mile and a half, Grandpa stopped the horses. I stood up to see what was causing this. An ostrich was blocking the road and would not move. There was some uncertainty about its behavior and that of the horses. An ostrich can be mean. Grannie finally took the buggy whip and went bravely toward the bird. It would seem that Grandpa should have done this but, if the ostrich charged, the horses would perhaps rear and panic and bolt. Only Grandpa could manage the team if that happened. I watched breathlessly as Grannie approached the ostrich. She did not want to get too close because they have long legs with a powerful kick forward, and the ability to strike with one leg, which could tear a person from top to bottom.

Now the big bird was waving its wings in a threatening manner, but she kept going forward slowly, then suddenly lashed out, not hitting him but causing a loud clap of the whip. The bird turned and raced away. We all breathed easier. "Good girl," said Grandpa as Grandma came back and calmly got back into the buggy, handing the whip to him.

Another half mile down the road we passed the kraal of natives considered not too friendly. The young black men were apparently having a drinking bash because we could see several behaving erratically. Their kraal was off the road to our right maybe an eighth of a mile away but sitting on a higher level than the road. This enabled them to see us approaching. Grannie and Grandpa made some remark to each other and he flipped the whip to make the team run faster. I was terrified because three of those naked men came running after us, moving surprisingly fast. Grandpa handed the whip to Grannie and she, half turning, flipped the whip at the one closest to her side of the carriage. Two of the blacks then returned to the kraal but the biggest one kept running and reached for me. I screamed and slid under the seat as far as I could. The carriage slowed and Grandpa rose to his feet and lashed out. The black turned and ran back.

I was terrified to see such a naked man in broad daylight and was almost ill with relief that he did not grab me. I started to cry; I was sure he meant to harm me. I wanted to get into the front with Grannie and Grandpa, but he did not stop the running horses until we arrived at the Trading Post. I was still shaking and wouldn't leave Grannie's side. Her arm around me was a comfort, but soon I was interested in watching Uncle Rob taking bread from his outdoor oven.

This was the first time I had seen an ond in action, although I had been curious about this little "house" upon previous visits. It was made of mud and I had thought it was a playhouse for his children. We watched him as he slid the long-handled spade-like shovel into the ond and pulled out the large pans of bread, each pan holding three loaves. The ond held eight pans at a time and he baked daily because he sold the bread in his shop.

After visiting with Uncle Rob and his wife, Aunt Edith,[2] Grandpa carried the mail sack out to the carriage and we headed homeward. I was apprehensive, as we again had to pass the kraal of the men who had run after us. It was a big relief to see no one in sight. Perhaps they were sleeping off their drunkenness.

When Len came in from work, Grandpa handed him a letter and said, "Here's your love letter." My ears perked up and I became very curious. What was a "love letter"? It was some weeks before I was able to find out. One day I was passing Uncle Len's room and, his door being ajar, I saw him finish reading a letter, then put it into a cigar box on his night stand. I wanted to read those letters, but how?

One morning at the breakfast table, Grandpa said, "Len, I want you to go with me to the navel garden this morning." Now would be my chance! After they left, I made sure the other uncles had gone to their appointed tasks and Grannie and Mother were busy. I told Jessie to come with me. We sat on his bed because it was a narrow room and there were no chairs. I opened a letter and instructed Jessie to fold the pages and insert them back into the envelope. She was five years old and I, eight. This was after I had started to school and I was not able to read well yet. Although I soon discovered the letters made no sense, I kept opening one and then another. Not once did I pay attention to what Jessie was doing. As I finished reading a page, I tossed it toward her. So absorbed was I that poor Sister could not keep up with me.

Suddenly a voice sounded and a shadow crossed the bed, and there was Uncle Len at the door! "What are you little devils doing?"

I gasped, "Jessie, under the bed!" We both slid off and under. Len would have to come to the bed to reach us so I watched his feet and whispered to Jessie to crawl toward the end and be ready to run, which is what we did. Uncle Len must have been speechless to see pages all over his bed, as Jessie had not placed

---

[2] Edith Ann Kirchoff.

one complete letter into any envelope. He didn't even try to catch us.

I expected to be severely chastised by Mother, for surely he would tell her. I also wondered why he was home before lunch. I was very meek at the table and tried to be preoccupied with my food. Not once did I look toward Uncle Len. I did learn that he had been suffering with a toothache and had to return home because the pain was so severe. Perhaps the pain, plus the surprise of seeing us two girls reading his letters, shocked him so much, he could not react as I had expected.

Mother never mentioned this incident and I wondered why. Years later, while we were discussing family events, I mentioned the "love letter" episode, remarking that I could see nothing in them do be considered so important. She was astonished to hear about this. It was then I realized that Uncle Len had never told her. She said, "If he had told me, you would have had a good spanking. I find it difficult to realize you did such a naughty thing, after my teaching you never to touch another person's belongings." She never knew how much I wanted to be like this uncle and do the things he did. Perhaps I loved him as a father figure, but I did lose interest in love letters.

The boys, as they were referred to, had a talk-session in the shop many evenings. I sometimes eavesdropped before making my presence known. One evening Uncle Len was talking about being caught short" as he was en route to the navel garden. Not knowing what he meant, I listened and heard him say, "I had an emergency and had to squat and chose a place under a large tree. I felt something touch my back two or three times but when I put my hand back I could feel nothing. After this happened again I turned to look and saw a big boomslang (a tree snake) coming down the tree. Believe me, I got up in a hurry, pulling on my pants as I ran!" I thought this very funny and laughed along with the uncles.

Those snakes had long, thick bodies and were usually harmless, but any snake can cause anxiety, especially when a person comes onto one unexpectedly.

I had a vivid mental picture of the whole thing and burst into laughter, totally forgetting I was not supposed to have been in hearing distance. I ran out of the shed as soon as I heard Uncle Len say, "Oh not you again, Edna. That damn little kid does the most mischief."

Uncle Clem[3] had no trouble from me, however, I did not have any feelings one way or another for him. This was, I'm sure, because he showed no interest in Mother or her three children. He was a sort of misfit in my life and, perhaps, in the lives of his brothers. I have no recollection of any togetherness radiating from him as was so evident in the rest of the family members at Smiling Valley.

Perhaps he was overwhelmed because of having a deformed foot. This was a cause for his being rejected when applying for military duty when World War I began. I overheard that as a comment at a much later time.

---

[3] Clement Gerorge Green, born 11th May 1893 at Smiling Valley Farm, was the thirteenth child of Robert Frederick Green and Louisa Jane Nash Green.

Chapter 18

Life on Smiling Valley Farm

The South African veld was a showplace in the spring when the flowers began to bloom. Wild daisies covered some areas like a carpet and along the ravine grew arum lilies. Those plants that grew taller with many flowerets formed large ball-like flowers, some as large as a small child's head, These, a gorgeous blue, were called "Lily of the Nile." Later, when Mother took us to walk beside the Bulugha River and sometimes to cross over at narrow places, we saw the white Lily of the Nile but only the blue grew in the ravine.

I particularly enjoyed the veld this time of year because then the myriad flowers popped up in the most unexpected places and I enjoyed examining them on my daily walks to and from school. The wild gladiola were my favorite because they stood tall, showing off their varied shapes and colors. It was interesting to look into the wide open florets at the lower flower and to wonder how those buds at the top could open. Sometimes a bee would come along and enter a flower.

My favorite pastime on days when there was no school was to lie in the grass and watch the clouds parade across the blue sky. I let my imagination run free, forming shapes of people or animals. One afternoon I saw what looked like an angel and thought long about it. Actually, I had no remembrance of having heard the word because our family was not church-oriented. I may have heard it when I went to Sunday School only once when I was four. As I lay there thinking of angels, one seemed to become real. I felt it would sweep out of the sky to pick me up. I suddenly became frightened, got up quickly, and ran home. This was my last time of lying in the veld and searching the sky imaginatively.

I often noticed that Mother would take a walk after the evening dishes were washed and go out of the yard, walk a short distance from the gate, and look toward the setting sun. I remember thinking she must feel as lonely as I often felt, but I never intruded on her solitude.

I took her stance one evening, however, to see what it was she might be seeing. I noticed how pretty the evening sky was as the sun slowly disappeared between two hills in the distance. I began to wonder what was behind them and what caused them to be there. My mind seemed to expand in consciousness and I somehow realized that the "world out there" was more vast than the farm area with which I was familiar. Many strange thoughts flowed in and I felt that some day I would know what was "out there."

Another evening, as I watched, the sun set and suddenly flared upward. I was excited and ran into the house, telling anyone who would listen that "the sun winked at me." My uncles roared into laughter and the grandparents had faint smiles. Mother just looked at me in wonderment. Years later I was to learn that she had psychic gifts and perhaps her wonderment was at my saying something she had herself witnessed.

In 1909 when I was born, seven cousins were also born, a good supply of grandchildren. Not all lived close enough for us to visit so often as we did with Cyril and Amy. Cyril was my age[1] although I was older by ten months. His sister Amy was the same age[2] as Jessie and often these two would return with us after school on Friday and stay overnight. This meant a fun time most of Saturday, like hunting for birds eggs.

This Saturday the four of us went on an egg-robbing trip. We roamed around the veld and followed the ravine for quite a dis-

---

[1] Cyril Hedley Green, born 10th November 1909 to Stephen and Martha Green.

[2] Amy Winnifred Green, born 31st July 1912 to Stephen and Martha Green.

tance. The little birds, called finches, wove pear-shaped hanging nests. These were intricate, having narrow entrances about an inch and a half long. The entrance to each nest was arranged in such a manner that the little eggs could not fall out. The eggs were small and white, with colored dots of blue or brown. As I recall, the finches were beautifully colored in blue, green, and brown outer feathers, with long tails and little golden chests.

Cyril and I were always doing things that were not right and sometimes we would try to see who could devise the most mischief. Now we took turns being first, meaning that he would rob one nest and I the next, and so on. Although the nests hung low on bushes, the two little girls were not tall enough to reach them so they were designated to hold the eggs. Our intention was to make a hole at each end and blow out the contents of the eggs so as to make a necklace.

In our excitement, Cyril and I lost count of whose turn it was and an argument arose. Being more of a pacifist, I let Cyril take the next turn. The nest was higher than he could reach from the ground so he climbed the tree part way, reached for the nest, and suddenly let out an awful screech as he fell to the ground. Mother happened to be in the yard and heard his screams. She ran down to the ravine and helped him to his feet.

"Cyril! what happened?" She was brushing off the dirt. Cyril's face was so white we all thought something drastic had happened. He tried to get his breath so he could talk

"A snake!" he gasped. "A snake in there!" He kept backing away from the bush. "I touched a snake!" He was still gasping. "Did it bite me?"

Mother looked carefully at his hand, then shook her head. "No, that snake didn't bite you. There's no mark on your hand." He sort of collapsed as she said that, then she went on. "Besides, the snake probably had eaten the eggs and was just lying there digesting them."

All this time the girls and I had been staring at first Cyril, then at Mother. Now she looked toward me. "Let this be a lesson to all of you! Keep your hands out of birds nests! Snakes do crawl in to eat the eggs!" We were a sober bunch of kids the rest of the day and we certainly had no intention of ever putting our hands into any more birds nests. We did not have any eggs to show the adults because after Cyril fell the little sisters threw away the eggs that they were holding.

Another Saturday we were together and again playing in the ravine. It was dry at this time from a drought. Two deep pools, however, still had water in them. We lay on our stomachs to peer into one of them. Cyril got to wondering whether it was safe to swim in one.

Jessie said, "You might drown."

Amy said, "What will I tell Daddy and Mommy if you do drown?"

I said nothing; so, as I did not challenge Cyril, he decided to roam elsewhere, with the two smaller girls following him. As I continued to lie there I noticed something moving in the water. It was an odd looking "stick." It sort of wiggled, stopped, turned, and finally slowly went down, down, and rested on a leaf of a bulrush anchored to the bottom. I thought the little bug was dying. The sun was shining in such a manner into the pool that I could see everything. I watched helplessly but I could not rescue the "waterbug," as I thought of it, without losing my balance and falling headfirst into the pool.

Then slowly, oh so slowly, the bug began to come alive again, but not as it was. Something else was emerging from that bug body. With great effort it began to move slowly up the stem of the bulrush. I watched breathlessly, wondering how a thin stick like that could move, knowing it was not my imagination. As the "stick" emerged out of the water, it crept up a bit farther. The sun shone hot upon it. Soon I saw wings appear and begin to flutter, while the back part of the "stick" began to take shape. A dragonfly with gauzy wings suddenly sat on that stem for a few moments and then flew away.

The miracle of metamorphosis was a stupendous experience for me, although I did not have the wisdom at that time to comprehend its significance. In later years when I saw a cocoon change into a beautiful butterfly, that experience did not strike me with so much awe as did the dragonfly experience.

One particular day I noticed an old wrinkled black woman sitting outdoors smoking a long-stemmed corncob pipe. Near her were two young black women, her granddaughters. Mother came out of the house and called me, then taking me by the hand she stood in front of the old lady and spoke at some length in Bantu. I noticed the old woman's eyes light up and her toothless mouth broke into a wide smile. She began talking to me but, of course, I did not understand her.

Turning to me, Mother said, "This is dear old Mickey. She took care of you when you were a baby for a short time right after you were born. Grannie sent her to Pretoria to help me." I asked Mother what Mickey was saying. "She is telling you that she used to change your napkins (diapers) and that you had a nice little bottom." I was very embarrassed

It seemed Mickey had been with Grannie when they lived in Port Elizabeth, had trekked with the family to the farm and had helped Grannie by caring for several of her children at birth. Thereafter, she had been a nursemaid and had this brief time with Mother when I was born.

I looked up at Mother, "Where has she been? I have never seen her before."

"She has been visiting some of her children who live far away and has just come back to the kraal here." Again Mother spoke to the old woman, who replied by nodding her head, then to the two girls who chatted for a few moments. I could understand none of what was being said.

Suddenly everyone got very busy and I was astonished to see them putting bundles of clothing on their heads. Mother was doing the supervising as more and more blacks appeared. Then she made the surprising remark that we would all go to the river to do the laundry. She handed Sister and me some soap, a bottle of bluing, and a few clothes pins, saying, "You girls carry those and I'll carry some of the bigger things." Then she explained, "We will be doing the laundry this way until it rains again. We have had so little rain that we can no longer use the water from the tanks but will have to wash at the river. You will even have your baths in the river."

Bathing in the river? What fun! I had never even given any

thought as to how our water supply was kept up. I knew there were three large round tanks at the corners of the house into which the rain water poured from the down spouts. I knew there were four or five strainers of different gauges that the rain water went through before it reached the tank; I also knew the corrugated roof guided every drop of rainwater into the gutters where it ran into the down spouts at each corner of the house and finally into the three big tanks. Water had always seemed plentiful when I wanted it So it was a surprise to be told now that we had a water shortage.

Then I recalled that for sometime the tanks had been locked, that Grandpa held the keys, and that each morning he had been dipping out water for household needs—enough for making tea and coffee and for cooking. Someone was always cautioning us children to drink all our water and not to waste a drop.

We arrived at the Bulugha River and Mother spoke to the young blacks who immediately went out in different directions and began to gather wood. Mickey had come to supervise her granddaughters who were now working hard. One of the girls began to dig a wide depression in the ground and to surround it with stones. Soon she had a small fireplace on which a five-gallon petrol can filled with water was placed so it would boil for laundering. Soon the other girl also had a fire going while young children continued to bring pieces of wood. The fires had to be kept burning most of the morning.

Mother was sorting the clothing, light colored in one pile, dark in another, heavy work clothes in still another, and bed clothes and towels into yet different piles. Now began the task of washing them in a small pool in the river, beating and rubbing and scrubbing.

I did not bother myself about all the proceedings but knew it was fun being at the river. Yet I did wonder why the water was not flowing. Jessie and I could walk on the rocks at almost any spot and Mother told us sternly to stay within sight. If we fell into a deep hole she could not see us and she had enough to do without worrying where we children were. Deep in me I felt that Mother was unhappy and I knew I should behave. But the day seemed so very long when I was thus restricted. There was really not much that Sister and I could do,

After the cold wash in the river, the young women took the wet white things and put them into the hot water for boiling. They were then transferred to the galvanized wash tub where they were rinsed. I had wondered where the clothes would be hung to dry because I saw no clothesline. I then found out that they were to be strewn over the grass and shrubs.

As the day progressed, the surrounding area was decorated with garments and linens drying in the hot sun, I noticed that Mother used a small watering can from time to time to spray the table linens. We always had a nice tablecloth on the dining table and we used cloth napkins because paper napkins were undreamed of items.

I watched her sprinkling the clothes. "Why do you wet them again?' I asked.

"The sun bleaches out the stains that don't wash out." Mother stooped over to pick up a dry dish towel. "Each time I wet them the stain fades a bit more." Carefully, she was folding the towel, to lay it in the basket.

Because the heavier work clothes took longer to dry, we had a bit of leisure time. Mother began pointing out the different birds and telling us about them. The secretary bird, to my eyes, was an astonishing sight: it was so tall, long-legged, and awkward look-ing, with a topknot that looked like pen quills over the ears. It ran so quickly into the thicket that I did not get a good look at its coloring. Mother said she was glad to see these birds were still around because they ate snakes. My reaction to that was, "Ugh!"

At noon we had lunch and it was a fun time for the black children as well as for Jessie and me. Soon the dry laundry items were being folded, the petrol cans emptied onto the fire—and the small parade started homeward, each person carrying some items of finished laundry.

Mother and her helpers did the family laundry this way for months; and our baths were done similarly. On Saturdays we would make the trip down to the river, affording us further. Mother would find a shallow pool in which to bathe. Because this was spring and summer, the water was not too cold for us.

Mother had spent much of her youth in this river area. Her brothers and sister Florence had often roamed here. We found evidence of this as the river kept drying up. One day we saw crabs minus their front claws. Then Mother was delighted when she picked up a crab and found her initials on the back. Some were initialed by her brothers also, and some even had the year scratched onto their shells. She explained that when rinderpest was killing cattle and robbing the farmers of meat, "We found that there were crabs in the river. We did not know how to use them but we robbed them of their claws and boiled them. Poor things! I'm amazed they kept living all these years."

We were able to cross the river at one point, as Mother wanted to see if there were any wild dates. We did not find any dates ripe enough to eat but did find some wild figs growing near the date palms. It was a low bush and had only two ripe figs but they were truly delicious. Mother said, "Wild ants usually get them first, so we are fortunate to have these." She took one and divided the other between Jessie and me.

A very large tree hung over the area where Mother had been washing at the river. This bore small fruits that Mother called "blue berries." They were the size of peanuts out of the shell and were tasty but stained one's hands, lips, and clothing with a purple stain. The center of the fruit was white. Along the river bank, in spots, were arum lilies and here the white and blue Lilies of the Nile grew in profusion. Also, the beautiful and unusual bird-of-paradise flowers were abundant. Of the many flowers growing in the area, these made the most impression on me. It was the proximity to the water that made them grow so well.

During breakfast one morning, we were aware of a loud chattering and went outdoors to determine what it was. The trees along the Bulugha River seemed to be moving but there was no wind. The men peered through their binoculars and reported that little brown monkeys were traveling along the river, probably heading to the Bulugha Mouth in search of water. This chatter kept up for half a day; hundreds of these creatures must have been on the move.

On another afternoon, during this drought period, we heard

a lot of squawking in the large orchard. Uncle Sid and Mother took us girls to a vantage point where we could see the trees, surrounding the reservoir, swaying from a large flock of strange birds. They, too, must have been migrating for water. Uncle Sid decided they were a species of the parrot family, all with brilliant green and bluish feathers. Their yellow beaks were somewhat curved. I did not see the tails, but Uncle went close enough to see that they were very long.

Much discussion was held about these two events occurring in one short period of time. Some wondered whether conditions up north were really so bad that these monkeys and birds would come this far south. Apparently this had never happened in all the years the Green family lived at Smiling Valley farm.

The topic of conversation began to center on the drought, its long duration, how much longer it might last, and what to do if it continued. The Bulugha River was actually dry except in deeper spots. The younger uncles, Len and Clem, had inspected the Kwelegha, which was much deeper, and they said it still contained a fair supply of water. After that, much activity went on in the work shop. Before long the uncles emerged with an invention they called a sled, upon which they had fastened two wooden kegs. Instead of using oxen, they inspanned a couple of horses, with the idea that they would go to the Kwelegha and bring home water for everyday use. A wagon, by this time, could not be driven over the road because it had become a place of deep, dry dust. The burden on the oxen, pulling a loaded wagon, was too much, so horses were used.

It was an event of some importance to the family when the uncles returned with both barrels full. A sense of triumph was theirs, for it was their idea that had worked so well; they then supplied water until the rains came again.

The drought lasted for three years. Had it not been for the water supply from both rivers, it would have been a disaster for the family. Uncle Sid was concerned about his apple trees, because they were farther from the river's edge. The windmill was not so helpful because there usually was not enough wind. One day he climbed to the top of it, with a can of oil, believing it might work even at the slightest breeze if it were well oiled. While facing the windmill parts to be oiled, he dropped a tool and bent over to pick it up, causing him to glance behind him. Because he was so high up, he could see a considerable distance up the river. He told us later, "I could not believe my eyes, as I saw a wall of water coming down and even heard the roar. Yet we had not had a drop of rain. I scrambled drown that ladder and by the time my feet were on the ground, the water began to swirl around my feet. What an unbelievable sight! I only hope the windmill stands. I'm sure we've lost many orange trees, probably all that were next to the river's edge."

The discussion went on and on; finally Grandpa and his three sons, Sid, Clem, and Len, walked to the garden to get an idea of the damage. The river was still at flood stage and as there was nothing to be done, all came home in somewhat of a gloom. More discussion about the possible damage continued. Because it still had not rained where we were, the uncles Len and Clem suggested they ride horseback to the beach (five miles away) to see how many trees might be lying on the ground. Grandpa and Uncle Sid returned to the garden.

When the younger uncles returned they reported that the Bulugha Mouth was now a wide channel right into the ocean. Oranges and trees were scattered over a large area, and natives were picking up the fruit on both sides of the newly made channel. Uncle Sid was happy that none of his apple trees had been even wetted by the overflow, but many of the orange trees had been utterly swept away. No one went to the upper garden where the bananas and naval oranges grew, but everyone was sure that many of those trees would be missing also. That evening brought much discussion about the terrific storm in the "up-country mountains." Everyone thought that surely rain would come soon.

This was in the early spring of 1917. We kept plans to spend Easter at the beach, which would be my second and last experience of camping at the seaside.

Once again we were trekking to the ocean. My expectations were not so high this time, as I knew where we were going and what to expect when we arrived. Also, there were fewer wagons in the final encampment. But it would still be a joyful time for all.

This time, until the mothers were ready, the children were forbidden to go to the Bulugha Mouth where we swam last year. They wanted to inspect the area to see if it were safe; however, we could go to the seashell area that was right in front of the wagon positions. It was disappointing to find fewer seashells. Whereas we had walked upon them the previous years, we would now be walking on sand.

The next morning several mothers decided to go swimming. They told us to wait until they changed into their bathing clothing, usually nothing more than an old blouse and a pair of bloomers. We tried to wait patiently, but it was not easy. Finally, they reappeared wearing their robes, and off we went. Our nice bathing spot existed no longer and I stared in amazement at the "river" that led right into the ocean. Mother told us children to stay only at the edge of the water. I held Jessie's hand as I turned to watch Mother and Aunt Florence drop their robes onto the sand some distance behind us. Because I was not looking ahead, I was not prepared when a large wave caught us and tumbled both Jessie and me over and over.

I had lost Sister! While I was spluttering because of the water over my face, I saw her being swept closer to the channel. I began screaming—oh, how I screamed! Aunt Florence immediately saw what was happening and I heard her yell to her son Sam to run for help. By now Mother began to react to my screams. I never saw two women run so fast. Both were strong swimmers but they had a hard time getting Sister out of the undertow. One of the uncles, which one I do not remember, soon helped the women bring Sister back to the beach.

It was a sober group of children and adults who looked on as Aunt Florence administered first aid to Jessie. I heard the word "drown" and began to realize how close we came to losing Sister. We no longer needed to be told not to go to that area. We contented ourselves with wading in the low tide pools and in paying attention to the sea life that they contained. Mother was giving us much more of her time now and often went wading with us, explaining to us what we were seeing.

The sea anemones were pretty and showed themselves in their various colors. To me they looked much like asters. I wanted to pick it one, but Mother said they might sting and that sting could be poisonous. She picked up a small stick and touched one to show us how quickly the "petals" folded, explaining they were open when the animal was hungry but when tiny sea animals swam close the jaws snapped closed, and that is the way the sea anemone got its food. This turned out to be good experience for me, as I learned something about sea life that would never have been my lot had the old swimming area been safe.

Mother showed us how some types of shells stuck to the rocks. Those she called "limpets" were the most plentiful. She showed us the little tracks left on the rock when a limpet decided to move to another place. It seemed they stuck so hard and stay so long in one place that after moving the outline of the limpet was still imprinted upon the rock. Their shells were brownish-green and slightly dome shaped.

The barnacle was another stone-hugging shell, with a very sharp or rough top. Mother said one of those never moved but would protrude a sort of tongue through the round opening on top, when the tide was high, to catch its food. To me they were very unattractive.

Periwinkles were a dark blue, almost purple, and had nice shapes. We pried the larger ones off the rocks and placed them in a bucket of water to roast in the evening's fire. There was other interesting animal life in those pools. We were thrilled to see something that looked like a sea horse. We also saw many tiny brown-colored crabs, some so small that if we were not watching closely, we missed seeing them.

One night we awakened to the sound of rain beating down and the surf pounding loudly. The rains at last! The sea sounded like a wild creature and I was fearful the waves would reach the wagons and wash us away. The next morning, however, was calm and after breakfast we all went to see what had happened on the beach. There were dozens of strange looking jellyfish, though not with their usual shape. They looked like elongated pyramids with long thread-like tails. They were a beautiful blue. Before Mother could anticipate her intentions, Jessie picked one up. Then she screamed horribly! The tail was a stinger, and it was now partly wrapped around her leg. Her leg was sore most of the day. This was a "man-o'-war," not typical of the South African beaches.[3]

During the night I was awakened because of a light in my face. I looked around to see its source and discovered it was from the full moon. I lay there, marveling at this great ball of light. As I had the previous year, I noticed its shining on the calm sea and imagined it was a path leading to the moon. The sea was golden in the area where the moon beams shone. In my imagination, I believed I could walk on that path right up into the moon! It was then I began to understand a song we learned at school:

> *"Lady Moon, Lady Moon, where are you roving?*
> *"Over the sea, over the sea.*
> *"Lady Moon, Lady Moon, whom are you loving?*
> *"All who love me."*

All too soon the women began putting the household things used at the beach back into the boxes, the men were taking down the sails, and the blacks were bringing the oxen and beginning to inspan. This activity was the announcement that we were returning home. As the wagons pulled away, I sat in the wagon bed, looking around and wondering if this would ever again be my experience. I felt sad because I felt that this was probably my last time at this beach.

Little could I know then that I would be sailing over the Indian Ocean to get into the Atlantic and eventually live close to the Pacific Ocean. Life and its changes were already in motion.

---

[3] The author's notes indicate that years later she searched for the explanation of these sea creatures and found in a public library an answer in a book called *Sea-Anemones* by O. H. Carlegran. "It was very technical, with many scientific words, so it was easier to remember the simpler explanation as that of a tube-like floating swimming colony; a muscular gas-containing sac that serves as a float on this tube-like sea creature."

Chapter 19

Journey to Ermelo

Early in August 1917, Mother received an invitation to visit her sister Lulu and family, whom she had not seen for several years. Lulu was the fourth of Grannie Green's children and older than Mother. She was married to Robert Bryson, a Scotsman, and they were living near Ermelo, a town about 95 miles east south-east of Johannesburg in the Transvaal, but 225 miles north north-east of East London in the Cape. They had bought a farm they named "Spriggs Rest" high up in the mountains; nearby was their trading post of the same name.

Mother decided to arrive there at the beginning of spring, which in South Africa was mid-September. This would give her time to make coats for us, something we never needed where we were living. She had to plan our wardrobe for all of three months. This meant she would be very busy sewing.

Jessie and I were delighted to look forward to going some-where. She did not remember our train journey from Pretoria three years previously. I tried to explain to our brother Leonard about the train but he could not understand. The time for our departure finally arrived and, after saying our good-byes, we were lifted into the wagon. Uncles Sid and Clem were taking a load of late fruits to market and now I began to anticipate another memorable experience at the rendezvous.

Our wagon was soon in laager. With the help of Uncle Sid, Mother got to the ground, then he went to instruct the cook. As she was lifting Jessie and Leonard out and before she could help me, a voice rang out, "Ivy Walker! What are you doing here?"

Mother turned quickly. I stared at the new arrival, a tall, thin handsome man coming toward the wagon. He reached us and continued, "How are you and where are you going?" They embraced warmly, then backed away and stood looking at each other. Both began talking at once, then burst into laughter.

Still standing at the end of the wagon bed, I said, "Mommy—Mommy!" Mother turned back to me. "Oh, Bob, this is Edna May! Remember how tiny she was as a baby? Edna, this is your godfather, Uncle Robert Matchett, who held you when you were christened. Say hello to him."

I had no idea what this meant. Because I was still in the wagon I could see eye-to-eye with him. We observed each other gravely. I liked what I saw in those blue-gray eyes. He reached out his arms, but instead of placing me on the ground, he hugged me tightly. He had a nice smell about him. I did not know what to say and could hardly understand his speech. He had the same Scottish brogue my dad had. Something about him seemed familiar, but not being used to being held I began to squirm. So he carefully placed me on the ground.

Taking Sister's hand Mother was saying, "This is Jessie who was born after you left Cullinan. She will be six next March." She put her other arm around Brother. "This is Leonard who has just had his third birthday.[1] He's been in the hospital, so he is looking a bit peaked. He was born after Sidney left us in April of 1914."

Uncle Bob squatted down so he could see each child eye-to-eye. He spoke to them but each eyed him solemnly and was silent. He stood up, saying, "A fine little family you have, Ivy."

Uncles Sid and Clem came over to greet Uncle Bob and they all began catching up on all the news, talking about what they had all been doing since seeing each other last.

Before long a servant announced the evening meal, so there was much bustling around getting logs in place for a family circle. While we children ate and Mother watched over us, she exchanged comments with the men. Most was beyond my comprehension although, as usual, my ears were ever alert. Then I heard her say, "Bob, what brought you down from the Transvaal?"

"Well, I've retired and I am planning a safari. This seemed a good place to start." They all talked about that for a time, then as

---

[1] This places the event in September 1917.

the other men drifted away, I heard Uncle Bob say, "Ivy, have you heard from Sidney?" Because Dad's name was seldom mentioned, for Mother never spoke of him to us, I listened intently. She gave a deep sigh before saying anything. She seemed reluctant to reply but finally she said, "Sid writes very seldom. When he does I wonder why he spends postage because he never gives any information that I need. He sends so little money that I feel I should do something to support my children. I just cannot expect help from my brothers and parents the rest of my life."

Neither said anything for a few moments, then Uncle Bob said, "Where is he now; do you know? This war is changing so many lives."

"He is somewhere in France—I think. When he learned he was to be conscripted he went to Jamaica but the British picked him up there because he is a British subject. I do have an official address to write to. He apparently enjoys wearing the kilt and being in the Canadian battalion called "The Ladies from Hell," because he makes reference to this in every letter.[2] Does he ever write you, Bob? You two were once good friends."

"That was a long time ago, Ivy. You know I never approved of his strike activities. I disapprove of any family man who jeopardizes his job when he has family responsibilities. What are his plans after the war is over? Do you know?"

"Because he can never get work here again, I think he intends to go to the United States. He was banned, you know."

Uncle Bob looked grave. "Yes I know. Has he ever spoken of sending for you and the children?" Mother looked thoughtful and unhappy. "He did make a vague promise once, but I just don't know. He never was a man of his word. I don't like to think about it. I sometimes wonder about other women in his life." She turned away. "If you will excuse, me I'll get the children to bed." She lifted Leonard, moved to the wagon and put him in it. Uncle Bob

---

[2] The only extant evidence of Sidney Arthur Walker's military service consists of the British War Medal and the World War I Victory Medal etched with his name, rank, service number, and regiment: "Pvt. Sidney A. Walker, No. 34408, 6th Bn KOSB." "KOSB" is The King's Own Scottish Borderers. He is buried in the Soldiers' Field, Woodlawn Cemetery, Saskatoon, Saskatchewan, Canada.

helped Mother herself into the wagon, lifted Jessie and then me. He held me closely and I could feel the warmth of his love.

We looked at each other silently. Finally he said softly, "Be a good girl and help your mother." Jessie and Leonard fell asleep a long time before I did. I had much to think about. I wondered about Dad and was puzzled by the last conversation between Mother and Uncle Bob.

There was also a nagging memory trying to surface. Suddenly I knew I had seen Uncle Bob Matchett earlier. The day of the rugby, match it was, when Dad had picked me up, tossed me high into the air, and said to an observer, "This is my big girl." He did that sort of thing so seldom I never forgot it. Later Mother verified what I was remembering.

This was the last time I ever saw this gentle, kind man. In later years I would receive many letters from Uncle Bob, none of which I kept. When Mother received news of his death she felt very sad.

When I awakened we were already in the city and we finally arrived at the station. Uncle Sid helped Mother with the baggage and we said good-bye. As we watched the wagon depart out of sight, I was suddenly worried. Were they going out of my life forever? "Mommy, will we see the uncles again?" "Oh yes, child!" she smiled. "We are not going away forever, only for a visit. They will meet us when we return." I felt relieved but did not ponder this too long, for the train was now approaching.

Now I wanted Brother to see the train, but his reaction surprised me. He screamed and frantically clutched at Mother's skirt so much that she had to lift him. Perhaps he thought the black, smoking, puffing, whistling engine was some kind of a monster! He clung tightly and would not let go until we were aboard and seated in our compartment. Mother had to reassure him over and over that everything was all right. With the exception of one piece which Mother kept with her, all baggage was placed under the seats by the porter. These seats would become our beds later, which I tried to point out to Brother.

The next morning I was anticipating food, as we had not had any since the evening meal. When a knock sounded the door opened and there stood the porter. I was happy to see him holding a tray with glasses of orange juice. He gave Mother a menu and she ordered our breakfast; then he left and I was anxious for his return. "Jessie," I said, "when that man comes back, watch him touch here." I was pointing to the side of the coach. "The table is there." Jessie eyed me strangely. After surveying the wall carefully, she said, "There's no table there." Finally the waiter brought the food Mother had ordered. As he reached toward the wall, I said again, "Watch, Jessie!" Both she and Brother became wide-eyed when a table was pulled out. We were all so hungry we did not talk for a time.

The train was now traveling through what had been a war-torn land, with death and destruction everywhere. The early settlers, 1791-1837, had fought bravely against the Xhosas in nine wars, besides several previous skirmishes to steal cattle. Later, the Anglo-Boer War, 1899-1902, caused even greater devastation, as the British burned farms, fruit trees, and homes. The train passed close to the area where British troops had kept thousands of women and children prisoners behind barbed wire, without shelter and with only a small amount of food.

Mother must have thought of this as we passed through this area, but we children were unaware of these tragedies. How safe we were now, traveling through this land even though another war to end all wars was being fought overseas. Men were still dying. Grannie had read the casualty lists just a few days before we left.

About mid-morning after our second night on the train, our porter came, saying, "Ermelo is the next station. I'll take your bags to the end of the car and see that they get off."

Mother thanked him and began helping us put on our coats and bonnets, putting on Leonard's last, then donning her own. Lifting Leonard, who was commencing to be alarmed again, she went out into the aisle, saying, "Hold onto the railing, girls, and follow me."

As the train stopped, the porter took Leonard, who was reluctant to leave Mother's arms, helped Mother down the steps, then Jessie and finally me.

We were here at last!

Chapter 20

Aunt Lulu & Uncle Bob

A strange man stepped forward and embraced Mother. By now I should have been used to the way she was greeted so often by someone who was to me a complete strangers but I never was. Then they both turned to us and Mother introduced us to our Uncle Bob Bryson,[1] a six-foot tall man, slim, and clean shaven. He wore a hat so I could not see much of his dark hair, but I did notice the kindly gray-blue eyes. He wore a vest beneath his coat. Across his middle was a chain, one end of which was in a left pocket, the other on the right, with an ornament half-way between. I wondered what it was for and Mother told me later this was called a watch fob. Just before he climbed into the buggy, I saw him remove his gold watch at the end of the chain to check the time, so my curiosity was satisfied.

Finally we were all settled in the buggy, one different from any I had ever seen: a two-seater, drawn by four horses. Mother must have made some comment because Uncle Bob said, "We have a long way to travel, mostly up a winding road, which is too much for two horses, so I have trained these four to work together."

Jessie and I looked around so as not to miss too much. We did not enter the small city of Ermelo, but went instead out onto a country road. There was no real beauty to see. The drought had been so long that the grass was still dry in appearance, the vegetation sparse. There were boulders everywhere. They were varied in size, most of them rounded and brownish In color. It was easy to

---

[1] Robert Bryson was born 16th March 1872; he died 8th November, 1950

imagine that a giant had stood on a mountain top and tossed them hither and yon. As we went along we began to see many little brown animals dart to and fro. At times one would sit upon a rock and seem to be scolding. They scampered so fast we really could not see them well but their antics made us laugh. Uncle Bob called them "dassies," which means rock rabbits. A few birds were much larger than any we had seen at the Cape. Only a few green bushes bearing either red flowers or red berries were scattered among the rocks. I suddenly realized there were no thorn trees! Grandpa Green's farm had so many that I did miss them. The trees we now saw were tall, with their leaves near the tops. Uncle Bob said they were the kind that grew on the mountains and he called them "pines." The "leaves," long and slender were really "needles."

The journey was coming to an end, for Uncle Bob was pointing with his riding whip to the distance, saying, "That bright green you see is our fruit garden, so we will soon be home." We arrived at an expanse of cleared, level ground where several people were waiting for us. The blacks took charge of the horses as soon as we stopped, while one took our baggage toward the house. Uncle Bob helped Mother down, then us children. She and Aunt Lulu embraced, and there was much talking and laughing as we children were introduced.

"This is your Aunt Lulu,"[2] said Mother, "and your cousins Violet, Thomas, and Harry." I felt shy but this was quickly forgotten in the warmth of Aunt Lulu's hug and the enthusiasm of the greetings by the cousins. Mother had last seen the two older ones when they were small. The daughter Violet was the eldest[3] and she was well named, for her eyes were like dark violets, gentle and shining. I was interested in the wide ribbon bow she wore at the nape of her neck, a bow that was attached to a looped coil of auburn hair. The bow was fashioned to look like a butterfly and she wore these daily, in different colors. The older son, Thomas, called Tom, was home from college. He was a handsome young

---

[2] Louisa "Lulu" Green, born 17th April 1877 was the fourth child, the second daughter. She and Robert married 14th June 1898.

[3] Violet was born 30th March 1900. She married Frank Hollis and bore three sons.

man, a duplicate of his dad in looks and appearance. Harry was two months my junior[4] and full of mischief, judging by his merry blue eyes. He had a mass of red hair and many freckles, adding to his charm. We would become good friends.

Although Aunt Lulu looked familiar, I knew I had never seen her before. Finally I realized she looked much like Uncle Clem, her younger brother. She had the same stature, tall and slim, with lots of red hair coiled on top of her head. She had a warmth that was absent in her brother and she had a quality of loving kindness that gave her an aura of serenity. We would eventually correspond for years. Through her I later learned much about family history, spurring an interest in genealogy. I felt akin to her, especially after I learned she suffered intermittent malaria as I did.

At last the greetings were over and Aunt Lulu led the way into the house. At the door stood a buxom, smiling Native woman. Aunt Lulu spoke to her in Bantu, then said to Mother, "Ivy, this is our head maid, Sara. She will show you to your room." Mother's greeting Sara in her own language seemed to please the maid, and we all followed her. She led us into a large bedroom, the entrance of which was a short corridor off the dining room. This was a pleasant room with double beds, a wash stand with a marble top supporting a pitcher and a wash bowl. Sara left us and Mother said, "Put your bonnets and coats on that bed," pointing to the farther one. "I'll put them away later. You girls can call that your bed."

She proceeded to change Leonard's clothing and freshen him, we girls had our turns, then she did the same to herself. By this time Sara appeared, announcing in Bantu that tea was ready. Mother led the way and we were all seated. Aunt Lulu was at the far end of a long table, Violet was to her left, across from Mother. Leonard would not sit on the chair provided for him between Auntie and Mother, so she held him on her lap for this time. Tom was across the table from Jessie who was sitting beside Mother, while I was seated at Uncle Bob's left, with Harry on his right. I learned

---

[4] Harry, then, was born in March 1909. He married Betty, and later worked at the Pilgrim's Rest gold mine.

that system, order, promptness, and ritual were to be a part of our lives while visiting in this home.

I eyed the place mat setting with interest, the first I had seen. Later I asked Mother what kind of lace was around them. "Tatting," she said. "It's made with something they call a 'shuttle.' I will ask Violet to show you, as she learned that at school."

When I thought no one was watching, I moved my hand along the edge of the table. I liked the smoothness of the wood. All other tables I had seen had square ends and sometimes felt rough or scratchy.

When tea was over, Mother suggested naps. I did not want one, because Harry had indicated he would show me the garden. So while Leonard and Jessie were taking their naps I went out with Harry. How small that garden was! There were only four to six trees each of apples, citrus, plums, and very interesting almond trees. The latter were unfamiliar to me because Grandpa did not have nut trees. Harry showed me how the nuts grew with a covering he called a purse. Later I would see how shiny smooth the inside of the purse was when it separated from the nut itself, and how fuzzy soft the outer part was. I told Harry in great detail about Grandpa's large farm. He had never been there, although this was also his Grandpa. He was impressed.

He then took me into what he called "the tunnel," a long grape arbor. He described its construction, pointing to the iron uprights on each side, four feet apart, that supported boards lengthwise. This had been covered with wire, fastened somehow onto the posts. These plants must have been old growth because the leaves were thick and the bunches of grapes forming were profuse. This would be our haven when we played hooky from school.

I was getting hungry, so I was glad when we were called for dinner. I noticed the dinner plates were placed in front of Uncle Bob, as were the vegetable bowls and the meat platter. After we sat down everyone was silent as though expecting something to happen. Then Uncle Bob said, "Let's bow our heads in blessing." I bowed my head as the rest did but I kept my eyes open and peeked around the table to see what was happening. Everyone sat very still, eyes closed and hands clasped in laps; all except me.

Uncle Bob said, "Amen," lifted his head suddenly and began to serve. A maid stood on either side of him. As he filled a plate he would pass it, alternately, to each maid, who in turn served Mother, then Aunt Lulu, and then the rest of us. This procedure, followed only at dinner time, was quite different from any I had been used to. Our farm aunties served "family style." As we finished eating, the maids cleared the dishes, then brought in plates and a platter, placing them in front of Aunt Lulu. She served the desserts. I thought much about this and somehow the word "elegant" came into my mind. After that I felt very special at the evening meals, as I had never been waited upon except by Mother.

When we were dismissed from the table, Uncle Bob suggested to Harry that he show us his treasures. So we left the big table and went to the end of the room where we sat on the floor with our legs stretched out under a small table. His treasures consisted of some picture postcards of wild animals and some of beautiful flowers. Jessie was fond of flower pictures and so really enjoyed these. Harry and I did much talking, in a subdued tone, so as not to interfere with the adult conversations. Before long Uncle Bob suggested we all return to the big table for evening devotions. We got up from the floor and took our accustomed places. I was astonished to see many adult blacks standing at the far end of the room, their children sitting quietly on the floor in front of them.

Uncle Bob, looking at Mother, said, "This is part of our family life, having devotions every evening except Sunday. Our servants usually visit their friends and go to church on Sunday and by the time they walk home it is too late to expect them to take part in our Bible time." He then read a lesson from scripture, offered a short prayer, read some more verses and spoke about them, in both languages (although I learned later that many of the servants also understood English), and then gave a closing prayer.

Violet left the table and went to the piano that I had not noticed before. Soon all except Mother's three children were singing *Praise God from Whom all Blessings Flow* as they gathered around the piano in a group. This was my introduction to hymn singing. I am sure that those older Natives understood more of the evening devotions than did any of us. We children had never been exposed to religion in any way. Transportation of twenty-five miles to the nearest church did not induce church attendance. The blacks began to leave, but one older man stopped to speak to Uncle before leaving, apparently to thank him.

We all slept well that night and were up early the next morning. After Uncle Bob asked the blessing for breakfast, I had one bad time. The maids served us with bowls of porridge, a very thick oatmeal mixture. I watched Uncle place his spoon in the center of his dish and let go—the spoon stayed in place, causing him to say, "Ah-h, this is what I call good porridge." (It seems his Scottish mother made porridge that way.) I was so absorbed in watching this performance that I did not watch my bowl. I had moved it too close to the table edge and the bowl tipped over. What an embarrassment! I moved quickly enough that it did not land in my lap, but crashed to the floor upside down. What a mess! I looked toward Mother who, for the moment, was speechless. Then, for the first time, I heard anger in her voice as she directed her words to me.

Uncle Bob saved the situation by saying quietly, "It is all right, Ivy. I'm sure the child did not do this on purpose and it won't happen again." He then talked about other things while the maid cleaned up the mess. Fortunately the bowl did not break. I was given a smaller portion and meekly kept my eyes on my plate.

Uncle Bob was a devout man, a good husband and father. His word was law and he demanded instant obedience. His strict discipline was needed in that area where dangers (snakes, unruly Natives passing through, or sudden storm) prevailed. The routines were orderly, imposed with kindness and understanding. His servants were treated with the same consideration and they seemed to know it.

As breakfast finished, Violet reminded Harry they would continue their class work and that I was to be included. Harry explained that his sister taught him when she was home because it was too far for him to go to school in the city. Violet had finished her formal schooling and was now home for awhile.

This "school" was held in her bedroom, a large airy room facing the front verandah. There was a window opening onto this and two windows on the outer wall. In one area of the room was a small desk, with chairs placed before it, and to one side was another small desk and chair which the "teacher" used. Promptly at eight o'clock class commenced and this continued for two hours, until morning tea was served. Then Harry and I were free the rest of the day. In the afternoon, Violet taught Jessie and Leonard, although I doubt that Brother stayed all through the session. He was still recuperating from his hospital experience and was very frail. He had become spoiled from the attention given him.

Most afternoons found Harry and me exploring the surrounding hill and other areas. When we decided where to go, we went to the shop and told Uncle Bob exactly where we would be. This first afternoon we roamed to the native huts that we had to pass to visit the pig pen higher up. A toothless, old woman, squatting in her doorway, smoking a long stemmed corn cob pipe smiled and spoke. Harry explained she was wondering if I would like to see her house. I hesitated, wondering if it were the proper thing to do. He said, "She might be offended if you refuse. She is the head woman and I've never known her to invite anyone before. I think you should say 'yes.'"

She seemed pleased when I nodded yes and got up slowly and stepped aside so I could proceed. What an experience! At first blackness was all I could see, not realizing this was partly because I had been out in the sun and my eyes were not yet accustomed to the gloom. There were no windows in the hut (rondeval), only slits high on the wall for fresh air. Finally my eyes adjusted and I was surprised to see nothing but bare walls and bare floor. Near the wall was a mound of rolled-up rugs. In the very center of the floor were ashes with a three legged, black pot standing astride. The odors from the cooking, the smoke charred walls and overhead thatch were overpowering. I told Harry I had seen enough. He spoke to the old woman and she replied, smiling and thanking me (he said) for honoring her with a visit. I was glad to escape as I was sensitive to odors and could not have stayed there long. I questioned Harry about the lack of furniture and the rolled up rugs.

"Those are their 'reeds,' as they call them. This is what they sleep upon. They sit on the floor and usually they are in their huts only to eat and sleep. On rainy days they stay outdoors too unless it is raining hard." (I noticed this family referred to these as "huts," while in the Cape they were called rondevals. They were made the same way.)

At length we arrived at the pig pen where I was delighted to see many tiny pink piglets. I wanted to touch, but Harry quickly pulled my hand away, explaining the mother would bite. The little ones had been born earlier in the morning.

We had to clamber up some rocks to get higher, really a rocky mountain hillside. I felt 1 could not climb another step when Harry surprised me by sliding down fast, saying, "Hurry after me!"

Breathlessly, I followed him and when he sat down, breathing hard, I said "What happened? You looked frightened."

"I was for a minute but I'm all right now. Whew, I did not realize the Abakwetha were this close!" He explained that when he reached the top of that rock, he was able to look down on a valley-like plateau. Here he saw the Abakwetha encampment. This is a private ritual of the Natives when they become of age and not supposed to be for other eyes. When I wanted to know more Harry either did not know or was reluctant to speak about them.

A few days later we were in the shop when some Natives came in. They were wearing white blankets and had white clay smeared on their bodies. As Uncle Bob talked to them they seemed happy at whatever he was saying, then made a few purchases and left, walking down the road, presumably returning to Ermelo vicinity. Harry had pulled me behind one of the counters. After the Natives left, Uncle noticed this and complimented Harry on being so discreet. I could not understand this and never found out the reason. These Abakwethas were not local Natives, so perhaps it was thought that they might not be friendly.

One school morning Violet had to leave the class room. She did not return immediately, failed to explain why she was leaving, and did not give us any instructions. Suddenly Harry said, "Come along. Let's do something else." He walked over to the open window, stepped through onto the verandah, and with me behind him ran into the tunnel grape arbor. He kept listening for Violet, but I became so busy eating grapes, now well ripened, that I paid no attention. We continued to pick and eat. Then, instead of waiting for tea, Harry ran to tell his father that we were going to the pine grove. The grove was not far from the house and there were no rocks. This apparently was a planned planting, because the pine trees were in rows. Harry said this was done by the former owner. There was a scarcity of underbrush and the pine needles of years made a spongy walk area. We sat down, ate our grapes and discussed what else we might do. It was quiet under those tall trees and so peaceful.

"It is like a cathedral, isn't it?" Harry's voice was quiet. "What's that," I asked. "Well—it's bigger than a church." I pondered this, then looking at him, I dared to voice the questions I had.

"Harry, who is this Jesus, God, and Holy Ghost your dad mentions and talks about at devotions?" Harry explained as much as he could and I was pleased he did not make fun of my ignorance. I asked many questions and I felt a sense of relief as he answered them to my satisfaction. We were quiet, then I was conscious of a different sound. It was not a bird call nor any sound I was familiar with.

"What am I hearing, Harry?" We both listened. "I bet you are hearing the murmur of the stream down there." He pointed straight across from us. We got up and walked over. It was a delightful, clear stream. I sat down and began taking off my shoes and socks.

Harry looked startled. "Why are you doing that?" "I'm going to wade in the water." "Oh no, you are not!" His voice was firm. "You will drown in the sand." I laughed. "How can anyone drown in the sand?" I finished taking off my socks.

"Look! I'll show you." He glanced around, found a short heavy stick and tossed it into the water. "Watch."

It slowly sunk out of sight. I was astonished. "What made it disappear?" "That is quicksand. If anyone stepped into it, the sand would drag him down as it did the stick. Dad showed me that a long time ago. When he bought this place, the former owner told him about it, so Dad put this fence up so no one would cut through here Once a man did get dragged down, in early days, and by the time his cries were heard and he was found, it was too late to save him."

I had never heard of such sand. I hastily put on my socks and shoes and said, "Let's go home." I never wanted to see that spot again.

One Saturday evening a discussion centered on going to Ermelo the following day for church. A special guest speaker was to be present. Aunt Lulu was not feeling too good so she said she would stay with Leonard and Jessie because they were too little for church. The buggy seated six so it was decided that Mother, Harry, Uncle Bob, Violet, I, and a servant to look after the horses would go.

I began to realize this was a special occasion as I surveyed the area, saw the many buggies and carts unload in front of or near the church and servants taking the buggies any. Adults, both men and women, all dressed in their best, interested me. The ladies were dressed in beautiful dresses, fancy hats, long gloves, and elaborate parasols. The men wore frock coats and top hats. I was used to farmers so this fancy attire was quite different. Uncle Bob cautioned me to be very quiet and not to fidget. I entered the pew first, Uncle followed, then Harry with Mother and Violet. This filled the row.

I had a difficult time keeping silent. Suddenly the church bells rang, followed by an organ's being played, then singing. I dared not turn around to see where the singers were. When this was finished, the minister in a white robe came and stood before the congregation. I thought he was wearing his night shirt, except I noticed the green cloth around his neck. This kept me silent, thank goodness.

(Once on the farm I had screamed much of the night because of an earache. Grandpa, dressed in his night shirt and a cap on his head, came to the door, holding a lighted candle, saying, "Ivy, can't you keep that child quiet. We cannot sleep with her crying.")

Fortunately the minister had no headdress or I might well have blurted out something regarding a night shirt.

All went well, as far as I was concerned. It was difficult not to squirm as the speaker seemed to go on and on. He finally sat down and ushers passed the collection plate. It was a blessing that Uncle Bob reached past me to receive the plate. Momentarily, I felt left out, as I thought the money was to be for us, until I saw Uncle Bob put money into the plate. I am sure I would have removed at least one coin had he not taken the plate when he did. Finally the service was finished and we were able to return home.

Harry was as outgoing as was his Father, speaking to the people who came to Spriggs Rest Trading shop in their own language. He could speak Native languages, of several dialects, and could also talk with the Dutch. By the time we would leave Spriggs Rest, I could do the same; not fluently, perhaps, but enough to talk with the Bantus on the farm.

One day Uncle Bob went to get supplies from Ermelo and when he returned he had a passenger. This lady was a nurse and still wore her uniform. Apparently she was a long-time friend of the family, as they all greeted her warmly and even Mother seemed to know her. She was referred to as "Nurse" and I never knew her name. She kept the adults in laughter with her many stories about the men who were victims of World War I, but some were sad. I tried to talk to Harry about what the war really was but he had very little information to offer me. At times I would eavesdrop, endeavoring to learn more about the war. Once I did overhear a story that sent Nurse and Mother into gales of laughter. I laughed to hear them, so much that Mother discovered my listening and I got a scolding I never forgot.

Nurse had said, "One old Boer was brought in with a back injury. I was assigned to work with this patient. As I gave him the usual bath, I told him to finish his bath, giving him the washcloth. One morning he said, 'Nurse, vhy you vash down to possible and up to possible but never vash possible? Always you say finish your bath. My back hurts too much to vash so far.'" Actually, I did not understand the gist of the story, but thought it funny enough to discuss it with Mother years later, and we had another good laugh.

When Nurse left to return to duty, I felt sad. I never saw her again. She was so jovial, a bit of sunshine always, and she had an inward joy that I missed very much.

Harry and I investigated the dry river bed many times. He always hoped to find a diamond in the white sand. At first I scoffed when he mentioned a diamond, having in mind Mother's diamond ring, and wondered how he could expect to find such a thing. He explained that this was the Transvaal and reminded me that many diamonds were found in that kind of sand.

One day we heard Uncle Bob calling urgently, "Come here at once!" We climbed the embankment, reaching him breathlessly, as Harry said, "What do you want, Dad?" Instead of answering, his father pointed to where we had been. In astonishment we watched the whole area become filled with water. Soon a turbulent, rushing stream carrying sheep, cattle, out houses, logs, and much debris went by. We stood watching it deepen and spread. Because we minded immediately we were safe as the bank on which we stood was high but the other side was flat land and the river flower outward for some distance.

Uncle Bob said, "A man upcountry sent a boy to tell me it was raining hard in the mountains. He needed some supplies that I gave to his Native."

It had not rained one drop where we were! This was my third experience where flash floods were concerned. After that, I had a deep respect for sudden storms happening in the mountains.

One day Mother began packing the suitcases and told us our long visit was over. "Are we going to see Grannie now?" I asked. She shook her head. "No, we are going to take the train to a place called Ida to see my sister Violet, your Auntie Violet and Uncle Frank Thornton. I want you to meet your other cousins.

It was sad leaving this loving family. I think the adults knew it was a parting forever, but I did not realize this.

Through correspondence, we would hear that Thomas finished his education. Because he had specialized in forestry studies, he and his Dad purchased a large wooded area nearer to Johannesburg, in a larger city than Ermelo, called Germiston. It was there they lived many years, not in a house, but in five different rondevals, to take care of the family needs.

They had many Natives working for them, and as trees were cut down, new ones were planted. It was a big business for many of these special tree trunks were needed in the depths of the mines.

They were to become sturdy uprights to support the ceilings, protecting the miners from cave-ins.

The Brysons were instrumental in establishing a school for the many black children on this farm. They believed in education for both boys and girls.

Another son was born to them after we left. Jack[5] was destined for military duty in World War II and became a prisoner of war in a German camp situated in Egypt. He was held for two years, a great time of heartbreak for Aunt and Uncle.

They were deeply touched by the love of their Native helpers, who had a deep caring for Jack and sorrowed when he was called to military duty.

One day a representative group, led by an old man, came to the main rondeval. The Brysons went out to see what they wanted. The old man made a speech, then presented his battered old hat half filled with coins. "This is to buy Jack back from that old Mr. Hitler. Please get our Jack back home."

Jack did come home and a week later his mother died. The relief and shock of having Jack safe at home, and having been weakened by malaria was too much for her.

---

[5] A fourth child, Jack, was born 22nd July 1918.
[6] Louise "Lulu" Green Bryson died 2nd June 1945 at Ermelo.

Chapter 21

The Thorntons of Ida

Uncle Bob Bryson and his son Tom took us to the station where we would board the train going to Ida, elsewhere in the Transvaal. It would not be a long trip, so by mid-afternoon we were once again helped to the end of the coach as the train slowed down. Ida was not a regular station stop but more of a mail stop. Therefore, there were no passengers to pick up unless the Thorntons were having visitors.

On the platform, waiting, were four women and one man. The older woman moved quickly to Mother and there followed a warm embrace between the two, then with the three young ladies. The gentleman merely shook hands as he greeted Mother. In turn Mother said to them, "These are my children," naming us, and to us, "this is your Aunt Violet and your Uncle Frank Thornton. These young ladies are your cousins, Louisa, Dorothy, and Madge." I felt shy meeting these cousins, for the others I had previously met and knew well were classified more or less as children.

The Thorntons lived quite differently from the other relatives I had met. Aunt Violet was Grannie Green's second child, her oldest daughter, and was twelve years older than Mother.[1] They were more affluent than we and their life style totally different. It might be termed "society." Their ten children either had attended or would attend boarding school and learn the finer arts of being ladies and gentlemen. Their home life was conducted on a more formal note than that in the majority of our family.

After being greeted as we got off the train, we moved toward a vehicle unlike anything I had ever seen. Uncle Frank Edward

---

[1] Violet Green was born 24th June 1873 at Bufflesfontein, Cape Province. She died 9th March 1955.

Thornton[2] called it his motorcar, one of the first bought in that area in 1917—but where were the oxen, I wondered? Uncle assisted his wife and our mother, who held Leonard, into the front seat, and his daughters, Violet, Dorothy, and Madge,[3] into the back. Jessie and I sat on their laps. Then he got behind the steering wheel, and with a chug-chug-chug, the car began to move forward, slowly at first, then faster and faster, much to my startled amazement. We probably were driving all of twenty miles an hour. By now I was no longer wondering where the oxen were.

We traveled a mile and a half on a straight road, toward a white fence. As the car approached, the gate suddenly swung open and as we passed I noticed two coloured children had each opened half of the big gate, making it seem like magic. They closed the gate behind us and eventually appeared at the house. A big white house had a broad stoep that this family called a verandah. With the assistance of a young man whom Aunt Violet introduced as their son, sixteen year-old Ernest[4], we all got out of the car, and Uncle Frank, still driving, disappeared around the house to the carriage house. Two other children, about our ages, joined us: Joyce was eleven, and John, six, the age of Jessie. We entered the house where a coloured maid was waiting.

"Please take my sister and children to the room we have assigned for them, Leona," said Aunt Violet. To Mother she said, "Leona will take care of your needs. All you have to do is tell her of anything you might wish."

We followed Leona down the hall to a big room on the right, a bright, cheerful room facing the outdoors showing an expanse of well cared for lawn. The day was sunny with a gentle breeze. This swayed the pretty flowered curtains which matched the equally pretty bedspread. Three beds and a large crib stood in this room. Beside each bed was a low dresser with glasses that I learned would contain water for drinking if we got thirsty in the night. There were two full-sized marble-topped washstands on which

---

[2] Frank Edward Thornton was born 17th November 1862 in Manchester, England; he died 14th January 1938 at Ida, the Transvaal.
[3] Violet Louisa, was born 29th September 1890; Dorothy Mary was born 6th November 1894; Marjorie Edith was born 26th August 1900.
[4] Ernest Harry Thornton was the 8th child, born 17th July 1905.

stood a large washbowl and pitcher. Leona said, "Madam, I will pour the water for you and the girls if you wish."

"Thank you. That will be nice." Mother was removing Leonard's outer clothing. "Girls, take your coats off and put them on this bed and I'll hang them up. Wash your hair and then wash your hands and faces."

Leona eyed us and the washstand, then spoke to Mother. "It is too high for your girls. I'll get another right away."

She left and soon returned with a lower washstand in which Jessie and I could take care of our own washing. She carefully poured the water into the washbowl which she had set on the lower stand. This was fun! We had never had such a pretty washbowl and someone to wait on us. The water was pleasantly warm. We children chatted among ourselves while Leona and Mother talked. Then Leona left with the high washstand, though in a few minutes returned to announce that tea was being served in the dining room. We followed as she led the way to the most awesome dining room I had ever seen.

To my childish eyes, it was huge in every way. The massive table, now set for ten adults, was long. I had never seen such an array of beautiful silver. Around the room were extra chairs, for this was a family that entertained often. Two older young men and our cousins Madge and Louisa came in to join the adults at the large table, while we younger children sat at a small round table just inside the entrance door that led into the pantry-kitchen. This table was low to the floor with small chairs and we sat with our cousins Joyce and John.[5]

Brother was not too happy being away from Mother but Leona talked gently to him, placing him between Jessie and me so we could assure him all was well. We did not talk much. All the strangeness of this tea time seemed to rob me of speech, and Jessie was never one to talk much. Neither John nor Joyce said very much. After we drank our milk and ate our little cakes, we were excused by Aunt Violet, who said "Joyce and John, take your little cousins outdoors."

We left the room, walked out onto the verandah, where John, as host, became very talkative. He and Joyce took us around the

---

[5] Joyce Muriel Thornton, the 9th child, born 6th July 1908; and Donald Edgar "John" Thornton, the 10th and last child, born 29th March 1911, one day before Jessie Walker.

front yard and to the right side as we walked out. Here were small chairs, tables, and a couple of settees, all made of iron and painted white. I learned this was where tea, both morning and afternoon, were served without the silver service. It was a pleasant place, framed by large oak trees, surrounded by a well trimmed lawn (their word for the green grass). John took us to walk in the grove of very old oak trees, very tall, with huge trunks. He showed us how to make "cups and saucers" from acorns falling everywhere. We soon discovered that only the brown ones would separate for our use, not the green ones. It was too early in the season for many brown ones yet. He showed us how to cut a small circle from the top of the acorn, scoop out the contents and fashion a handle for a cup and set it back in its saucer, the bottom part. I did not learn the art of placing the handle and soon became bored with the whole thing.

We wandered around quite a while, then were called into the house and told to prepare for dinner. It had been such a long time since afternoon tea that I was hungry. On the farm we had been used to having the evening meal about 5:30 or 6 o'clock. This formal dinner in this home was served between 7:30 and 8. We went to the bedroom with Mother where she told us to lie down and rest. She did likewise, all of which seemed very strange. After resting, we were told to put on our best dresses. "Are we going to a party or something?" I asked.

"No, Edna, but in this house we must dress up for the evening meals. It is the way Auntie wants it."

In later years, I wondered how Mother felt that evening, because she never had a formal gown during her whole life. It was fortunate she had a long white skirt and a fancy blouse with her. She wore the old stand-by green corded sash with the long tassels at each end around her waist.[6] She had worn this when she went to the ball in Cullinan. I'm sure that the family realized we were poor relations, as we had the same "best" for every special occasion.

We finally were ushered into the living room. I was amazed to see so many lamps lighted and a candelabra on the table. All the elegant gowns worn by the women of this family and formal attire

---

[6] Edna May's notes indicated that she still had the sash long into the 1970's.

of the men was something I could not comprehend. I felt very subdued and could never recollect much of what the meals were. The adult table was served by two colored maids and we children were served by Leona. I liked this woman, as she was warm and loving to all of us. She was a born mother type person. She had the knack of saying the right thing to make Jessie and me feel more at ease. In fact, she seemed the only person present aware of our feelings.

The maids in this home were not Blacks. They were called "coloured" because they were descendants of the Malays who were brought into South Africa years before, to work in the sugar cane fields of Natal, a Province of South Africa. They were a brown race of people, of short stature, with black straight hair.

While any meal was in progress, the children did not interrupt the adults. We could talk among ourselves but not to the adults.

There was music after dinner, but by this time we children were so sleepy Mother excused herself and put us to bed. Jessie and I each had a twin bed all to ourselves and Mother had the big bed to herself, unless Leonard fussed too much about sleeping in the child's bed. When we awakened at our usual early hour, Mother said, "Stay in bed, girls. This family does not get up early, so do not talk too loudly." This was indeed a change. We had always been told to get up and get dressed. We never had robes and slippers until we old enough to purchase our own. It was always get undressed and go to bed; get up and get dressed. And now we were told to stay in bed.

I was on the point of saying, "Oh, Mother, I am so hungry," when we heard a rap on the door. "Come in!" Mother called. A maid wheeled a small cart into the bedroom. She served tea and toast to Mother and orange juice to us children, but Mother shared her toast with us. We were to have this in-bed service each morning while we were there. I do not know whether this was that family's custom or if Aunt Violet ordered it for us because she knew we had been early risers. Mother thought it was the former because they always had a late breakfast.

At last it was time to get up and get dressed. Mother reminded us that the maid would soon come to call us for breakfast. It was often a subject of discussion between Jessie and me that we had juice and toast before we ever got our nightgowns off. Some of our farm cousins would scoff at our telling this later. I am sure this was a first time for Mother also. She who had to be the first up, to start the kitchen fire, to prepare the breakfast for her parents, brothers and children, now was a lady of leisure to have tea and toast in bed.

We joined the family for their 8:30 breakfast. After finishing eating we were told to go out and play. John took us to the other side of the house where we saw a large fruit garden of apples, guavas, grapes, peaches, and some fruits that were strange to me. Later we would see many trays made of screening set upon wooden supports called "horses" to keep the trays off the ground. Many servants under the direction of one of the eldest daughters, Madge, washed and sliced apples, peaches, and other fruits to be dried, placed them on the screen trays, and put them on the horses to be preserved by drying in the hot sun. The trays were moved from time to time to get the benefit of the sun's rays. Young girls would stand by, wafting large fans back and forth to keep the flies off.

Madge was the second daughter in this family of ten children. She was a quiet person, though one who had a unique hobby. She was greatly interested in photography, a rather strange occupation for a young lady in those days. She enjoyed taking pictures and developing her own prints. She surely knew her work well, for I still possess some of the prints she made of us in 1917.

Those cousins were so much older than the three of us that I never got to know any of them very well. This was the first and last time I was ever to see them. The older sons were managing different phases of the farm and were only home for meals. They were the age of the uncles on Grandpa Green's farm and, of course, did not pay much attention to us. Even Joyce, nearing twelve years old, thought she was too old to play with us small children. John was fun and we got along fine, because Jessie was just one day younger than he. They seemed to enjoy each other and talked more together than I did.

In a way it was a lonely time for me, because I sensed I did not fit in very well. I was a strange, moody child; often occupied with my own thoughts and seeming to know things that I could not name. I could not express my feelings or my thoughts to anyone. Mother was a good person and took care of our material needs, but she was not one I could cuddle up to and talk about things. So it was here that I began to brood about something being not quite right. We really did not fit into that family and I began to wish we could leave.

Mother was doing something she had never done before, namely cautioning us children to behave, almost on a daily basis. Did she, too, feel uncomfortable? Did she feel our family style was not blending in well? The next year held the answer.

Uncle Frank was in the sheep-raising business. He had many shepherds working for him and one day John announced that it was going to be sheep dipping day. He asked permission of his father to take us to the dipping shed, something I knew nothing about. We went through a small gate into the largest pasture I had ever seen. It had gently rolling hills. It had no big rocks as Spriggs Rest had; nor did it have thorn trees as Smiling Valley farm had.

John pointed to a covered shed with open ends and said that was the dipping shed. As we got closer we heard baaing and bleating from the sheep as the shepherds rounded them up and put them into a fenced paddock. From this a small gate opened into a long runway. We moved closer to the covered area and smelled the strange pungent odor of what John called sheep dip, something black mixed with water. This was in a long trough-shaped channel. A big lead ram was being forced to go through this first. John said he was called "Judas" because he was betraying the sheep. (It would be many years before I would understand what he meant by that remark.)

Now the Judas ram went into the trough with the black liquid, swam several feet, with other sheep following, and climbed up and out into another paddock where all the sheep would then dry in the sun. The purpose of the dip was to rid the wool from fleas or other parasites. With hundreds of sheep, it was a long drawn-out process.

Uncle Frank's sheep were merinos, a variety of sheep valued for its long, fine, silky wool. They originated in Spain but in 1789 four ewes and two males were imported into South Africa. Sheep shearing time was quite an event. John went with us when Mother took Leonard and Jessie and me to see the shearing. The sheep seemed docile enough after the actual shearing started but at first it seemed nothing but confusion, with the men getting the sheep bleating and sometimes kicking, into the shed. Finally, as a shearer caught an animal and got his arm around the neck and began to run the clippers over the body, it lay quietly enough. I asked Mother if it hurt and she assured me that it did not. After the wool, like a big mat, fell away from the sheep's body, the man let go and the animal staggered to its feet, a bit unsteady for a moment. It then slowly walked away or sometimes leaped away. The shearing took a long time because there were so many sheep to be sheared.

Swimming was something the Thornton children liked to do and they could swim well. A large round pool in the backyard was fed by an underground spring and many afternoons were spent here. Jessie and I could not swim so we stayed at the edge just paddling. As I was watching the other children swimming and having fun, I noticed they sometimes caught a big overhanging branch of a tree and bounced up and down in the water. I waited until they went to the other side of the pool, then I caught some of the overhanging willow fronds to bounce as they had done. I failed to grasp enough of the small branches, and the weight of my body caused these few to break. Suddenly I was going down, down, down. I panicked! It was a frightening experience, as I felt I was in a dark pit and drowning. I thrashed around until my feet touched a part of the sloping bank and I started grabbing. Then I managed to climb out of the water and saw that everyone was still on the opposite side and no one was aware of what had happened to me. I never tried to swim again.

I did not believe that our visit to the Thorntons was too successful. We children were not permitted to roam hither and yon. The Blacks were having some internal troubles, and the adults of the family cautioned us to always be in sight of the house, though they never gave any explanations.

One day a group of Abakwethas approached the house from the rear. I saw them and went into another part of the house. Cousin Harry Bryson had told me never to look at them when they had their initiation garments on. I was fearful because they certainly were wearing something different. Jessie happened to be in the kitchen, a place she enjoyed because one of the maids helped her make cookies. When one Abakwetha approached and asked by motions for a drink of water, Jessie gave him a drink. The maid seemed afraid, perhaps because she had never seen such a one. Jessie, being a child and unafraid of anything, gave the water without any qualms. I found out it was unusual that they should come to the house when covered with the white clay, wearing their peaked straw headgear and their white blankets.

One evening dinner became a special ceremony. It was the custom in the Thornton family to have a "graduation" when a child became old enough. This meant that Joyce, now twelve years old,[6] could be seated at the big dining room table instead of sitting at the children's small table. Thereafter only John sat at our little table with Jessie, Leonard, and me. I often thought of poor John sitting all alone after we left.

He had a birthday the 29th of March, the day before Jessie's. After our dinner a beautifully decorated birthday cake with seven candles brightly burning was placed before him and the family sang Happy Birthday. This was a new experience for us as we had never had or seen a birthday cake.

The next evening, then, the 30th March, was Jessie's birthday. She was so disappointed when a plain, white frosted cake, without the birthday candles, was placed before her. Leona said a quiet "Happy Birthday," but there was no singing and no family notice. This crushed Jessie for a long time. She once said, "I was so disappointed. It is the only memory of that whole visit I have. I had wanted the same kind of pretty decorations, and all I got was a plain cake." This may have been an oversight. It may have been a last minute remembering that Jessie had a birthday, too. It might have been because we were "nobody." After all, we *were* poor relations.

The only time I recall going to church while visiting there was to a special christening one afternoon. This child, whose name I do not remember, had been wanted for a long time, and his arrival was an occasion for a joyful celebration. I think he was related to Uncle Frank's side of the family. The christening took

---

[6] It would appear that Joyce would not be twelve years old until 6th July 1920, after Edna May had left for the United States.

place with only the family members, Mother, and me present. The minister spoke at some length and I thought he would never finish. For some reason we all stood throughout the ceremony.

As an adult held the child, I noticed the christening robe almost reached the floor. I wondered why such a long dress was necessary on such a small baby. I stared at the dress for a long time and finally realized that the minister was reading the names the child would be known by. I forgot my manners and blurted loudly, "Mother, how will he remember all those names?" Poor Mother! After all her admonitions as to how we were to behave while with those relatives, I now ruined the whole performance by embarrassing her in church. Mother knew that everyone would be unhappy over this incident. I noticed her face was very red as she stared down at the floor.

Later I asked her about that. "Yes, my face was red! I could feel it burning! You embarrassed me terribly and I was horribly mortified. It is so rude for a child to speak out in church, or for anyone, as far as that goes. That was such a solemn occasion." She did explain that this was a long awaited child and because the parents did not expect another, the boy was named for his four grandfathers and his own father. Five names to remember! It seems such a big burden to have so many names. I thought of that baby for a long time.

Once again it was time to pack suitcases and to be on our way. I was greatly relieved to learn we were going to be leaving this home and take the train again. This time we would return to East London and back to Grannie and Grandpa Green and the uncles. I was a happy child to learn this and I think Mother was also feeling a sense of relief. We never saw any of those cousins, again but would see Aunt Violet and Uncle Frank. They would come to Smiling Valley farm once, and their reason for coming would cause a break between Mother and her sister that would last for years.

Unhappy times lay ahead for Mother and her children, but we did not know that the day we boarded the train at Ida, to return to Smiling Valley Farm. It was going to be difficult for Mother to look forward to any more brighter tomorrows.

Chapter 22

Return to Smiling Valley Farm: A New Gloom

It seemed wonderful to see Uncles Len and Sid waiting on the platform as the train slowed down at East London depot. We joyfully met them and basked in their obvious caring about us. This time Uncle Sid did not carry me to the wagon as he had done on our first arrival. Instead he picked up Leonard. Uncle Len placed our luggage in the wagon, and even Jessie and I greeted the Xhosa voorloper as he smilingly approached and greeted Mother. Soon we were on our way through the city streets, past the market that had been teeming with wagons and produce earlier, now empty and somewhat forlorn as the wind swept small whirlwinds of dust over its expanse. It did not seem such a long journey past the Nahoon River and into the usual outspanning place, as we chattered almost continuously relating what we had seen and done while in Ermelo and Ida. Mother and her brother Sid spoke between our chattering and there seemed to be a serious vein to their conversation.

As I became aware of this, I began to talk less, partly out of the concern I was feeling and never expressed and also because I wanted to hear what was being said; but I did not learn anything. We were soon outspanned and the evening meals were being prepared. After we all ate, there was the usual small talk, tobacco odors became noticeable, but the laughter of previous outings seemed to be missing. Many conversations had a bearing upon the war still going on, and some of the people mentioned the loss of son or friend. I heard Uncle Sid tell Mother of one who would never return, so perhaps there had been many casualties, tales of which were the cause of the gloom. Further, perhaps the food prices were down and fewer shillings were being taken home.

Some of the musical instruments were brought out, but I

noticed that none of my three uncles brought out their instruments this time. The music was not played so long a time as usual. When Mother put us to bed in the wagon earlier than usual we did not protest because it had been a long day with all the traveling. I awakened during the night, thinking I heard Mother weeping. This disturbed me and I lay awake thinking about it. Did I really hear her or did I imagine it? As it was so dark, I did not rise from my sleeping space to find out; I could not see where Jessie and Brother were sleeping. I had a sudden sobering though that our returning to the grandparents might not be so happy an experience as I was anticipating. I had many questions but no answers. I drifted off to sleep with my mind troubled and did not awaken until the wagon was just beginning to pull onto the main road, homeward bound. I noticed that other family members were still asleep. Mother awakened after a short time, and Uncle Sid who had been walking climbed into the wagon beside her when she said, "Good morning."

They apparently continued to talk about something they had started the previous evening. As we passed the schoolhouse and entered the farmland of Smiling Valley, I began to lose my apprehension and my feeling of something wrong. I was looking forward to meeting the grandparents again. Once again the little Xhosa children opened the gate for us and soon Uncle Clem called a whoa to the oxen, and the lead riem was placed over the horns of the lead oxen. The young blacks put the baggage on the stoep, returning to take their places beside the ox team as Uncle Sid lifted us to the ground and helped Mother down.

Was it my imagination, or did there really seem less joy at our return than we experienced four years previously? I was not wise enough so to determine but again I had a sense of anxiety. Grannie soon put me at ease. She suggested we go searching for eggs and take a walk around her flower garden. In my happiness to be with her again, I became less aware of troubles. I chattered, telling her about the garden at Spriggs Rest and the way cousin Madge Thornton had preserved the different fruits at Ida. I told her about the sheep and what I thought of several happenings. She seemed to be interested in the news she otherwise would not receive.

Our daily routine became normal. I still had chores to do, really a pleasure to me. By this time I learned to climb up the trunks of the gum trees to pull down the loosened bark that had not dropped normally. I found this way of gathering the chips for morning fires filled the wood box more quickly than hunting for the fallen pieces over a larger area.

One lunch time Grandpa announced he was going to visit his older son, our Uncle William,[1] who lived a mile away.

"Are you going to ride Prince?" Grannie asked.

"No, I'll walk. It is no use taking Prince and tying him up while I talk to Will. His barking dogs make Prince nervous. I will walk both ways."

Grannie cautioned him, "Watch out for that ostrich they have."

I walked with them to the gate and Grannie and I stood watching as Grandpa walked away. She said, "Let's walk down into the old paddock where the herbs grow and we can watch him as he walks most of the way to Uncle Will's."

So we walked down the seldom used front yard and could see Grandpa until he disappeared over the ridge to the shallow valley where the house was built. We returned to the house and I noticed that Grannie was thoughtful. Later she walked to the front stoep and looked toward Uncle Will's for a few minutes. It was getting to be late afternoon, and I thought she was worried, especially as her three sons had returned from the gardens and Grandpa was still gone. Grannie finally walked over to the shed and talked with the uncles. Uncle Len came out with her and I heard him say, "I'll go, Mother, although I'm sure he is all right." To me he said, "Hey, Bully, come along. You might be of some help."

I followed him toward the paddock where the donkey Jacob was roaming. We walked through the gate and down the length of the paddock to the barbed wire fence that penned the enclosure. As we arrived at the fence, Uncle Len reached for the bottom strand. Lifting it, he said, "Now watch how I put my hands between the barbs and then lift the wire. I want you to do this as I lie on the

---

[1] William Robert Green was born 5th October 1871 at Bufflesfontein, Cape Province, undoubtedly named for his grandfather and his father. He married Annie Whittington about 1899 and sired four children: William, Emily, Robert, and Herbert John.

ground and roll under. Pull as high as you can, so I'll not tear my shirt on a barb." The fence had six strands of wire.

I did as he instructed and he rolled under to the other side. I watched him walk some distance when he suddenly turned and ran toward me, waving his arms and shouting. I thought I heard him say to get Sid. He needed help for some reason. So I ran to the shed to call the other uncles. Uncle Sid ran with me to the paddock fence. He and Uncle Len began talking and I heard something about Grandpa's being on the ground. Uncle Sid ran back to the shed, soon appearing with two long poles, each having a loop at one end. I had never seen these and could not imagine what they were for.

He tossed them over the fence, then lay down on the ground while Uncle Len held up the bottom wire. By now Uncle Clem, following slower with his bad foot, had joined me in watching as the two men ran toward Uncle Will's. All this commotion had attracted Mother and Grannie and three blacks who had not yet departed for their kraal. All looked worried. Grannie said, "Do you think they will be able to rescue him?" Rescue him? What did they mean? Rescue him from what? Clem and Mother both reassured her. I began to realize that something out of the ordinary was occurring.

Uncle Clem spoke. "As long as Dad stays under the thorn tree he'll be safe. That ostrich can be extremely treacherous, so I hope the kid (Uncle Len) will keep his head." Why was Grandpa under a thorn tree and what connection was there between an ostrich and a tree? I looked at the women and decided against asking questions right then because they appeared so worried.

We finally heard a shout and saw two figures coming toward us. Grandpa was being helped by Uncle Sid and they were moving very slowly. In the meantime Uncle Will had been alerted as to what was happening and he arrived at the scene just as Uncle Len got the loop around the ostrich's head and pulled it toward the ground. An angry ostrich is helpless when its head is down. It cannot see from a down position, hence the need for a pole at least seven or eight feet long, with a loop at the end.

As Grandpa and Uncle Sid reached the fence, many helping hands held up the lowest strand so both men could roll safely underneath. Uncle Clem and Mother helped Grandpa to the house, with Grannie following. I stayed to see if Uncle Len would return. When he did, he said, "Will took that darned bird home. Now maybe he'll think twice before he lets it roam free again." When we all got into the house, Uncle Len said he had noticed the ostrich running round and round this one tree and he surmised Grandpa was underneath. He could do nothing except get help. Grandpa said, "I saw the bird come toward me so I had no choice except to get under the thorn tree as quickly as possible. There were no trees around to climb."

This was a painful experience for him, as the thorns, which are about an inch long, are very sharp. He had crawled on his stomach beneath the low hanging branches. This meant the thorns scratched his head and neck, his hands, and some went through the material of his clothing. But at least he was safe from the ostrich. He said he had not expected the ostrich to keep running around the tree and it was a long hour before help arrived.

To sustain even one scratch by such a thorn is painful, so Grandpa's many scratches and punctures must have caused him much discomfort. Perhaps Mother's first aid and some of Grannie's herbal salves eased him somewhat.

I looked out the bedroom window one morning and saw several strangers in the paddock near the barn. I noticed a black man held the tail of a bull, pulling it toward him, while two other blacks were holding a riem that went through a ring in the bull's nose. The uncles and Grandpa were present. The bull seemed to be very angry and pawed the earth, bellowing loudly.

"Mother, what is the matter with that animal and why are the men holding him that way?" I asked. "Edna, don't go near that paddock today. When the blacks let go of him, he will be very angry and try to hurt someone. Don't you be anywhere near, do you understand?" She said this so sternly I meekly nodded my head,

At the lunch table I paid attention to what the men were discussing and learned that the bull had been borrowed from the Schultz farm to "sire the cows," a term that meant nothing to me.

Two or three days later, the same strangers came and took the bull. I forgot all about this until a few days later when I had an experience that was rather startling.

Grandpa announced at lunch that he was going to the naval orange and banana garden and said, "Len, I want you to go with me." Before they left, Grandpa said, "Louisa, I'll take the short cut home, and I should be back in about two hours."

Much later than that I happened to be roaming in the paddock, hoping to see Jacob and wondering if I dare try to get on his back again. He was not close by so I walked to the end of the paddock but I still could not see him. Suddenly I looked beyond the fence and was astonished to see Grandpa running, with a black bull some distance behind him. Grandpa waved but there was no time to run to get help. If I shouted, it would do no good, so I simply stood and hoped that he could reach the fence in time.

He had his right hand pressed against his right side. This told me he was having pain, as I had noticed him doing this once before and had asked Mother why. Now I became very anxious. Thank goodness Uncle Len had shown me how to pull up that bottom strand of wire. I stood ready, then exerted all my strength as Grandpa threw himself on the ground. He rolled under the fence and lay breathless at my feet. I was looking down at him as I heard a snort and looked up to see the bull collide with a fence post so hard that the ground shook. He stood pawing the ground for a moment, then backed away and began to graze, apparently satisfied he had done everything he could do.

Grandpa, still lying on the ground, said quietly, "You saved my life, young lady." He finally regained normal breathing and held out his hand for me to help him up. I could help him to a sitting position but did not have the strength to help him stand.

My presence seemed to give him added incentive and at last he did get to his feet and limped slowly toward the house, his hand on my shoulder. I began yelling for Uncle Sid who was astonished to see us together. Realizing something out of the ordinary had happened, he rushed toward us and put his arm around Grandpa, helping him the rest of the way home. That evening he sat in his rocking chair on the patio instead of in the dining room as was his wont when Grannie read the newspaper and casualty

list. He had been telling us, including Aunt Libby[2] who had been
asked to stay for the evening meal after a late visit, about the bull
chasing him.

Mother was doing the dishes and soon brought in a stack to
place in the pantry. As she again crossed the room en route to the
kitchen I saw her give Libby an odd look. Next time she came in
she was carrying a straw broom and suddenly she slammed it just
above Aunt Libby's head, much to the shocked surprise of the
family. "How dare you try to strike me!" screamed Aunt Libby.

Mother pointed to the floor where a dead tarantula had fallen.
She did not need to say a word. Aunt Libby gave one look and
fainted dead away.

All the adults knew the bite of this kind of a tarantula was
very poisonous. Had Mother spoken or had Libby made a sudden
move, the big spider would have jumped because they always jump
at any moving object near them. Mother had to act first.

This was a new experience for me, as I knew nothing about
these huge spiders. I asked Uncle Sid about them and the next
morning he took Jessie and me out before breakfast when the dew
was still on the grass. Looking around intently he finally pointed.
"See that web on the ground? That is the web of a tarantula spider
that lives in the ground. Every morning while the dew is still on
the grass I want you to look for the webs. When you see one, call me
and I'll show you what I'll do. Wait here." He hurried toward the
shed and brought back a can with a long spout. He squirted some of
its contents into the hole, then lit a match, talking as he did so. "Now
I'll put a match to the petrol and the bugger will be burned up."

For several mornings Jessie and I were on the lookout for
webs. While one stood near the spot, the other would go to call
Uncle Sid and he would come and get rid of what we had found.
We did not find too many tarantulas because we looked only close
to the house and did not go far afield to search.

Early one morning I noticed the wagon was placed just beyond
the dairy and Uncle Sid was washing the body and the wheels. "Why
are you washing the wagon, Uncle Sid?" "Because I want all the dirt

[2] This may be Elizabeth Ann Nash, married to Herbert Arthur Green,
born 22nd May 1884, the 8th child of Robert Frederick Green and Louisa
Jane Nash Green.

off before I start painting." He seemed to be scrubbing in spots. "The designs are getting faint and the wagon needs a new dress." He grinned as he said this. "This old girl has to look pretty, you see, and I can make her look that way."

I was silent as I pondered the word "designs," as I had no idea what this meant. Finally I said, "What are designs?"

Look here! See this pattern around the body—a wavy line indicates the hills and valleys, the colored flowers are the veld and this rounded shape represents the fruits Grandpa hoped to grow when he came here."

"Did Grandpa make the wagon?" I liked to keep up a conversation with Uncle Sid. He was always patient, sometimes funny, like calling the wagon "old girl," and I learned much from him.

"By the time Grandpa decided to leave Port Elizabeth he had to have a wagon, so he went to a man who made wagons, telling him what he wanted. This wagon is four feet wide and twenty feet long, the extra length being for his big family. The wagon maker drew the design according to what Grandpa indicated. It is one of the prettiest I have seen. He sure had an imagination."

Uncle Sid bent down to wash the spokes of each wheel and I tried to absorb all the information he had given me. "Are you going to paint the spokes too?"

"Of course! I could never do a halfway job. Everything done right is a task well done, you know." He looked at me and smiled. "Just remember, young lady, that you must always do things well. It saves your needing to do it all over again."

The wheel washing did not interest me much. After they were all washed he began to feel each spoke and check to see if it was sturdy. He said, "Before I paint these I must be sure they are strong and not cracked. A wagon wheel is only as good as its spokes and rim. One has to be careful because a wheel broken while on trek could ruin the whole wagon if it fell over."

I had to ask one more question: "What is a rim and where is it?"

Uncle Sid pointed. "See this iron around the wheel? That's a rim. Usually it is about a quarter inch thick but Grandpa had it made wider and thicker because he was uncertain how the roads coming to the farm would be. Of course the wagon would be used for years, so it had to be strong. Sometimes wagons carry loads of a ton or two and its strength depends on the wheels, rim, and spokes." He patted the side. "This wagon is made of wood from a tree called ironwood: it is very strong. That's a good name, don't you think—ironwood? Wood as strong as iron." He chuckled at my puzzlement.

He put the wet wash rags in a pile. After the wood was dry he picked up the small cans of paint, taking the blue one first, and a small paint brush: then he painstakingly dipped it into the blue paint and carefully followed the lines already on the wagon. He went over the blue design on each spoke of each wheel. When he finished, he carefully rinsed the brush in turpentine and closed the can holding the blue paint. As each color dried on the wagon, he got out the red, the yellow, and the green colors, applying each with a different brush. His hand was slow but steady as he finished all this on the body of the wagon. He finally stood up, cleaning the brushes and closing the cans, sighing in relief. "That is painstaking work, Edna. I'm thankful it is finished. This will last for another three years at least."

Grandpa came out of the house, walked around the wagon, smiled, and said, "You have done a good job, Sid. The wagon looks as it did when I first bought it." Uncle was pleased at the praise.

As Grandpa returned to the house, Uncle Sid said to me, "Did you know the seat is really a box?" I shook my head so he lifted me into the wagon, climbed aboard, and lifted the seat, showing me it was, indeed, a box. "When my parents came to East London, there were three of these boxes in the wagon. One on each side," pointing to right and left, "and one in front. One was for adults' clothing, one for the children's, and the third for tools. Two of them are in the shed now and we use them to store things. Wagons were always made in such a manner so all parts could be easily removed. The old time trekkers had to travel over mountains so it was necessary that wagons could be taken apart to go down the steep hills, then the pieces put together again."

I looked up. "Did Grandpa have to do that?"

"No," Uncle shook his head. "But the wagon is made that way anyway. Grandpa did not know what all he would have to travel over; he did have to cross rivers but there were no mountains." I asked, "How is the sail put on?" looking upward and pointing. "The wagon maker put these ribs on after the wagon was built." He touched several as we walked to the end of the wagon. He leaped to the ground and lifted me down.

"See these hooks?" He touched one. "These are all around the wagon, matching the rib positions." We were walking along one side. "The canvas, or sail, is fastened to these hooks. Two sails are put on, both painted white and both thoroughly dried, one over the other. This not only makes it waterproof, but with three layers of paint the sail is hard enough so that a Zulu assegai cannot penetrate it. When the first sail is placed in position on one, it is thrown over and men on the other side pull it tight before they tie it in place. It is painted and dried before the next sail is thrown over. A final coat of paint is put on the second sail and dried, then all is ready for traveling. Now you know all about it." He smiled down at me and I nodded.

We went to the house for lunch and after lunch I followed Uncle Len out to the shed where he had been working. "Uncle Sid said you might show me what you're doing," I said. "I watched him paint the wagon this morning."

"All right, Bully. We're making new riems, the black and I." He nodded toward a tree where a black man was tying the end of a long thin strand of skin around a large stone. "You can watch but don't get in the way."

The other end of the strand was attached to an overhead branch of the tree, under which the men worked. They both pulled on a stick that was inserted somehow in the top of the skin near the tree. They walked around and around in a circle, bringing up and up the end of the rope that was held by the stone. Suddenly they let go of the stick, causing the riem to be pulled down, thus stretching it.

They did this again and again as the hot sun dried the slender piece of skin. They repeated the twisting upward, and the sudden downward swing of the stone prevented the skin from drying into a curled, useless mess. This would become a riem, used for whip and used also as part of the harness in spanning the oxen together.

For once I did not know what questions to ask, so I watched without bothering the men. Uncle Len and the black man were too busy to pay any attention to me so did not notice when I suddenly had to sit down. I did not feel well but dreaded the thought of another malaria attack.

Chapter 23

Illness; Adventure at the Nahoon River

The next morning Mother told me we were going to town with Uncle Len and Uncle Clem, who were taking a load of produce to market. Although I was beginning to feel quite ill but did not want Mother to know, I was happy to be going. It never dawned upon me that she could see something was wrong by my actions. Also, I saw her looking at the calendar, which meant she was believing that I was about ready for another malaria attack.

It was a surprise when we got to the wagon to see it would be pulled by a span of 18 pairs of donkeys. I had not realized that donkeys could be used this way, nor did I realize there were that many on the farm. When I asked about it, Uncle Len explained the load was smaller than usual, that the donkeys needed the exercise, and the change would give the oxen a rest.

We had not gone far when one of the lead donkeys decided to rest. It was an old donkey Uncle Len said as he got out of the wagon and loosened the attaching riem so the other donkey would stop protesting by snorting, twitching its ears and braying. The yoke was too tight with the old animal down.

"There is simply no use trying to hurry that beast," said Uncle Len as he stood beside the wagon. "He just rebels more if we try to force him so we let him do his own thing."

"Why don't you hit him?" I asked. "Goodness, child, we never hit our animals. They have feelings too, you know. Grandpa would half kill me if he thought I would hit one of the animals."

As I pondered this, the blacks sat down on the wayside grass, and Mother talked with her two brothers. I was feeling worse and worse, so was very quiet. Half an hour later, the donkey suddenly jumped up as though nothing had happened and stood patiently while Uncle Len and the blacks reharnessed him to his companion. As Uncle climbed aboard the wagon again, he was shaking his head. "There is simply no way to understand that donkey's actions or reasons for such behavior." We proceeded without further incidents and the usual activities took place at the rendezvous for the evening. I discovered I was becoming less impressed with all the activities that occurred. They was no longer mysteries, but a sort of human experience.

When we arrived at the market next morning, Mother took me by the hand and informed me we would go shopping. We stopped at a tea room and had a nice breakfast, later going into various shops and making several purchases. The most interesting place we went to was a book shop. I had no idea so many books existed! The only ones I had were "school books" and my horizon of awareness about books expanded in leaps and bounds!

"You may choose a book of your own," Mother said. A lady came to ask Mother what she wished. I was shown some children's books and my choice probably was more expensive than Mother could afford, but it became my treasure, *A Child's Garden of Verses*, beautifully illustrated with scroll work on the pages in a vine-shaped pattern of many colors.[1]

When I was again happily walking beside Mother, she suddenly turned into a large building on which I read, "Medical Building." I began to be apprehensive. We entered a "lift" and the man inside asked us to sit down on the bench. As he closed the door, the light went out. I think Mother was as startled as I, but the man quietly said, "The light will go on when the door is opened. This is a lift and the purpose of it is to take you to a higher floor." At that moment we stopped moving upward, the door opened, and the light went on. We walked down a hall and Mother reached for the door knob on which I the words, "Dr. Nangle." My apprehension increased.

Soon we were ushered into another room and Mother began telling the doctor of her concern about me. I did not understand

---

[1] Edna May's notes indicated that she kept the book until her days in Omaha, Nebraska, when she lent it to an eight-year-old. She found it a week later, torn, tattered and rain-soaked in her yard.

much of the conversation. Finally, I was lifted to a table and the doctor started his examination. I was soon asked to lie down; he began to push gently into my tummy, asking, "Does this hurt?" It did! but I recalled one of Mother's often-stated words when she was upset with me, "If you are not a good girl, I'll take you to the doctor and he will cut your tummy open; so take this castor oil like a good girl."

All I knew of doctors was that they "cut your tummy open" and, in my ignorance, I did not realize a person was put to sleep first! So, no matter how much the pushing hurt, I kept saying, "No, it does not hurt." I must have been a good pretender, because the doctor finally stated, "I really see no reason for this child's being hospitalized, Mrs. Walker." Mother related in detail my several malarial experiences and how she had kept notes on calendars at their repetition. "And so Doctor, she is due for another attack and I simply cannot handle another of these anxious experiences. I'd prefer that you to put her in the hospital."

He looked at Mother, recalling how many weeks she had been at the hospital, sitting beside my brother Leonard when he was just eighteen-months old and hospitalized for surgery in 1916. He had been so critical after having two and a half ribs removed in order for them to clear the pus from his lungs. "Is Mr. Walker still in the War Zone?" he asked.

"Yes, he is in France now and probably will be to the end of the war."

"In that situation, we can hospitalize Edna without payment. My fees, however, will have to be paid." And so it was settled. We left the doctor's office after he gave Mother some papers to sign and one she had to give to the Admittance Office. We walked a short distance and Mother turned toward a large, low, white building, on which was written, "Frere Hospital. "

Several things happened to me that were rather bewildering and I cried when Mother left saying she would "try to get in next week to see you." I realized I was all alone in this strange world! There were nine beds arranged on one wall, and across from me were another nine. Children occupied some, but I was not interested then. I noticed that my bed was near the main entrance. During the night I was chilled and restless, and by the morning I was feverish again. This particular experience, however, was some what different. I vaguely wondered why I hurt so much all over. I was aware of many adults in white coming and going and some talking; then I remembered nothing.

My entrance to this world of mystery was the 8th July 1918 and it would be late September before I would know who and where I was. I had developed a typhoid fever experience!

At times I'd hear a voice saying, "Missy you must drink," and something was put in my mouth. As time went on, I began to focus my eyes on a dark face. Once I even saw the "thing" in her hand, which she put into my mouth. It had a large teapot shape, but had an extra long spout. "You must drink the soup," the dark face said. I obeyed, but I have no recollection of anything else that was done to me.

One evening, I was able really to look at the dark face that belonged to a young girl, dressed in a calico garment with a bandanna over her hair. I refused the soup and amidst her protestations that "You must drink," I exclaimed, "I want fish!" The teapot was put down carefully, while the girl of about sixteen years of age, clapped her hands, went into a little dance, and said, "Nurse, she wants fish." A nurse came on the double, followed by a man, presumably the house doctor and again I voiced in a demanding manner, "I want fish."

The two medical people consulted and the maid was told to go to the kitchen for fish. I ate this with relish, to the obvious delight of my young maid who had been helping for the several weeks I was unconscious. Soon Dr. Nangle appeared and after hearing all that transpired, decided "She can have all the fish she can eat." No one, however, expected a child, so long without solid food to keep on demanding more fish! The young house doctor finally told me very firmly, "You cannot have any more fish to-night. Perhaps tomorrow you can have more, if you would want it. We are so happy to know you are getting well. You have been ill a long time."

During the early evening hours, several nurses and men with white jackets kept coming in to see me and to look over the chart that they took from the bottom of my bed. I then noticed all the beds I could see on the opposite side had charts hanging on them as well. I did not realize my returning from the near dead was considered a miracle. I began to improve steadily and in early October was helped to a standing position. My legs would not hold me up for a time, but soon I was helped to start walking again.

I passed a mirror as they took me toward the women's ward. I was startled to see I had lost all my hair, and began to weep. When the nurse realized why I was crying, she assured me, "Your hair will grow again. You lost it all because of the fever." I felt sorry for myself for a short time at this loss and the realization I had to learn to walk again, "Like a baby," I said to the nurse.

I soon became aware of other children, one in particular. Diagonally from my bed was a boy of my age named Joshua, which I thought to be a strange name. His mother visited him daily, with a basket of goodies. I envied him, as my Mother had not been able to visit me. He was termed "a miracle child," for he had recovered from lockjaw, having fallen on some metal that cut his thigh deeply. He was a noisy child, but in a pleasant way. He loved to sing, and the louder he sang the more enthusiasm he put into his songs. His favorite was "It's a long way to Tipperary," which he voiced with gusto! We finally got to talking across the distance and it was then I learned more about the "WAR" that had been a mystery to me. He said, "My Daddy is coming home from the war," and made up a tune that conveyed these words over and over. I learned from him that the war was almost over, but I was not aware enough to understand all these words conveyed to him, to the world, and, in a way, to me as part of the Walker family! Did it not mean, too, that my Dad would be free from the war? Of course I had not given any thought to that. I would not have known Dad was *not* coming home.

The ward was a very quiet place when his mother was told to take him home. There was only a thin partition between our ward and the women's ward. Just behind the partition, which did not rise to the ceiling, was a very sick lady. So Joshua went home happy, and left me sad. He was a city child and seemed to know so much more than I.

It was during this recuperative time that I became more ac-

quainted with my Aunt Florence[2], who was five years older than
Mother. She would come to the market with her son Harry, five
years older than I,[3] and while he was busy she would take time to
visit me in the hospital. I liked this buxom, smiling woman, with
the flaming red hair piled high on top of her head and held in
place with tortoise shell pins and combs. Her special comb was a
large one with a flared top, filled with green rhinestones, absolutely beautiful against her red hair. I felt she cared about me because she brought me little gifts, usually sweets (candies). Sometimes these were in containers I could keep. I still possess a small
green ceramic pitcher and washbowl and a blue patterned washbowl, both of which had been filled with chocolates, my first experience of having such sweets.

One day in November[4] Mother came to visit and I was permitted to leave the hospital with her. I had been there four months,
so was eager to get to the farm again. But it was not to the farm
she took me; it was to her sister, my Aunt Alice Elizabeth Green
Gager[5] instead, who lived in East London. Mother explained that
because I had been so ill I should be close to the hospital. Aunt
Alice could take me quickly, if necessary. When she left I felt
quite deserted.

It was summer[6] and Aunt Alice thought I needed a lot of
sunshine. After breakfast she would tell me to play in the sandbox. This was great for a day or two, as I had never had a sandbox,
but I was too much alone. Her two children played outdoors only
occasionally. Kathleen was two years of age and Robert Frederick

---

[2] Florence Ethel Green, the sixth child of Robert and Louisa Jane, was
born at Buffelsfontein on 10th October 1880. She married Adolph
Sonnenberger, a native of Budapest. See Chapter 10.

[3] Harry was their third child, born about 1904. He married Bertha
Steyn.

[4] Perhaps 1918.

[5] Alice Elizabeth Green, born 29th October, 1891, at Smiling Valley
Farm, was the twelfth of the fourteen children of Robert Frederick
Green and Louisa Jane Nash Green. She married Horace Albert
Gager.

[6] Remember, this is the southern hemisphere.

was just four;[7] perhaps Auntie thought they were too little to play outside without her supervision. During those few weeks I felt very alone and began to feel quarrelsome. I was nine, so I might have known better. Yet I resented the pretty clothes Kathleen wore and the devotion both children received from their obviously caring mother. I did not, of course, realize that Aunt Alice was expecting her third child.

One evening when Uncle Bert Gager[8] returned home from his work as a railroad official, I overheard Aunt Alice say, "Bert, you must take that child to the market tomorrow. I can no longer tolerate her disturbing our children. It is time Ivy came for her anyway." In a way this was good news, but I felt more unwanted than ever and was quite miserable. I went out to the sandbox and just sat, idly turning shovelsful of sand and feeling sorry for myself. Aunt Alice awakened me early the next morning to have breakfast with Uncle Bert. She told me he would take me to the market so I could go back to Smiling Valley farm with the uncles. I was not happy at the thought they did not want me, but I was happy at the thought of going home.

I lost some of my misery as I enjoyed the sounds of the clop clop clop of the horses hooves on the cobble-stone street. Soon other buggies and horsemen passed us and this added to the many sounds. As we entered the city I was interested to see that the streets were wet, though it had not rained. Men in white clothing, with long pigtails hanging down their back, were scrubbing the streets, swishing dirt and water into the gutters. Some were sweeping the sidewalks and spaces near shop doors and some were washing and drying the big glass windows, all getting ready for the shoppers who would come later.

As I had not talked much with Uncle Bert, I kept my questions to myself. He had, however, apparently noticed my observing the activity so he finally said, "Those men are called coolies. They keep our streets clean." I later learned that the coolies, with their long queues down their backs, some pigtails reaching to their

---

[7] Robert Frederick Gager was born 12th May, 1914; Kathleen Gager was born 3rd October, 1916.
[8] Horace Albert gager was born in August, 1886.

knees, were from East India and had been imported years previously to work in the sugar fields of Natal, later drifting into the cities of Cape Colony. They did the menial tasks in the city and the shops and some worked as servants for city dwellers.

Soon the carriage was stopping at the market place. Uncle Bert tied the horse securely and then lifted me down, saying, "One of your uncles will be present and he will take you home." Holding my hand, he carried my suitcase to the space where the uncles usually parked the wagon and showed their produce. No wagon from the farm was there! This must have been of concern to Uncle Bert, because he had to get to his office and had no time to return me to his home. He spoke to a Xhosa in charge of the Bauer farm, the one just east of Smiling Valley. The black man said he would care for me until the Green brothers arrived, smiling at me and motioning me to stand behind him near the wagon. He had everything displayed on his wagon and ready to sell, as had the other wagons.

No matter how closely I searched with my eyes, there was no wagon from the farm. It made me unhappy and a little bit frightened, but each time my eyes met those of the Bauer black, his smile reassured me. I presume he was just as anxious to have that wagon appear as I was. I began to wonder what his thoughts were when it was obvious he would have the responsibility of caring for me.

I enjoyed observing the individuals who approached the wagons to buy vegetables or fruits. One lady looked at me a long time, then at the Xhosa, opened her mouth as though to speak, then walked off. I had hoped she would give me an apple or something to eat. Breakfast had been early and now it was late afternoon. I was terribly hungry and uncomfortable.

Apparently the black man did not think of food for himself and perhaps he thought I had some in my suitcase. As the suitcase was in the back of his wagon, I could not reach it nor could I climb into the wagon. As the afternoon worn on and drivers were beginning to pack boxes into their wagons, I wondered what was going to happen to me. Would I be left behind? Would Uncle Bert come to see if I was safe. I decided he would not come because he had been sure one of the farm uncles would be at the market.

I watched the Bauer Xhosa packing the empty boxes into the front of the wagon. The young herdsmen were returning with the ox team. As they were inspanning the animals, their father motioned to me to go to the back of the wagon. Oh, he was not going to leave me behind, and I felt better. He lifted me into the wagon, climbed in himself, then folded some gunny sacks and motioned me to sit down. He said something but I understood only two words, "Big Baas," and I was comforted. He was telling me he would take me to the Big Baas, which always meant Grandpa Green, as he was called this by all the natives, even those who did not work for him.

As there had been no place to sit, and I had been standing all day, at times leaning against the front wagon wheel, it was wonderful to sit down. Actually, I had not moved from that wagon since Uncle Bert had left me, so I was terribly tired. The driver must have done a lot of thinking about this unusual predicament that he was in. Never in his life had he been left a white child to care for. He would have to deliver her to Smiling Valley farm, and this would make him late in returning to the Bauer farm. I am sure we were both wondering why none of the Greens had appeared, as it was very unusual for them to miss a day. We were soon to find out.

The Bauer wagon was the first to leave the market place. Other wagons had been ready first, but there seemed to be a pattern for their arrival and departure, although I had not previously been aware of this. I hardly recall leaving the market area, as I soon went to sleep on the gunny sacks. Suddenly I was awakened by loud voices and realized the wagon was not moving. I sat up, then stood up as I noticed the lead oxen of the wagon behind us were almost touching the end of the Bauer wagon. Men from wagons farther back were walking toward us. Something was wrong.

I turned and looked toward the front and saw an unbelievable sight! The Nahoon River was in flood and there was nothing but a rushing, roaring broad expanse of water ahead of us. In all the previous times of this crossing, I had seen only a trickle of water. Once I heard the uncles and Grandpa discuss their inability to cross because of the flood and having to return home, but this was my first time to see such a thing. At that time the produce wagons were held up for several days. After the farmers protested to the city, demanding a bridge, a good sturdy cement bridge had been built. Now nothing could be seen of that bridge; it was under water. Or had it been entirely washed away?

I marveled at the change. The rushing sounds of the river, the mooing of the cattle, the loud shouts and gestures of the men, all brought a keen sense of suspense, yet a mingling of fear and excitement.

So this is what Mother meant by a flood, I thought, completely awed by the whole thing. It couldn't happen, but it was happening. As I stood on the wagon bed, I could see wagons and people on the other side of the river. Everyone was trying to decide what to do—those who were going and those who were coming. The Bauer Xhosa driver seemed to take charge, perhaps because ours was the first wagon returning from town. His oxen were getting nervous and showing this by restlessness. Some of the other herders stepped along the side of the Bauer oxen, calming the animals as they rubbed and patted them.

First, it had to be decided if the retaining walls of the bridge were holding. Two young black men from each side of the river volunteered to find out. This was true bravery, for the native mind had many taboos, one very strong one, a fear of the "water witch" who often dragged a person down into the water forever. Ropes were tied around the waist of the young men who had volunteered, with many other men holding the ropes firmly to keep the two from being swept away. They must have been strong swimmers, because before long they indicated that the bridge was still in place and the walls were holding on both sides. It was safe for crossing.

Now began a lot of activity. Each driver hurried to his own wagon and slowly the wagons were backed up, to enable the oxen from the wagon immediately behind us to be loosened. These were then placed in front of the eight pairs of Bauer oxen, which meant this wagon had to be backed up in order to have space for the extra eight pairs of oxen in front. At last sixteen pairs of oxen were ready to take the wagon across, each ox having a human hand on its side as the men swam with the oxen. While all the hitching of the teams was going on, the Bauer driver climbed into the wagon, stacked the boxes high and tied them, then indicated by voice and motions he was going to place me on top. I nodded and he lifted me up and tied a rope around me, hitching it to one of the ribs of the covered part. Taking my hand, he placed it on a rib and motioned me to hold tight.

I held tightly all right. I wanted to be ready for anything. Sitting as I was, I could not see what was happening up front so I kept my eyes on the empty wagon bed. Finally, I could feel the oxen making headway, then felt a bump that was frightening at first, until I realized it was the wagon bumping against the side of the bridge. The rush of the river had shoved it against the side. I held my breath, wondering if it would hold, then forgot this as I saw the water swish into the wagon bed. Now I was afraid we were going to be washed away.

We were not. I heard shouts and twisted my body to look ahead. I had a grandstand seat from where I could see men shouting and waving their arms. I then noticed we had two drivers, one from the wagon behind us. By now the lead boys and oxen were apparently walking on the bridge floor and soon I could feel the wagon wheels also turning. I gave a sigh of relief—we were across. We then pulled out some distance from the river's edge so some of the oxen could be outspanned, the ones that would have to make a return trip to help the next driver across.

All the drivers were going to be helped in this way. The Bauer driver watched, as we all did, until the second wagon reached the other side. By then it was assumed that each driver and team would make a safe crossing, so our driver went on to the rendezvous.

It was soon apparent that the men waiting for the early morning trek into town were unaware of the problems they might face. The Bauer driver was surrounded by men as the word spread. It must have been an exciting time for him to have this unusual happening in his usually uneventful life, and to help others with his knowledge.

I was pleased to see the cooking fire get started and hoped I would be given some food. I would never ask for it even though I was very hungry. At last the driver showed me a box to sit upon, left me, then returned with a plate of food. It was unlike any I had eaten previously but oh, it was good! I looked up into the eyes of the black man watching me eat, and he began to grin, apparently wondering if I would eat the Xhosa mealie-meal. I smiled at him as I continued eating, and he soon went about his own meal, satisfied that I was enjoying what he had given me.

Later he came to retrieve the plate and said, "Good Missie," which told me he was pleased. He then motioned toward the wagon, again lifting me up, and arranging the gunny sacks one upon another. This was my bed and I was thankful to lie down. Although it had been a tiring and exciting day, I would not have missed it for anything and was sure that up to that time it had been the most exciting day of my life. Thinking about it, I was soon asleep.

I was awakened by the jostling of the wagon and realized we were nearing the school house because I recognized the terrain. Then the driver turned into the road that led to Grandpa's place, so I knew I would soon be home, smiling again on Smiling Valley farm.

Yet a sudden surge of alarm went through me. What would the family think of this situation? No one expected me home; and how would Mother react to having a black man bring me home? No doubt the Bauer driver was wondering himself about this very thing.

As the wagon came to a stand in front of the house, the adults appeared. The driver came in back to help me down, giving my suitcase to Uncle Sid as he explained what had happened. I quickly ran to my speechless mother, who gathered me up in her arms. Grandpa then walked over and talked with the driver and everyone began to talk at once. I heard something about Uncle Clem and Uncle Sid not trying to go to town to market because of the flooding river, which Uncle Bert and Aunt Alice didn't learn about until too late to keep me with them.

Soon Grandpa went into the house, returning with his gifts of appreciation for the Xhosa and his boys, tobacco and beer and whatever else. Mother carried me toward the black man and told me the necessary words in Bantu to thank him personally. He seemed to be pleased that I said a few words in his language. Mother spoke at some length with him before he finally left. We all hoped that Mr. Bauer would listen to the explanation for his late arrival.

Mother wanted to know what I had done to cause Aunt Alice

to send me to the farmers' market. I was hesitant to tell her I had been a naughty girl, but she seemed to be more understanding than I expected. She knew that Aunt Alice was expecting a child in a few weeks,[9] so I was not scolded, giving me a sense of relief.

I did ask Mother why the river was so flooded when it had not rained in the city. She explained that after a drought, with rains suddenly so heavy in the mountains, this caused the rivers all along the way to flood without warning as the water rushed to the sea. Many people and animals were caught in these floods.

"Remember two years ago when Uncle Sid was on the windmill and saw the wall of water rushing down the Bulugha River when we had not had rain for a long time? Remember how it washed out many of the fruit trees?"

"Yes, I remember." I also remembered the flood at Spriggs Rest and now this Nahoon River flood. And I thought of the flood that had killed John Sievert, the man my mother was engaged to, before she married Sidney Walker, the man who became my father.

Yes, I remembered. This was enough floods for a lifetime.

---

[9] This would be Doreen Gager, born 22nd December, 1918. A fourth child, June, was born 2nd June, 1924.

Chapter 24

A Schoolhouse Home

The year of 1919 was to be a year of changes for us and much sadness for Mother. I began to sense tension between Mother and Grandpa. One evening they both went into the dairy, an omen that caused me much concern. This was Grannie's private domain and she had already cleaned the separator and closed the building. Now she was walking back and forth on the stoep as she held brother Leonard who was ill again. I was as usual curious as to what was being said in the dairy, because occasionally I could hear sharp words coming from there. I wondered how I could eavesdrop.

At that moment, Grannie said, "Lennie is asleep so I'll put him in his bed."

As she entered the house, quick as a flash I ran to my favorite tree and climbed into it and out onto the branch that overhung the dairy door. The voices were getting more angry sounding. I felt safe from being seen because the leaves on the tree were thick. It was a bit difficult to hear from my vantage point, as the voices were not loud all the time. Suddenly Mother raised her voice and I heard, "But I have to have some money. How else can I get any? I have to pay Dr. Nangle! This is an opportunity for me!"

It was then I recalled the doctor's telling her that my hospitalization was free but that he had to have his money. Dr. Nangle's statement had much bearing on Mother's decision to earn some money. Grandpa then said, "It is not my wish for you to do this, Ivy, and had Sidney been a real man, he would have stayed and taken care of you and the children instead of traipsing off and getting into the war."

This was all I heard because at that moment Grannie called my name. Looking down I saw her standing beside the dairy and motioning downward as she said, "Come down, right now!" She did not raise her voice, but her very quietness made me obey. She gently led me into the house, then sat down and, holding my hands, looked right into my eyes for moment. Finally she said quietly, "It is very wrong to eavesdrop. I hope I will never see you do this again."

I felt chagrin, but I did not ask Grannie what it was all about and it did not stop my curiosity about the conversation in the dairy. I never saw Mother and Grandpa talking together again. If they did, it was done when I was out of sight.

About three weeks later we had unexpected visitors. I was surprised to see Aunt Violet and Uncle Frank Thornton, whom we had visited in Ida. They were in the longest motorcar I had ever seen and when they got out both were enveloped in long dusters. These were worn because the car was open and clothing had to be protected. Most of the roads during that period were unpaved, especially in the country areas. I do not recall how long they stayed, but I remember their departure because of the way everyone talked. It was not the custom of this particular couple to speak when children were present.

Uncle Frank, standing ready to get into his motorcar, said, "Well, Ivy, have you definitely decided? We made the long journey from Ida and purposely bought this new touring car in order to take you and the children home with us." I looked at Mother and we all waited for her answer. Her face was not the usual friendly looking one.

"I thank you for your thought, although I recognize a selfish motive in it. I know you would never give my children and me free room and board until they are grown. I will not be a slave in your home, as I am here, where I have to do everything without servant help in order to earn our keep. I can at least get away from this place if I have to. If I were at your home, I would never, never be free."

Aunt Violet in the car was looking straight ahead. Uncle Frank turned to her, saying, "Violet, I want you to look at your sister for the last time. You will never communicate with her from now on." Aunt Violet's eyes were sad as she looked once at Mother. He turned once more. "Is that your last word, Ivy?"

She looked as though she might cry. "Yes, it is!" Her voice also sounded as though she might cry.

"Very well. You heard what I said. Do not write to Violet. I'll not allow you two to communicate or see each other again because you choose to disgrace the family by working at the school. We thought you would appreciate our help."

Having already said good-bye to Violet's parents and brothers, he got into the car and slammed the door. The grandparents turned and arm in arm went toward the house. Uncle Clem did a very unusual thing. He took Jessie and me by the hands and said, "Come on, girls. I'll take you with me." As the motorcar drove off we turned, leaving Mother with her brothers Sidney and Leonard. This was the only time I recall Uncle Clem's paying specific attention to us girls. I never knew what Mother and her brothers talked about, but I am sure they tried to comfort her.

A few days later Mother began hastily to pack our clothes and some other items. I tried to find out why, but she just pinched her lips together and said nothing. Jessie and I could not understand what was happening. This did not look like a "brighter tomorrow" move, but Mother would not say anything. As she finished each bag and box she would put it on the stoep, and I began to wonder who was going to pick up the things. I did not see one member of the family, a very strange situation. Grannie had gone to her bedroom and was staying there; this must have been a pain-filled situation for her, whatever it was.

Several black women appeared and Mother talked with them. Then they picked up the suitcases and boxes, put them on their heads, and walked off. Mother, Jessie, and I, each carrying whatever we could, with Mother holding Leonard by the hand, followed, trudging down the pathway that led to the schoolhouse. We were moving, but where and why? It was not in a wagon or a train this time, but on our own two feet, with black women helping. It all seemed very strange, and I kept wondering why Grannie and Grandpa did not appear. It did not occur to me that I might never see them again.

As we all trudged along behind the black women, I ventured a question as to why we were leaving. It was only then that Mother explained we were going to live at the schoolhouse and work for Mr. Rankillor until a rondeval could be built in the front yard of Aunt Libby and Uncle Bert's place, where we would live later.

Little did Mother realize that she was walking from the frying pan into the fire! As Aunt Libby and Uncle Bert[1] had room for one extra person, Mr. Rankillor would live with them until our new home was completed, then he would move back.

We reached the schoolhouse and saw that the teacher's suitcase was waiting near the front room doorway. He had three rooms in which to live while teaching school, but now we were going to stay in these quarters while Mother would cook, wash clothes, and do general housekeeping for all of us. He would take his clothes and live with Aunt Libby and Uncle Bert during this time.

After we finished the evening meal, we all walked half way toward Uncle Bert's home with Mr. Rankillor, watched him until he was out of sight, then returned to our new home. Each evening, after dinner, this routine was followed. He ate breakfast with Aunt Libby and Uncle Bert before coming to school to teach. Mother would serve lunch for all of us and later dinner, then he would leave for the night. It was this situation that caused the rift between Mother and her father. She was working for money in order to pay Dr. Nangle because of Leonard's and my doctor expenses, so it was really our fault. This gave me a very odd feeling, thinking I was to blame, even though it was something I could not help.

My grandparents, being proudly British, felt disgraced that a daughter of theirs should feel the need to have to earn wages, something not done by daughters in the better families. It was bad enough that Mother had returned to their home, but now it was very awkward indeed that she was going into the home of a bachelor, even a bachelor so highly respected as our teacher, Mr. Rankillor.

But what else could she do? Dad was not sending any money. Usually families automatically receive a soldier husband's allowance but we found out later that he did not even put Mother or us children down as dependents.[2] British soldiers did not receive large pay at that time and he probably thought we were at least

---

[1] This was Uncle Herbert Arthur Green, born 22nd May 1884 at Bufflesfontein, the eighth child, Ivy's next eldest sibling. He married Elizabeth "Libby" Ann Nash, born 1886, a daughter of Harry Nash.
[2] A puzzling script marginal note here says "not true" of this sentence— but what is the untruth? And who wrote it?

eating and sleeping safely with Mother's family. Learning more about him in later years, I suspect he no doubt felt elated to be free from the bondage of a family.

One Saturday we spent some time at our home-to-be near Uncle Bert's home, because he had told Mr. Rankillor that their Xhosas would start building the rondeval that day. After lunch Mother took the three of us and we watched the beginning of this very unusual project. First, a large circle was marked on the ground and the dirt within the circle was dug deeply. A group of men got into the center, while others poured water onto the dirt. They then went around and around, stomping and singing, as the natives always turned any activity into a dancing, singing time, thereby making the work less tedious for them. It fascinated me to see these black feet oozing the good old mud, to get it as soft and deep as possible. As soon as the consistency seemed right, they stepped out of the circle. Two men, one at each end of a long board, smoothed that surface. This was then left to dry in the hot sun.

At the outer edge of this muddied circle, holes were dug at intervals and sturdy tree trunks were placed in each hole. For the outer wall, about two feet farther out, another circular stand of tree trunks was placed in holes, alternating between each two of the former.

In the meantime, women had been making many trips to and from a nearby dry waterway, where they had cut some slim trees and also picked up branches that had been cut from the larger tree trunks. They brought all these to the area where the men were working and began to twine them in and out of the uprights, tying them with special reeds where they met the next branch. As soon as they reached a certain height, possibly three feet, the women wove the outer edge in the same manner in the outer wall.

Other blacks had been digging dirt outside of the yard and mixing it with water. They would then dump this mud into the area between the two walls, mixing it into parts of branches already tied with reeds. Because this all had to dry thoroughly before more work could be done, the day's work was finished. More mud was put between the walls each day, drying each time before more was added, and at last the required height of the rondeval was reached.

On our next visit we saw the inner and outer walls being

plastered with additional mud by the men, while the women were sitting down tying bulrushes together. They were tying these reeds together with strips from certain trees, with each layer being entwined with other layers tied to the first. This was the thatch that would be the roof covering, and several women were working at this while others brought supplies from the nearby creek. The men were tying boards to the first row of tree trunks, spanning the mud-filled center and on up to the center pole that would be the peak of the rondeval. These were all tied in place with thongs of tree strippings and reeds.

The women then tossed a layer of thatch to the men who were on ladders. They began laying the thatch in circular fashion, returning to the beginning and working in circles to the peak. Then they placed another layer of thatch onto the first one, so that there was an overhang of about eighteen inches. The reason for this overhang was to prevent the rain from splashing against the walls. Because they were made of mud, a constant rain would gradually dissolve the mud walls. This overhang also prevented the rain from coming into the doorway, and afforded a dry space all around the rondeval. Thatch, when properly placed, would keep the interior waterproofed for years.

After the blacks had been paid for their work and were gone, the room was not yet quite ready for occupancy, as the floor had to be finished. Mother and I would do that, although I was squeamish about it at first. Mother picked up a pail and said, "Come along, Edna. We are going to gather chips." These chips were dried cow manure, not the kind I gathered for Grannie's stove. I also had a pail, and soon we had our pails about three-quarters full and carried them to the water tank. I stared as Mother poured the water into the pails, then put her hands in to show me how to dissolve these chips into a messy mixture. It was important to get the texture just right. She kneaded and pressed and squeezed, waiting for me to do the same, but I just stood watching her. How could she put her hands into that? How could I put my own hands in?

Finally she said gently, "This is the way Grannie smoothed her floor in their first rondeval. I learned to do this when I was a little girl." She smiled at me. "You can get used to it." I took a big breath, putting in one hand and then the other. By now the chips in my pail were water-soaked and soft. I squeezed one slowly and almost threw up, then I gritted my teeth. If Grannie and Mother could do it, I could too! I kept squeezing until my pail was one gooey mess, as was Mother's. Actually, it was something like making mud pies, so I finally tried to do exactly as Mother was doing, thinking of it as just plain, old dirt mud. Only it was a dirty yellow!

I watched Mother applying it to the dirt with a cupping motion of her hands, and I tried to do the same, smoothing it out as best I could. She taught me how to smooth this, how to knead it onto the bare ground. This had to be done correctly, otherwise the result would be an unsightly floor when it peeled and loosened. When this mixture dried, the surface had a glazed look of dull yellow. There were two purposes in using this method for preserving the surface of the floor; it prevented dust arising from our footprints and it eliminated the possibility of bugs working their way up from beneath the dirt floor. Insects did not care to inhabit a room that had manure floors! (Not to mention what some human beings thought, although I did not mind it after a while.)

This procedure had to be done every second Saturday and I was assigned the task. I came to enjoy doing the work because it pleased Mother and I liked the praise she gave me. I would hear her say to visitors, "Look at the floor. Edna really has a knack for doing this cleaning. It never peels."

As soon as the floor was dry, two beds, a four-drawer dresser, and a couple of chairs were placed in this room, which was to be our home for more than a year. It was a happy time for us children, as we had cousins Gladys and Arthur to play with, their both being the same ages as Jessie and me.

Finally, the teacher returned to his own rooms at the schoolhouse, meaning that Mother was no longer earning a wage. It was then the truth of her dilemma became evident. Aunt Libby informed her in no uncertain words that she would have to do all the household tasks in return for the privilege of having a home. "You cannot expect Bert and me to support you and your children," saying this one day when Uncle Bert was away from home.

Mother could not tell her brother about his wife's demands, because she did not want to cause trouble between them. Aunt Libby was not too well liked among the family members. She was a person who had tantrums, was mean to her own daughter Gladys, and spoiled her son Arthur. Her partiality toward her son was very pronounced.[3]

Mother asked us not to enter that house except at meal time because it was best we play in the yard or stay in the rondeval. We did have to enter at meal times because we all ate at the same time. We three children and cousin Gladys all learned to be silent at the table. Aunt Libby was sweetness itself when her husband, Uncle Bert was present.

Aunt Libby thought Mother too lenient with her children. At times Libby would speak harshly to one of us and Mother would defend us. Mother believed in quiet reprimands and an explanation, whereas Libby demanded and expected unquestioned obedience from Gladys, though not from Arthur. Sometimes, for no apparent reason, she would vent her ire upon Gladys. She would reach for her shambok, a rawhide whip with a short handle. This was the signal for Gladys to go outdoors. She never ran, just stood with her hands over her face, while Libby whipped and whipped her. Apparently this had happened so often, the child knew better than to run or to scream. The first time this happened while we were there, we three looked at Mother who just pointed to our rondeval. We all entered in shocked silence. Mother sat on the bed and cried, and we children were too frightened to say anything. Mother had never even slapped us, let alone beat us, so we could not understand this situation.

One Saturday Arthur, then seven, climbed a tree and not holding tightly enough fell and broke a shoulder. We girls and Leonard were on the opposite side of the yard. Aunt Libby saw us when she heard Arthur screaming and ran to pick him up. She became like a wild woman and blamed us girls for deliberately knocking Arthur out of the tree. I protested but it did no good. She went into the house, only to return with the shambok. Gladys took her usual stance while we girls and Leonard hurried toward the rondeval. Mother protested and tried to grab the shambok. This made Libby so furious she went out of her mind and whipped Gladys all the

---

[3] These children were Gladys Ann Green, born 3rd April 1910; and Arthur William Green, born 6th November 1912

harder. Mother was still trying to take the shambok from Libby as we girls screamed louder and louder. Then Libby hit Mother.

Our screaming reached the ears of Uncle Bert in the garden, about an eighth of a mile from the house. In the midst of Mother's struggle with Libby to make her stop hitting Gladys, Uncle Bert with three of his black men appeared on the scene. It was a very dreadful experience for all concerned, as Libby was hysterical and now completely out of hand. As Uncle Bert took over, Mother gathered us all, including Gladys, into the rondeval where we all cried and cried.

Uncle Bert finally came in to speak to Mother and learned what had been happening. He had to get Arthur to the hospital so he asked Mother to pack a bag for Libby, as he was taking her away from the house for a time. I am sure this was a rude awakening for him, as he apparently had no idea that Libby had been mistreating their daughter so terribly. Gladys had never dared tell him because this would have meant more beatings by her mother. It was an incredible situation.

With Mother cooking and taking care of the house, we had peace and harmony for several weeks while Aunt Libby stayed with Arthur at the hospital and later took him to Port Elizabeth for a time. I overheard Uncle Bert tell Mother that Libby was under treatment, although I never learned what type of treatment it was. Eventually she returned and I noticed Mother was not happy. I learned much later that Aunt Libby was persecuting her with words, sly innuendoes, and sometimes unkind remarks about "that Sid Walker." Mother bore all this in silence for the sake of us children and because she did not want to add to her brother's burdens. This was the only experience Mother ever said was one of the most unhappy situations of her life.

Another difficult time faced us as Uncle Bert came down with the Spanish influenza, which had reached the cities earlier but only now, in early 1919, was reaching the farm areas. He must have been very ill, because we children were not permitted to go into the house but ate our meals out doors. Between the care of Mother and Libby he got well.

It was fortunate he did, as all of the five children and both women then came down with the flu at the same time. Uncle Bert had to be nurse and cook for all of us. He was kept busy caring for our needs and dosed us on a regular basis with a tablespoonful of whiskey for each child and a double dose for the each of the two women. We children recuperated first, then Aunt Libby. Mother, however, was so ill I was constantly watching by her bedside, feeling relieved to see that she still breathed. It was a time of apprehension for me even though I was only ten. If Mother died, what would happen to us children? I certainly did not want to live with Aunt Libby the rest of my life. It was a happy day indeed when Mother could at last sit up in bed and act as though she was interested in what was happening around her.

One morning we were told we did not have to go to school that day because some unfriendly Xhosas were on the warpath. Uncle Bert said, "Children, you are not to leave the yard at all today. Stay close to the house because we must know you are safe."

Mother added, "The Xhosas at Xinza Beach stole a girl from the Bantus near the Kwelegha River and the men from that kraal are going to fight the ones at Kinza. Because they will be angry as they march to the beach, we have no idea what would happen should they see anyone along the way. This is the reason Mr. Rankillor decided to have no school today."

Uncle Bert spoke again. "I am staying home today as is Uncle Steve, and our own workers are staying in their own kraals." I did not believe this because I did not see how this information was received, there being no telephones. Yet I knew some information got through in some way when Uncle Bert got down the guns and laid out ammunition. I learned later that mounted policemen had alerted all the farmers to the uprising. No one knew how big this affair would be.

We children played out in the yard and I had been hanging around near the gate because I wanted to see the Xhosas. About ten o'clock Uncle Bert called us to come into the house. He was going to lock the doors. The rest of the children went in, but I quickly climbed a big tree that gave me a good view some distance down the road. Then I saw them coming! How fierce they looked! I changed my mind about staying there and looked toward the house, but Uncle had said the door would be locked, so there was nothing to do but stay in the tree. I flattened myself along the limb, hanging on tightly. I was beginning to tremble and was glad the tree was heavily leafed. If only none of the blacks would look up.

None did! There were many of them, but I was too scared to count them. They wore war paint, designs of white and red painted on their faces and naked bodies, except for the loin cloth. They carried shields and assegais and were chanting a battle tune of some kind. I had never seen Xhosas wearing such strange head-dresses made of brilliantly-colored feathers and plumes. I held my breath as they passed not ten feet away from where I was hiding, afraid they would hear my breathing. I stayed in that tree until Uncle Bert finally came and told me to get down and, of course, I received a lecture for disobedience. But I felt very brave, as it was an experience none of the others had. The next day, however, when we children were told to stay near the house and then to come in, I gladly stayed with the adults. I had seen all I wanted to see. The Xhosas returned on their way home but I did not watch this time.

We learned later the battle near Kinza Beach was so fierce that several men were killed.

In contrast to Aunt Libby's and Uncle Bert's unhappy home, another of Mother's brothers, Uncle Stephen and Aunt Martha,[4] had a very happy one. They eventually had five children and all were encouraged to talk and enter into activities with adults. Cyril, the older boy, was my age, his sister Amy was Jessie's age, and May was Leonard's age. Harold Green was born in 1918 and Enid was born after we left South Africa.[5] We all got along well and Cyril and I were much alike, in that we enjoyed getting into mischief.

I loved both Aunt Martha and Uncle Steve and it was a joy to visit in that home. Aunt Martha was a laughing person, with snappy brown eyes and brown hair piled on top of her head in the current

---

[4] This was Stephen James Green, the seventh child and fourth son of Robert Frederick Green and Louisa Jane Nash Green, born 26th February 1882 at Bufflesfontein, and his wife, Martha Hoffman, born 26th October 1886. They were married 1st June 1909.
[5] The children were Cyril Hedley Green, born 10th November 1909; Amy Winnifred Green, born 31st July 1912; May Elizabeth Green, born July 1915; Harold James Green, born 3rd June 1918; and Enid Green, born 7th February 1924.

fashion. She always wore an apron and was forever hovering over her stove baking something good. She specialized in crullers, deep fried twisted dough. She enjoyed her children as well as Mother's, always happy and playing jokes on all of us. After Harold was born, I was there as often as possible because I loved to hold the baby. Auntie never cautioned me to be careful, as mothers often do. She just trusted me. Before he was a year old he had whooping cough and she later said, "I'm sure Harold got well because Edna took good care of him."

He was a fat baby, compared to my skinniness. On warm days I would take him outdoors by holding him around the tummy with his back to my chest. Aunt Martha was highly amused when I gravely said, "He must get some sun if you want him to get well."

Some Friday or Saturday evenings Mother would permit all three of us to stay overnight at this home. Aunt Martha would place a mattress on the floor and we would all sleep on this, lying side by side. We could make all the rumpus we wished until she came into the room, saying, "That's enough, children. Be quiet now and go to sleep." We knew then she meant it and we quieted down.

Uncle Steve, with his full red beard, red mustache, and thick red hair, was almost as fun-loving as Aunt Martha; only I spent more time with Auntie and knew her better.

One morning when we gathered around the breakfast table we seemed to have a stranger with us. Certainly the man at the table was no one I ever remember seeing. We children were quiet, waiting to learn more about him. Aunt Martha and he exchanged several amused glances, then she smile at us. Finally she leaned over to him and whispered something. I felt uneasy and wondered what had happened to Uncle Steve and why she was being so friendly with this stranger. Finally, he spoke. "Children, why are so quiet this morning?"

We all gasped and shouted. It was Uncle Steve himself, now clean shaven! Aunt Martha had cut his hair after we had gone to bed, then he had shaved. Now he looked like a different person. Only his voice was the same. Aunt Martha thought this was great fun. She had wanted him to cut off the beard to see how the children reacted, and she had found out. She was the most fun-loving mother I ever knew.

Later Uncle Steve reported that he would take a load of watermelons to market as they were now ready to pick. He looked at Cyril and me and said, "You children stay out of the watermelon patch. We'll be picking tomorrow."

I had never been to this garden that was shared between uncles Bert and Steve. Aunt Libby had forbidden us to go out of the yard unless we were going to school, and I'm sure that Cyril was not in the habit of going to the garden. As soon as we were outdoors I told Cyril I had never seen a watermelon and I wanted to know more about them. I told him that Grandpa had not raised watermelons. He suggested we go to the garden and he would show me.

Because I wore shoes, he asked me to take them off and go barefoot. My shoe prints would let his father know we had disobeyed. I took them off and he showed me how to walk like the blacks who always walked with the great toe separated from the others. He said his dad would think that a Xhosa had been walking in his garden, perhaps one of the black children, as my footprints were so small. His prints were only a little larger than mine. What we did was shameful, so shameful I still cringe today when I think of it. Because we had no knife, when I wished to taste one of the watermelons, Cyril picked it up and threw it onto another, resulting in the breaking of both. We continued to do this, not once thinking of the damage we were doing.

That evening during the dinner hour, Aunt Martha noticed that Uncle Steve was downcast and unhappy. "What is wrong, Stephen?" She looked very concerned. He sighed deeply, sadly shaking his head. "Well, Martha, I counted on making money on the sale of watermelons, but someone got into the garden and damaged too many."

"Do you think any of the children did it?" Aunt Martha glanced quickly at Cyril and then at me. He shook his head. "No, I don't think so. I examined the footprints and decided it must have been the blacks." I let my breath out slowly and could not look at Cyril. Why had we done such a thing? I am sure he felt as guilty and sad as I did. Until Uncle Steve said he wanted to sell those melons, I had not realized fruits, vegetables, and going to market meant money.

Money was something we children never handled. We simply had none. Perhaps we should have been told something about the economics of the family, but there was no place to spend even a penny so no one thought it was important that we know about it. This was the only incident of my childhood that made me feel guilty and unhappy and I often wanted to tell Aunt Martha I was so sorry about what we had done. But I dared not because that would incriminate Cyril and I could not do that. I was too fond of him.

If we wanted toys, we learned to create our own and to entertain ourselves. Cyril decided he would make a wagon from scrap wood and four old wheels he found. This was a flatbed wagon, with plenty of room. When he finished it, he wanted us four older children to go for a ride. We went over near the Kwelegha River where there was a flat place. The area had more of a downgrade than Cyril anticipated, especially when the rope he was using to guide the wagon, broke. He was frightened and kept saying, "I don't know what to do! I don't know what to do!" I was seated in the front half with him, Jessie and Amy were behind us. I soon realized we were careening too fast toward the river and would go right in if we didn't do something. No one would ever know what happened to us.

I threw myself off, grabbing desperately at the front wheel. It turned just enough that the wagon upset, throwing the three other children in different directions! What a howling! Jessie and Amy set up such a crying and screaming that I was sure someone would hear them. They were, however, more scared than hurt, although we were all bruised. Cyril said, "Let's go home and leave this thing here." He turned and walked away, limping slightly.

We all limped back to the house, with our bruised knees and skinned hands and all considerably shaken by the experience. We did not try to explain the episode but Aunt Martha had very sharp eyes. She could not accept the fact that we all had fallen down to get our knees scraped in the same manner. She laughingly wanted to know if the wagon had been a successful venture.

Chapter 25

A School Holiday Visit

One morning as I was ready for school, Mother told me, "When school is out this afternoon, you are going home with Sam,[1] Ivy, and the other Sonnenberger children. I've packed a few things for your needs and when the children return to school after the holiday, you can return with them, and, of course come home after the school session ends.

I was so excited! I had not stayed with this family except for an occasional Friday night to Monday morning. This was a ten day Easter holiday time.[2] It was a wonderful experience to be with such a large family of eight children at that time. It also meant I was to see Aunt Florrie. I also would meet, and get to know Uncle Adolph.

I had seen him upon two occasions when they visited the grandparents, but we had never spoken. He was Austrian by birth and quite different from my English uncles, somewhat severe, possessing some apparently unloving ways. But he also could have a twinkle in the eyes and a little smile, discerned below his somewhat straggly mustache. He had bushy eyebrows, but was clean-shaven. He was more on the blond side, which seemed strange to me as most of my uncles were dark-haired. He could become very angry, if obedience was not prompt. If there were any specific instructions given out during the breakfast hour, they were to be

---

[1] Edna May would have known the following Sonnenberger children: #1—Merle, #2—Ivy, #3—Harry, #4—Sydney Samuel, #5—Bessie. Children born later were Ivan, Myrtle, Victoria, and Victor.
[2] Easter Day was 4th April, 1920.

totally adhered to, as he would check by evening. He was also quick to praise something well done.

For example, one morning he told Cousin Sam to bring a certain cow into a special barn as she was due to calve during the day. Sam was my favorite in that family. He was about four years my senior. For some unknown reason, Sam chose not to obey, even though he had been reminded by some family member during the day. When Uncle Adolph came back from a conference with one of his neighbors that late afternoon, he naturally checked at the barn. The cow was not there, so he searched for her in the fields and found her calf had already been born. It was a healthy calf, but I later wondered what would have happened to Sam had the calf died. Uncle Adolph's fury against Sam seemed to me unnecessary. Cousin Ivy must have known I'd react, as she stood behind me. I started to protest and quickly a hand covered my mouth while she held me as I struggled to be free. My thought was to go to Uncle and tell him to "Stop!" Had I done so, it could have been rather disastrous for me as well, as I learned later when I asked Ivy about it all.

Aunt Florence and Cousin Mabel put the food on the table, all got into their chairs quickly and quietly. Food was eaten in silence, during which time Sam lay on the floor, weeping I suppose. I had ambivalent feelings toward Uncle after that. I also was better able to understand then why Sam had so many stripes on his skin. I had seen those on his back when we were at the beach, and once I asked him why he had them. He gave no reply. Apparently he was somewhat defiant, as a youngster, and so was recipient of several beatings in this manner.

Had I been beaten, I'm sure I would have hated my Dad or the one who beat me. Strangely enough, in later years, Sam was the best friend and helper Uncle Adolph had in the years preceding his death.

While at this farm I learned there were hives in which the bees collected their honey. This was a commodity we never had at the Bulugha farm.

Aunt Florence always milked certain of her dairy cows, and one in particular was "special for the children." We lined up at milking time and each in turn had milk squirted into his or her cup. It was so pleasantly warm! Auntie would sometimes ask the smaller children to get on their knees and she would squirt the milk right into our mouths. We thought this great fun and often laughed aloud, causing "Old Bossie" to turn around with her big eyes, seemingly wondering what was so funny about her being milked.

We played often below "Kwelegha Krantz," a high wall of rock beside a place where lay a natural clay pit. Here we spent hours forming the figures from clay. As a team project, we started to form a wagon with clay, complete with wheels and the spokes, a desselboom, and finally an inspan of four pair of oxen with their curved horns. We all felt great pride as we finally stood up and observed the finished project. Sam had made the yokes so carefully. Each piece was sun-dried before it was all assembled.

"Let's take it home to show Aunt Florrie," I suggested. "No," said Sam and Ivy, "It needs to sit in the hot sun one full day before it can be moved." I never saw it again because the next day we all had tasks around the yard and house and thus never returned to the Krantz.

Sam and I often climbed a tree somewhere so we could talk in private. We were mutually conversant. We shared our dreams for the future and had some other fantasies about life in general and some people in particular.

One early evening the corn crib was filled with corn cobs, and as I liked to climb, I suggested to Sam that we climb onto the top. It was forbidden by our parents, but as both of us were adventurous and somewhat inclined to disobedience, he climbed up first, showing me how to put the bare feet about the corrugated iron circles. (The corn cribs were all made of corrugated iron in a circular pattern.) Sam pulled me up the final few inches. We sat here and felt grand as we watched the children running around below us.

As it was beginning to get dark, Sam suggested we get down while we could see. He was used to doing this, apparently, and had no trouble getting down first—so that he could "catch you if you fall." I then began to be fearful as I could not see exactly where to put my feet, and there seemed nothing to hold onto as I began to slide. I must have screamed, even though Sam caught me, and this alerted the family. We were seen after all. Sam got the brunt of the reprimand, but neither of us was spanked, for which I breathed a sigh of relief.

These few days with this family knitted us into a close relationship, for I was soon never to see them again. But we never forgot each other and later would correspond for years.

I did not get to know Merle very well, although we too have corresponded. She was the eldest in the family. Cousin Ivy and I remained close all the rest of our lives. Cousin Harry was the quiet one. He and I were the two in the family who experienced a healing because of the knowledge of a witch doctor of the native tribe that helped the family with their farming needs.

Harry was kicked by a mule when he was a few months younger. The blow landed on his left ear. A peculiar pear-shaped lump began to grow and hung out of his ear. The medical people could not understand why this grew and did not know how to treat it. Apparently, it was not painful to him. But, how could he go through life with this protuberance so noticeable?

Of course the Xhosa workers saw it, as the older children also had to work in the fields. No doubt they conversed about it, perhaps one even asked the witch doctor to do something. All these workers on "Springfontein Farm" had a good feeling for Aunt Florence, as she was counselor, friend, nurse, and helper in many other ways.

During our preparations for breakfast one morning, we heard chanting. All went outdoors to see what was the occasion. We saw a large group of natives coming toward the farm gate. Many had fantastic head dress of plumes and feathers together with much bead work. I was a bit frightened, but no one else seemed to be so. We children held back, as did Uncle Adolph; Aunt Florrie met them. Speaking in their language, she inquired the purpose of this early morning visit. The witch doctor and Aunt Florrie carried on their conversation for some time. She soon seemed satisfied and called Harry to her. She explained to him that these were the tribal chief and his counselors together with the witch doctor who wished to heal the ear.

The sun was not yet above the horizon, but it soon appeared. At that time the chanters began and a ritual dance was performed. The witch doctor in his strange robes and face marked with clays placed a hand on Harry's head, just over the ear, and began to speak with authority in his native tongue. He then made gestures over the child and the ceremony was over. Speaking to Aunt Florrie again, he made it known that they would return at sunset and again the next morning. The same ritual was performed that evening just as the sun went down. The following morning the chanters, the council members, and the witch doctor returned. They seemed more joyful, if that was possible.

Harry was placed before the witch doctor and lo! the strange lump was no longer to be seen. It was odd that none of us had noticed this as we prepared for breakfast. It is likely that most of us younger children were still half asleep, our rising time in this household being rather early. We each had appointed tasks to get ready for the breakfast and each of us must have been concerned with getting these done. At any rate, that unsightly lump was gone forever! The Xhosas danced, shouted with more abandonment, and raised their assegais and spears, which were carried as part of their attire, though not always for war or battles.

Many of the South African witch doctors were women, called "sangoma" in their native tongue. These were usually called to the healing arts. The male witch doctor, who inherits his profession, is called "inyanga" or "naka." The sangoma are trained over a period of three years and have to take certain initiations or steps in this period of time. They all have a basic knowledge of herbs and roots and learn what each is best for healing physical problems. The secrets of this is carefully guarded, lest anyone use it wrongfully. Should any sangoma fail one of the testings, she is no longer permitted to proceed with the lessons. To be thus disgraced is a sore trial and so each exerts herself to the utmost to attain perfection.

The vacation was soon over and off we trudged the three and a half miles to school. After school, I bid these cousins farewell, thanking them for a happy time. I went home with Gladys, Arthur, and sister Jessie. It was good to see Mother again, too.

Chapter 26

Farewell to South Africa

We were well into year 1920 when one Saturday in May, sitting on the edge of the bed, Mother was talking seriously to us three children. Even before she told us the latest news, I had a feeling that our lives were once again going to change in some way. She was looking thoughtfully at a letter in her hand. It was hard to tell how she felt, but I soon realized she was feeling relieved at what was in the letter. Finally she looked up.

"This will be your last full month at school, because we are all going to America to live with your Dad. He has sent us some money for the trip." Now she held up the letter. "We will travel on a big ship that crosses the ocean to England, then to the United States, where we will go by train to a place called Omaha, Nebraska. There he will be waiting for us."

I was not too impressed, because Daddy was not a very real person to me any more. I am sure he was even less real to Jessie who had not seen him since she was two years old. Certainly Leonard, born 4th September 1914, five months after Dad left, never even knew him.

I thought of school and hoped we would not leave before the Inspector came to give us our tests. I certainly wanted to pass into the fifth standard. But now Mother was talking about leaving and what she hoped America would be like.

"Will this be 'the brighter tomorrow'?" I asked. She smiled and looked pensive. "I hope so, I do hope so," she said slowly. "It surely cannot be any worse than my last two years have been here. 'A brighter tomorrow?' I wonder." She said the last so softly I hardly heard her.

The following Monday morning, Mr. Rankillor made the

announcement that the Walker children would be leaving school in the middle of June and going to the United States of America. This led to a number of things, including a new geography lesson showing just where we would be going. During lunch hour Maria Hill, the oldest girl in the group, stood before the map of the world, pointing out the expected route the Walkers would take as they left South Africa. "From East London, they will stop in Port Elizabeth, then on to Cape Town, to the Maderia Islands, then to Southampton, England. They will change ships and go to Newark, then by train to Omaha, Nebraska." The teacher nodded as she gave this information.

Someone asked where Omaha was and Maria said, "Somewhere in the middle of here," pointing triumphantly below Chicago, which she could plainly see on the map.

At this moment I began to feel excited and loudly exclaimed, "I'm not going to Omaha, I'm going to Seattle!" Startled, everyone looked at me but I was not daunted. I was positive I would end up in Seattle, although up until then none of us had heard of Seattle, Washington. I have no recollection of previously hearing the name of that city, so that statement was surprising even to me. I just knew I would eventually go to Seattle to live. All my life I have had strong intuitive feelings from time to time, although I knew nothing about intuition.

Unfortunately, I was not able to attend the last three weeks of school nor to take the exams given for passing into the next standard. I was once again sick during that time with the malaria that has plagued me all my life. I overheard Mother and Aunt Libby discussing my dilemma as they stood at my bedside. Aunt Libby said, "What will you do if she is still too ill to travel when you are ready to leave?" Mother's reply was too low for me to hear, but I vowed I would get well because I did not want to stay with Aunt Libby. I was afraid Mother would leave me behind.

On a bright sunny afternoon in early June, the school children arrived to wish us all good-bye. It was then the reality of our leaving truly struck me.

The day finally arrived when we left our rondeval and said good-bye to cousins Gladys and Arthur, to Aunt Libby and Uncle Bert Green. We would, however, see them a few days later when we would be at the Springfontein farm where Aunt Florence and Uncle Adolph and their eight children were planning a gala farewell dance for Mother. Mother and we children went a couple of days before the dance so she could help in the preparations and have a few hours with Aunt Florence.

As Uncles Sidney, Clem, and Leonard, Mother's younger brothers, formed a trio of significant uncles with whom I had a relationship, so Aunt Florence and Uncles Steve and Bert formed a trio of her immediate older siblings with whom I had a relationship in the last several years.

Soon people began to arrive, some in covered wagons, some in horse-drawn carriages or buggies, some on horseback. The gathering was a repetition of the gatherings I had seen for weddings and trips to the beach and at the rendezvous. Relatives and friends came from farmlands and the city, some who had known Mother since childhood. The yard became a scene of much activity and confusion, with Xhosas to handle and care of their respective spans of oxen or horses. Many of the wagons arrived by mid-afternoon, because evening travel was difficult. Social events were so few and far apart that any such event was something special. Families came, planning to stay overnight, sleeping in their wagons after the strenuous dancing that lasted until the small hours of the morning. Children learned to dance when adults took time to teach them, so it was a fun time for everyone.

Naturally, Mother was the belle of the ball. She had little time to sit and eat, as someone was always wanting "this last dance with Ivy." She had always been a favorite with everyone, and this festive occasion was both a joy and a sorrow for her. The realization that these dear friends and loved ones were gathering in her honor for the last time and that she would never see some again caused her many mixed feelings. I really, however, had no concept of the emotional experience Mother had, and we never discussed it. I only knew that I felt her moments of sadness, even as she laughed while dancing. I was almost always very perceptive of Mother's feelings and moods, so when I was not dancing I watched her closely from the sidelines.

It must have been painful for her to face the fact that this was truly a farewell to all she held dear. The future in a strange land, once again to be with the husband whom she had not seen for six years and one with whom she surely had many difficult times, could not be a joyful expectation. The die was, however, cast. There was no way out of this situation. I am quite sure that if she had only herself to consider, she would never have left the land she loved and the ones she held dear. With three young children to consider, no doubt she thought they needed their father. Now here we were, having one last party for our going away, and I wondered if I would ever see any of these people again.

Soon mothers were telling children it was time to lie down and go to sleep, and many went reluctantly. Others were already nodding their heads before being tucked into the wagons or on the floor inside one of the bedrooms. We three children, along with cousins Bessie, Myrtle, and Victoria, Aunt Florrie's youngest children, were better situated, as we all were on a soft bed. We had one bed for six children; we slept crosswise with our heads against the wall, six little kids with feet curled up for those who were longer than the bed was wide. Bessie and I were at one end of the bed, closest to a window that opened out onto the verandah. A faint light was showing from the hallway into the bedroom. We were whispering quietly, as the smaller children were already asleep.

Suddenly I heard the sound of a galloping horse, the quick thud of a horseman hitting the ground, and steps running until they were at the window. Someone was looking through at us, a man who was very thin and wearing a tattered felt hat. He looked sick. "Who is that, that man on the verandah?" I whispered. Bessie raised herself on one elbow. "I don't see anyone, but I heard him."

"Who?" I spoke softly. "I don't know." She lay back down. "Those sounds have been happening for a long time. We all hear them, but we never see anyone."

"But, Bessie, I did see him! He was looking in the window, then he turned away." We then heard receding footsteps, the rattle of a bridle, and the galloping of a horse. It seemed to upset her that I insisted I had seen the man, but she did not say anything more. Soon we all were asleep.

The next day a neighbor, taking a wagon load of produce to the city, took Mother, us children, and our baggage to deliver us to a downtown hotel in East London where we stayed for three days until the ship sailed. While there, I told Mother about hearing the horse and seeing the face at the window. Mother then explained that Auntie had told her about this strange visitor who came about once a month for several years, then gradually discontinued his mysterious visits.

It seemed that Aunt Florrie was often called to be a midwife. At that time a neighbor several miles away was expecting her child, but unfortunately Aunt Florrie was also expecting one of her own. The husband of that woman rode horseback to fetch Auntie to assist his wife, not realizing that she could not help this time. He then returned home, only to discover that his house was in flames. He never knew how the house caught fire, but it burned to the ground and all was lost, including the pregnant wife. He died from grief and a short time after his burial. Aunt Florrie and her family began to hear this galloping horse. Auntie was gifted with "second sight," so she understood the reason for the galloping rider after he was dead.

Our three days at the hotel was a great wonder to me as many visitors, unable to attend the dance, came to see Mother, to bid her good-bye. Some relatives came from Queenstown and other surrounding towns, so she had little time to ponder our future. Sometimes one of these guests would take us to the dining room for lunch and we always went there for dinner. Mother would dress us girls in our new white dresses and Leonard in his white suit. She always cautioned us to behave properly.

I enjoyed entering the dining room, as Mother made a striking figure with her slimness, and all four of us dressed in white. I also enjoyed the attention of the waiters and looked forward to the food that was served so differently from what we were used to. The last evening there our host was Mr. Rankillor. I sensed this was a special occasion, but did not know why. Perhaps it was the contrast of his dark suit against the white attire of the family, plus the white table linens. Perhaps it was the sensing of a deeper emotion between the adults. Certainly it must have been a time of gratitude on Mother's part to this one person who had given her an opportunity to free herself from debt.

We had just become seated and our food was served to us when without warning the silence was shattered by a loud howl from Jessie. Shocked, we all stared at her as Mother tried to quiet her. Jessie kept her hands over her mouth in between howls. The waiter as well as the maitre d'hôtel hastened to our table.

Finally, Mother shook her by one shoulder and Jessie took one hand from her mouth long enough to point to what looked like a small dish of mashed turnips. It was some very strong horseradish! Hastily, Mother picked up her glass of water and made her take a sip, and then another. This probably did not help much, but it did give them something to do, until the waiter reached over and buttered a small roll that Jessie took and started to eat. The awful burning sensation must have lasted a long time. Later I took a tiny nibble of that horseradish with my meat, which was very tender, and even that small amount was potent enough to make tears come to my eyes. Although I had sympathy with Jessie, the rest of the diners apparently did not. The English are very proper in their dignity. To have a howling child disturbing their dinner hour was unthinkable. Although Mr. Rankillor was very sympathetic, Mother was terribly embarrassed and I am sure was very glad when that meal was finally finished.

The morning of Saturday 12th June 1920 finally dawned bright and clear. Mother had us up, dressed, and finished with our early breakfast. When we returned to our room, I noticed she often hovered at the window, pulling the curtains apart and peering out. This window looked down onto the street where horsemen hitched their carriages. Motorcars were not too often seen in 1920 in East London.

About eleven o'clock I heard Mother gasp. Hurriedly she went to the door and soon we heard her exclaim joyfully. Grannie had arrived! What a joy it was to see her, as we had not seen her since we left the farm in the last days of 1918. We children scrambled around her, quite forgetting that Mother and she were eager to talk. It was a tearful time for both women, a reunion and a final good-bye, a wrenching experience for both.

"Will Dad come up to say good-bye? Will you be at the jetty?" Mother was asking. Grannie sadly shook her head, then replied, "No, Ivy, I'm afraid not. I begged him to see you, as it will be the last time, but he was adamant. At first he refused to bring me into town, but I told him I would walk if he did not." She would have done so, too! The twenty-five miles would not have kept her from seeing her daughter for the last time. It must have been very difficult for her not to have seen any of us for the preceding nineteen months.

At last Mother said, "Kiss your Grannie good-bye, children." I noticed she kept wiping her eyes as she said this, and Grannie had tears in her eyes. I did not fully comprehend that this was a final good-bye. Mother and Grannie embraced and there was strong emotion by both being held in check. I could only imagine, in later years, the deep drama of this episode and the very deep sorrow of my mother.

After Grannie had gone downstairs, Mother stood at the window looking longingly at her father sitting so erect in the buggy and waiting for Grannie. The tears streamed down her face. The fact that his pride would not permit him to say a last good-by caused her deep grief, although she had consolation in the fact that he did drive all those twenty-five miles to bring her mother into town for a last good-bye. I often wondered at the conversation that went on between these two grandparents as they were homeward bound.

A porter came to take our baggage and we followed him to a carriage that served as a taxi. Soon we were at the jetty on the Buffalo River. Way out in the bay we could see the two-masted ship and I wondered how in the world we could get aboard when there was such an expanse of water between us.

Mother must have felt forsaken as we stood there, with not a soul to tell her good-bye, while people around us were being hugged and kissed. Then we heard a voice calling, "Ivy!" Mother's face lit up like a sunbeam. She turned, and there were Aunt Alice and Uncle Bert Gager with Bobby, now six years old. Then Uncle Sid, Uncle Len, and Uncle Clem appeared, together with Aunt Florrie and cousins Ivy and Mabel, also a couple whom I did not know, though known to Mother. Now there was a lot of talking and laughing and passing out of gifts.

I eyed these with anticipation. Bottles containing sweets of different colors appeared and our farm uncles gave us children each a bottle. (It happened we never ate a single piece. Seasickness kept us from that enjoyment.) At that time the Buffalo River was not deep enough for an ocean liner to be docked at the pier.

Later the harbor was deepened by dredging; and today Buffalo River harbor is an industrial shipping lane.

My curiosity as to how we would get aboard that ship was soon solved. A small boat came close and much activity began, with people moving closer to a man in uniform. He said, "All of you who are leaving on the *S.S. Saxon* be ready when the horn blasts. Only those traveling will be permitted to go aboard. Please step forward as I call your names." Then he pointed to what, to my childish eyes, looked like a huge basket. "Family members stay together and you will enter the bucket alphabetically." As our name was Walker, Mother knew we would be among the last. So we stood watching with interest as more and more people entered and a big crane lifted them, ten at a time, into the small boat.

As the group on dock dwindled, Mother was being hugged and kissed and people were crying. It suddenly dawned on me that this was not a happy time, after all. I sensed a feeling of foreboding and finality that made me very uncomfortable.

At last "Walker!" was called and Mother maneuvered us into the basket-like thing. We stepped over its threshold and I tried to look over the wall but it was too high. The door was locked, we clutched Mother as we were lifted up, up, up; then swaying gently, we were lowered to the deck and the door opened. The sides of the boat were too high for me to look over, but Mother was waving one last good-bye.

The boat began chugging and we finally came alongside the ship, the *S.S. Saxon*. The basket process was repeated and we were lifted, then lowered to the deck where I saw my first sailor. I thought his uniform was very funny, with his funny little white hat. A man in uniform with a different shaped hat, said, "Mrs. Walker?" When she said yes, he added, "Please follow me and watch your step as we go through doors and down the stairs." He was a steward and we would see him often for the time we were on the ship because we were assigned to his section of the cabins below deck.

I had not considered that our baggage was not with us until I saw it in our stateroom. It had all been taken on board before the passengers.

Chapter 27

First Ocean Passage

It took awhile to become used to our small cabin space. Sets of bunks lined the walls, leaving a narrow walking space between. At the farther end, opposite the entrance, was a wash basin, with a mirror above it. Our baggage had been placed beneath the lower bunks. Mother decided I could climb the ladder easier than could Jessie, so she assigned me the upper bunk on the right of the entrance. She could lift Leonard to the one opposite, while she and Jessie took the lower bunks. She put the precious jars of sweets by our pillows, but we would not eat them because we wanted to show them to Daddy. Actually, we had not been used to sweets of any kind and hardly knew what they were. (Later, when Mother was very seasick, she could not stand the sight of these, and one day she opened the porthole and threw them out into the ocean! We were all so seasick we did not really care.)

But now we were trying to get settled. Our conversation was disrupted by a sudden loud noise, the ship's whistle. Our startled gazes met Mother's and she smiled faintly. "That is just the signal to let us know we are leaving East London." Now she wasn't smiling as she hastily brushed away a tear. We children were silent as we listened to the strange sounds of the swishing of the ship moving through the water after anchors had been noisily hoisted. We stood near Mother who was sitting on her lower bunk.

Suddenly our conversation was interrupted by a knock on the cabin door. She rose and opened the door. An officer stood smiling. "Mrs. Walker, I am Mr. Scott, your cabin steward. Would you like to have a short tour of the ship's facilities so you will know your way around?"

"Oh yes. May I take the children?"

He nodded. "Of course. Just follow me, please, and do watch your step as we pass from one area to another. It is easy to stumble over the high doorsteps when one is not used to them." I had already noticed the height of the step at the first door we had entered, because Leonard, with his short legs, could hardly step over. I found out later this height was to keep water out of outside rooms when the seas were rough and the ship was rolling. Even some of the inner sections of the ship were divided in this way.

Now the steward was pointing to rooms along the corridor, all having numbers on them. "These are your fellow-passenger cabins. This is the bathroom area that you will share with them." We walked on a bit farther. "Here is the dining room, as you can see. Dinner is served at seven." He reached toward a small stand, removing a sheet from each of two piles of schedules, saying, "One is a schedule of meal times and the other gives events in the recreational area. You may wish to refer to them later."

Walking on ahead through the narrow corridor we came to the recreational room. "There is entertainment here each evening," he said, "which includes card playing and dancing." Then he pointed to his left. "Notice over in the far corner are small tables where the children are supervised by an attendant. You can bring them here evenings and relax yourself, knowing they will be well cared for. You are welcome to go above deck any time, but it is too dark now to see anything. I'll show you that area later when it is light."

The conversation was at an end, so Mother thanked him and we returned to our cabin. That brief visit to the dining room was the only time I would be there in all of the next four weeks we were aboard the *S.S. Saxon*!

We were awakened early the next morning by a knock on the cabin door. Mother opened it to a steward who held a tray of juice, teas, and toast. They said good morning to each other and he placed the tray on a small table he drew down from the wall. "The dining room will not be open until seven this evening for dinner," he said. "We will soon be in Port Elizabeth to pick up more passengers. You may leave the ship if you wish, but you must return by three o'clock because we leave for Cape Town at four."

Mother thanked him and he departed, leaving us to eat our food. I did not feel hungry but the juice tasted good. Mother then told us to put our hats on and we all went to the upper deck where many people stood waiting, some with baggage though most without. Mother said that those with bags were getting off the ship at Port Elizabeth. "We'll get off," she said, "but not to stay, only to visit. My Aunt Louise, Grandpa Green's sister, lives here."[1]

Just then the ship's hoarse whistle boomed out and talking was impossible. I watched the sailors doing things with ropes. As the ship slowly moved to the pier, those ropes, both at the bow and at the stern, were thrown to the longshoremen on the dock, who secured them to huge iron, double-pronged things protruding up from the edge of the dock. The men pulled the ship slowly against the pier and quickly secured it by wrapping the ropes tightly around the double prongs, making figure eights as they did so. Other longshoremen had been standing by with the gangplank, ready to shove it toward the ship, dropping the far end onto the deck where part of the rail had been swung back. It was now made secure by sailors standing by.

Finally, passengers going ashore were allowed to descend and we slowly followed. As we reached the bottom of the gangplank, I heard someone calling Mother's name and she rushed to one side, with us following, to a woman who embraced her warmly. "Oh, Ivy! It is good to see you! So good!" Mother could not seem to say anything for a few moments and kept brushing tears away. At length, she introduced us, and our Great Aunt Louise led us to a waiting carriage taxi. She took us to a tearoom where we ate sandwiches and drank tea. Now I was hungry, so it tasted good.

The two women ignored us more or less because they were trying to catch up on news and activities in their lives. This did not matter to us, for we were all busy eating. At last Aunt Louise said, "I'll have to leave you now because I have some appointments. I am thankful we had this little chat; we may never see each other again because you are going so far away." We left the tearoom and Aunt Louise stood waiting for a carriage. She and

---

[1] Sketchy family records indicate that Robert Frederick Green had two brothers, Philip and Matthew, and one sister, Sarah.

Mother looked at each other, silently, embraced, and then this great aunt of mine bid each of us children good-bye and hugged us lovingly. We watched her drive out of sight. Then Mother hailed another carriage and we drove off.

For a short time Mother was silent. Then she said, "We are going to see an old friend of your father's, a Mrs. Hartley, who took care of him a long time ago." She added, "She saw you, Edna, when you were little, but she's never seen Jessie and Leonard." Mrs. Hartley's house was big and white. As soon as she ushered us into the parlor she and Mother began to talk. I looked at the sofas, the big chair, the many paintings on the wall, and a piano with several photographs on top. Some of the furniture was covered with red velvet. I was awed by the entire room. I heard Mrs. Hartley say, "Would you like to see him? I'm sure he will be pleased to see Sid's wife and his children."

We followed her down the short hallway, where she turned left into a large, hospital-like room smelling of medicine. In this room was a strange bed, strange because a long board overhung the bed from end to end. Hooked to this board was a chain and hanging from the chain was a bar. My eyes then traveled down to the occupant. He was a man, clean shaven, rather gaunt, with dark hair and a wan smile. He seemed to come alive when Mrs. Hartley said, "Alex, I have a surprise for you. Here are Ivy Walker and Sid's three children."

Mother went to him and he withdrew from beneath the covers a very thin arm and a hand that was almost transparent. He must have been ill a long time. Mother held his hand and they talked quietly together. I stood at the foot of the bed watching his facial expressions and wondering what was wrong. He finally looked at me and, letting go of Mother's hand, beckoned to me. I refused to move, even when Mother said, "Come and speak to your dad's nephew. This is your cousin, Alex."[2] I still stood silent.

---

[2] It is not clear who this Alex is. He appears to be the only Walker, other than Aunt Agnes Robinson Walker, whom Edna May recalls meeting as a youngster in South Africa. Her father, Sidney, born 10th July 1886 at Uitenhage, was the youngest of twelve; his close brother Ivan Lawrance Walker, was the eleventh child and was born 7th November 1883 at Uitenhage. Several of the others appear to have died young without issue.

"Ms. Hartley took care of both of them when they were young and ran away from home." I still refused to go near him.

Finally, Mother said, "Alex, I'm sorry this visit is so brief. We are going to America to meet Sid and live there. I'll tell him I have had a little visit with you. Be of good courage." She leaned down to kiss him on the forehead while he held her hand. "We have to be aboard the ship at three o'clock so we must go."

We once again were in the parlor and both women were crying. Mrs. Hartley was saying, "I know he has been suffering a long time; he was badly wounded in the war and has never walked since. He is like a son to me and I hate to part with him. But for his sake I hope his ordeal will soon be over." Mother agreed and promised to tell Sid about this visit and talking with Alex. This kindly woman kissed each of us as we said good-bye and left the house.

We were all silent as we rode back to the boat and climbed up the gangplank, going immediately to our cabin. I was very tired and Mother had much to think about, so there was little conversation. She suggested we children rest as she also wanted to lie down.

I was soon fast asleep. When it was time for dinner, Mother did not awaken me but had some fruit for me later when I awakened. I was, however, to asleep until morning. The ship was moving when I awoke. As I had missed breakfast, Mother gave me fruit and fruit juice. We were headed for Cape Town, two days' journey from Port Elizabeth, and all this time so far I was not feeling good.

Rather than leave the ship at Cape Town, Mother decided to stay aboard. because it was late afternoon when we arrived. We all went above and watched the passengers disembark and the sailors unload large boxes and crates, cranes lifting them from the hold of the ship. At length, we returned to our cabin.

Mother looked at me sharply. "Edna, are you feeling all right?" It was hard for me to tell how I felt. I just nodded my head and crawled into my bunk. I promptly fell asleep and did not

---

Two sisters survived to adulthood: Alice Walker, the third child, born 8th July 1865 at Port Elizabeth, married Henry Acker. Agnes Robinson Walker, the sixth child, born 12th July 1871, was mentioned earlier in Edna May's story in Chapter 3. The eldest of the Walker children appears also to have been an Alexander, born perhaps in 1860. He remains a mystery.

awaken until morning, when I was given some breakfast right in the cabin. After eating, we prepared to go ashore. I did not feel like going, but I did not say anything. I was still very tired.

Ashore we were met by a Mrs. Steffens, a friend of the family. She didn't seem too friendly to us children because she and Mother were busy talking to each other. She took us first to a shop on Adderly Street because she had a purchase to make, then the women decided to walk to the tearoom. When we stepped out into the street, I was surprised to see such a hard surface to walk on: a sidewalk of cement! As the two women walked along arm in arm, Jessie, Leonard, and I walked behind holding hands. Then I let go.

I began to feel strange and my legs did not maneuver properly. I felt as though I could go no farther. Why I did not call out to the adults, I don't know, but gradually I dropped behind and stood watching as they entered a shop on their left, a shop with a golden ornament above it. Later I learned the ornament was a symbol of the type of bakery foods they served, something Danish. Soon I could stand no longer and I sat down by a lamp post. Two strange ladies stopped and spoke but I did not understand them, so I shook my head. I could not understand why I could not see them very well, My vision was playing tricks on me. I sat with my head in my hands.

I felt a touch on my shoulder and a voice saying, "What is the matter, little girl? Are you lost?" I looked up, trying to focus my eyes on the bobby (policeman) who stood before me. Again I shook my head. "Where is your mother?" I am sure he knew I was not a waif, because I was well dressed and clean. I tried to speak, but all I could do was point to where the women had gone, saying, "Tearoom." Then I fainted.

I did not know that Mother had missed me as they were being seated in the tearoom and came running to find me. Fortunately, she arrived just as the bobby was going to put me into a carriage, apparently to take me to a hospital. I did not regain consciousness for three weeks and have no recollection of being on the ship. I was sometimes semiconscious and once I heard the doctor tell Mother, "There are no facilities aboard for a hospital case. We will just leave her here and I'll check on her. Mrs. Walker, I must prepare for the possibility of her being buried at sea. She is a very sick little girl. She has rheumatic fever, as far as I can diagnose, and I am helpless to help her."

I can recall that Jessie came to my bunk, climbed the ladder, and put something in my hand. This turned out to be crackers and cheese, the only solid food I can remember eating. She said she got them each evening and wondered if I could eat them.

There came a day when the steward carried me, bundled in blankets, onto the upper deck. Many individuals came and spoke to me. There were for the children music and games in which I could not take part. All the time Mother hovered over me. Finally, I became so chilled that the steward took me back to the cabin.

As I began to get better, I found that by raising myself upon an elbow I could look out the porthole and watch small boats laden with fruits, linens, and people going and coming. Once a body flashed by and went into the water and I wondered what that was all about. Once Jessie rushed into the cabin. "I wish you would come up on the upper deck." Pointing out the porthole she said "People from Maderia Island, have brought many fruits and pretty things to sell."

As we talked another body went into the water. "Why are people diving into the water? Where do they come from?"

She had also seen it. "They are called divers and they dive in for money that people throw in, trying to catch the coin before it reaches the sand. I hear people talking about it. I can't see over the railing, and no one will lift me up. I'll go up now and see if I can bring you some fruit." As she went out I peered out the porthole, watching for a few minutes, but soon became too tired and lay down again.

One day Mother brought in some food and, sitting beside me, she said, "Edna, you must eat all of this. We will soon be in Southampton to get off the boat, and I cannot carry you. Eat this, and you will begin to feel strong enough to walk." After that I began to eat more, thinking of what Mother said. I could not disappoint her. At any rate, I wanted to be able to walk off the boat. In spite of the fact I was now better, my being so sick, however, was to cause some unforeseen problems.

In the late afternoon before our next day's arrival at the Port of Southampton, England, the ship's doctor made a final visit to see me. He turned to Mother and said, "Please understand that you cannot leave the ship without a notification signed by me, because Edna has been so ill. I'll bring you the paper in the morning." But—he never brought that paper! We waited and waited, with Mother's becoming more upset all the time. She even left the cabin door open to await his approach. She was in tears when a cleanup person came to our cabin. He stared in disbelief, then exclaimed, "Madam, why are you still here? Everyone is off the ship!"

Mother explained about the doctor. "But, Madam, he was the first one off the ship! He always is."

"Oh, oh! Whatever shall we do?" Mother almost wailed. "We have a ship connection to make because we are going on to the United States."

He dropped his cleaning things. "Better come with me." He began picking up our baggage. I'll see if I can find some help for you."

We followed him up the steps. Setting our baggage down, he darted off and soon we saw him with one of the ship's officers approaching quickly. "Madam, I'm so sorry this has happened! You had better go ashore and get through customs before they close."

We trudged quickly down the gangplank, along a wooden passage, into a room that read "Customs," and Mother told her story to a kindly man in uniform. When she explained about the ship we were to transfer to, asking which way to go to reach it, she listened in consternation when he said, "My dear lady, your ship left the harbor fifteen minutes ago! How unfortunate that you were delayed."

Mother almost fainted. "Oh, what are we to do? My husband is expecting us to arrive on that ship." To our great dismay, Mother burst into tears, while we children huddled together. The officer called someone to him and said, "Take this lady to the Red Cross office."

When we reached there, the middle-aged woman listened carefully to all that Mother had to tell. She then asked for Dad's address. "We shall send him a cablegram that you are delayed. When you book passage on the next ship, let the Red Cross know and we shall again send a cablegram to tell him when to meet you."

She turned to reach for a slip of paper, handing it to Mother as she said, "Here is the address of a woman who takes in people in your situation. Go out that door, and a carriage will take you to this address. Just give the driver this paper and you will not need to pay him." She smiled at Mother. "Don't worry. We shall do some checking to find out when the next ship leaves for New York."

We arrived at the address given to Mother. The lady led us upstairs to a lovely bedroom. After she went out and closed the door, Mother said, "Children, do not sit or put your clothing on the bed." She began lifting the bedclothes, suddenly throwing them back. She gave a gasp and replaced the covers after searching carefully around the mattress. I didn't know what she was looking for. "Oh dear," she said, turning to us. "We cannot sleep in that bed. It is full of bedbugs. Pick up your things. We'll go back downstairs." We obeyed as she pickup our suitcases.

As we came downstairs the lady came out of another room and Mother said, "Madam, I want permission to leave my children here near your fireplace. My older daughter has been very ill. I have to go out but should not be long." The woman eyed us, the baggage, and Mother, then said, "Why didn't you leave your baggage upstairs?"

"Bedbugs!" said Mother shortly. "I'm sorry, but we cannot stay in a room in which the bed is full of bedbugs. I will need to look for other lodging."

The woman looked surprised but said, "Very well. Yes, your children can stay here but there will be a charge, you know."

"I'll pay when I return," said Mother. Looking at us, she added, "Children, be brave and behave. Stay right there and I'll return as quickly as I can." With that, she left the house.

We were silent all the time she was gone and kept huddled together. I began to wonder if she ever would return, she took so long. At length, however, she did return and later told us how she had walked in one direction, then in another, until a carriage for hire came along. She told the driver about our situation and he promised to take us to his sister who had rooms.

Mother paid the lady who was not very pleasant in telling

Mother what she thought about our leaving, but Mother paid no attention. We gathered our things and walked out and soon we were being delivered to another home, closer to the downtown area. The driver stopped, helped Mother out, then she helped us down as he picked up our baggage. We followed him to the house. The door opened and a smiling, buxom woman said, "Well 'Arry, and now what 'ave we 'ere?" The driver explained, then Mother explained in more detail our situation, as we were served tea. The big woman was delightful as she waited upon us. "The young ones must be 'ungry for sure."

As the driver was ready to leave, he said, "Well, Ma'am, I'll come around tomorrow and take ye where ye needs to go, so don't worry. Sis, here, will take good care of ye." Mother felt better, I'm sure. After a hearty evening meal, we all went upstairs. Again, Mother checked the room, saying, "Thank goodness, this bed is clean." The day had been a traumatic experience for her, and I heard her sigh deeply as at last we all got into bed.

The next morning, after breakfast, our hostess said, "Now, Dearie, ye go along wi' my brother and don't worry about ye'r little ones. I'll watch them, all day if necessary." As Mother left the house, we watched out of the large window. Most of the afternoon had passed before the carriage returned, and we were happy to see this kind man bringing Mother back to the house. The lady threw the door open and asked, "How did it go?" Mother came in, hugged us children, and said, "Very well, except we will need to stay here three more days, if you don't mind. I booked passage on another ship that will leave England on Thursday 15th July. We leave early that morning." Then she asked the driver if he could take us to the dock at that time. She also added that the Red Cross was sending her husband another cablegram as to when we would arrive in New York. The man touched his hat, a gesture he often performed, "Yes, Ma'am. I'll take ye. Ye can always count on 'Arry." How relieved and thankful Mother was for these two kind people who came to her aid in a time of such stress.

Chapter 28

A Second Ocean Passage

Our driver showed up early the morning of the 15th and we bid farewell to his good sister. Soon we were en route to the dock where the *S.S. Lapland*, a Belgian ship, was moored. We walked up the gangplank. An officer, after looking at Mother's paper, handed them to a sailor, asking him to show us to our cabin.

What a contrast to the ship on which we had arrived in Southampton! We walked down, down, down three flights of steep steps that were more and more dimly lit the farther down we went. It turned out to be in sub-steerage, below regular steerage! "Oh no!" said Mother in shocked dismay. She turned to talk to the sailor who had brought us down but he was already gone. We three children just stood huddled together staring around. Because of the poor light, at first we could not see exactly what we had gotten into. Mother was aghast when she saw where we were, below the waterline in what was the steerage below the steerage. The gloom was alarming to me but the odors were just too awful.

When we finally did get used to the gloom, we discovered that our cabin had room for six people. Jessie was the first to speak. "This isn't like the other ship." Her voice quavered a bit. "Do we have to stay here?"

Leonard added his thoughts. "I don't like it here." He was clutching Mother's skirt.

I was watching her. Had she run out of money? Why were we in such an awful place? True, I had been so sick on the other ship that I didn't remember much about it except that Jessie had told me later how much fun she had and that there was even a place for children to be cared for and to play. But this! If only I hadn't been sick, if only the doctor had remembered to give us that permit!

Mother was staring around in disbelief. We could now see that our accommodations were dark, dingy, and dimly lit by the single bulb in the center of the ceiling and the bunks were all in shadow.

Two women in very short skirts entered the cabin at that moment to share the other two bunks. They were smoking cigarettes and were unlike any human I'd ever seen. One had such red hair that it looked unnatural. The second had hair of straw color. Both had painted faces. In fact their eyes were so surrounded by colors that I could barely keep from looking at them. I did try not to notice so much bare leg above their knees! Mother was more distressed by their foul language, and they seemed to quarrel continually. They had a sneering attitude toward Mother, who learned later that they were prostitutes and felt this was the ultimate in degradation.

Mother, usually not talkative around us children as to reasons for or against anything, said, "This is terrible, terrible! When I agreed to take this ship because it is the first one leaving for America, I never dreamed it would be like this in steerage, the only space they had left. I thought only of getting there. But this is terrible!" She rubbed one hand over her forehead, "If only that doctor had remembered to give us that permit, or I hadn't waited so long, or—or so many things."

She turned suddenly, grabbed Leonard's and Jessie's hand and said, "Come, children, we are going up and I'll talk to that officer. Maybe he can do something." But our once having a first-class ticket from South Africa did not help at all. If we wanted to travel now, it would have to be in steerage or wait another week. "But we can't wait another week," she told the officer firmly. "I do not have that much money."

"I'm sorry, Madam." He turned away. Nothing could be changed. We slowly went down the steps again and returned to our cabin. It was dreadful to think of being in that place for the six days of the trip.

We went into the dining area. Long tables had baskets of food stuffs strung out over the top. These belonged to steerage passengers who had boarded the ship at Antwerp, Belgium. Most of these people were refugees going to the United States to get away from the war-torn Europe of World War I.

As we had not brought any food aboard, there was nothing for us to eat except coffee and bread furnished by the ship. And because we children had never learned to grab, our politeness meant others snatched the bread away before we could even try to take any. Were we going to starve?

As we stood staring at the long table piled high with baskets of food belonging to the passengers, Jessie wrinkled her nose and said, "Mommy, I don't like the smell. I want to go out." Awful smells were indeed strong. Odors from unwashed bodies, malfunctioning toilets, and spoiled food we saw on the floor were unbearable.

"Come!" said Mother suddenly. "We'll go back to our bunks."

Back in our cabin, Leonard said plaintively, "I'm hungry." Mother stood undecided for only a moment, then she pressed her lips together. "I'll get you some food if it is the last thing I do! Come with me!"

She reached over and jerked a blanket off the bunk and started for the door. We trailed after her as she went up the three flights of steps. The fresh air was a boon! She found a sheltered place on deck and as she spread out the blanket, said, "Stay here! Don't move away! I am going to see if I can find some decent food for us. If you move, I will not know where to find you. Don't talk to anyone! Do you all understand?" We understood all right. With all those strange people milling around we were not about to move among them. I silently hoped she would not be gone too long. I wondered, too, at her commanding tone of voice, as she had never spoken so severely to us!

"Oh there's Mamma," at length cried our usually silent brother and he rose to his feet and ran to meet her. I began to realize that he, too, had worried about her even though he was only five. Something different was happening within myself. I sensed Mother was very distressed as she looked more harassed than I had ever noticed. I wished there was something that could be done to change our situation, but felt very helpless. I did some deep thinking, and suddenly thought of Uncle Bob Bryson's talking about Jesus. I did not know how to pray, but thought of Jesus and believed he would take care of us. Uncle Bob had often said that Jesus cares. Perhaps I breathed a prayer? I'm uncertain about this, as I had not been taught to pray. Nonetheless, I felt more at ease.

So Mother came back, looking somewhat harassed, but she did have biscuits and fruit. How good it tasted! Apparently, for steerage passengers, there was a sort of shop where food could be purchased. It must have been a very difficult thing for Mother to have to spend what little money she had for this extra food. Mother said, "We will just sit here all day, children. We must learn to wake up early as we must not stay in that awful place more than necessary. If we get up early, we can always find this space and claim it first; this is one reason we must not all leave here at the same time. I will take you one by one to the lavatory. We are sheltered here and no one can come from behind, because this storage place protects our backs."

After that, we returned to the cabin only when darkness was descending. We did not eat in that steerage dining area for the entire six days.

Our fellow passengers were a mixture of many languages, none of which I understood. Quarrels flared up very quickly, and this was one reason Mother appreciated our protective space. One day two young teenagers began quarreling early, and as the day progressed, so did their words. Soon they were physically combating, first with shoves and kicks. Finally anger flared to such a degree that each drew a knife. I was terrified to see this, as one slashed the other on the forearm. When the blood started to flow, the cries of the watchers were loud. Quickly two older woman went to the boys, each putting arms around them, while two men went toward the ship's officers who demanded to know what's going on.

We did not understand the language so could not know what was said. Apparently the two dads answered favorably, as no action was taken against them. The officers moved away and quiet was heard for a time. Thereafter, when boys began quarreling, their respective adults were quick to put a stop to the fracas. Each family was afraid it would be deported from the "land of freedom and a new life," as Mother explained. She went on to say, "You remember your Dad was in the War? Well, these people lived in that war-torn land and these young ones probably were so aware of fighting that they are still filled with hatred. War makes far too much hatred among people."

That day was beautifully sunny and warm and soon two young men, probably about thirty years of age, approached Mother and said, "Excuse us Madam, we are wondering if you are English. We have heard you speaking to your children and are amazed to find you here among all of these." He looking all around and with a wave of his arm, included all the Europeans.

"I am Harry Green and my friend is George Graves. We are from England and traveling second class; sort of slumming it now, as it were," again gestured to the crowd, laughing.

"Sit down gentlemen and I'm sorry not to have chairs." She gathered us closer to her. "Sit down on the blanket." They all laughed while the men sat, tailor-fashion. Mother introduced herself and each of us. I liked these men because they were so happy. I could see Mother brighten up as she exchanged conversation with each. Mr. Green did most of the talking. He had dark hair, wore a dark suit; Mr. Graves was a blond, a little shorter, and more rotund, but dressed casually.

The conversation between Mother and Mr. Green became more animated when he mentioned he was born in Cambridgeshire and said, "My family have been there for generations." Mother quickly said, "Oh, my dad said *his* family had been there for generations. We could be related! I had a brother named Harry.[1] Dad and his parents left England in 1850, or so." They concluded there could be a family connection though no real facts were established, then or later. (These two young men would visit us in our home in Omaha.) These men were a great blessing and help to Mother.

---

[1] This was the other uncle Edna May could not have known. Harry Matthew Green was born 29th August 1889 at Smiling Valley Farm, the eleventh child of Robert Frederick Green and Louisa Jane Nash Green. He died of a heart ailment on 11th April 1902 at the age of 12 years $7\frac{1}{2}$ months.

They came daily with food items she could not get at the little shop on this part of the ship. Their conversations gave Mother a boost in morale after the bleak days in Southampton and on this ship, with all its inconveniences and odors of stale foods and un-washed bodies. Both young men were going to visit relatives in the northeastern part of the United States and would try to find work there.

On our third day, missing a piece of lingerie, Mother locked her suitcase that she had been using daily. When we arrived in our cabin that night, the two women were sitting on their bunks and reeked of cigarette smoke and liquor. The redheaded person was more obnoxious than usual. Her foul language made Mother cringe and, fortunately, we children did not understand a word. It was with great effort that Mother remained silent when she referred to us children as "damned brats." When Mother continued in silence, the redhead was eyeing her carefully and finally said, "You shouldn't be wearing that diamond ring, Dearie. Someone might try to get it away from you." Again Mother remained silent.

Brother was already asleep and Mother lay down, getting beneath the covers. Jessie was almost asleep. I lay beside her. Mother had decided to use the lower bunks only, as she could not see how clean the top ones were. They were too high for her to lift the two younger children and because there was no ladder, I could not climb up. Our cabin was lit by one tiny lamp bulb in the center of the ceiling that burned all the time. This did not hinder sleep as the bunks were shadowed. I lay facing the opposite bunks and, through half closed eyes, watched the redhead. There was some-thing about her that chilled me. I thought about it and, suddenly, the peculiar feeling assailed me and I knew, inwardly, she planned to harm Mother. But how? I could not understand. I was very rest-less, determined to stay awake and watch, but sleep overcame me. The next day, when we were sitting on deck, I mentioned this to Mother. "Oh, no, child, she cannot possibly harm me. I am much stronger than she."

"But, why did you look so funny, Mother, when you opened your suitcase?"

"I noticed the things were not so neat as I usually leave them and noticed that the beautiful gown Aunt Florrie had given me was gone."

"Do you think she took it?"

"Well dear, I did not see her take it, so cannot say yes. But it was gone and that is why I locked my suitcase. We cannot trust everyone as we once did. Remember that."

Mother must have thought the redhead's remark about the ring was valid, for she did not have her ring and brooch on the next day. I remarked about this, only to hear her reply, "I put them in my suitcase and locked it." I did not say anything but thought a lot. I was uneasy, but she was "mother" and knew more than I.

As we were getting ready for what would be our last night on that Belgian ship, that particular woman said, "Well, Dearie, I see someone got your ring. It is not on your finger." Mother made no explanation and tried to ignore her. I watched the redhead with mounting distrust, and suddenly recalled the deadly red-lipped snakes that Jessie and I had been saved from years ago. Now I saw this woman with her painted lips and face and felt she was just as deadly. What would she do to Mother? I could not imagine, but knew fear.

Unfortunately, after using her cosmetics, Mother did not lock the bag again. On our last morning we were not awakened as usual by loud voices. At first Mother was relieved to see that the two women were gone. Then she noticed the baggage under their lower bunk was also gone. Hurriedly she searched her own bag and discovered the ring and brooch were both gone! We crowded around Mother as she was so anguished and started to cry.

"But Mother, how could she when you locked it?" I said.

"Oh, Edna, I did not lock it last night. I remember that Leonard needed attention when I had it open. In my hurry I neglected to relock it. They left quietly and early. Their suitcases are gone. Oh, dear, Sid will be so angry at my carelessness! I should have kept it on my finger. The brooch is gone, too, the only thing my brothers ever gave me. And she stole the only beautiful gown that I ever had." With this she burst into uncontrollable sobbing. We tried to comfort her. I was to realize, much later, that it was a blessing our trip did not last longer, as Mother surely had more than she could bear.

With her characteristic optimism, Mother just as suddenly, smiled and said, "Well children no use crying over spilled milk. We will never see them again." I did not know if she meant the women, or her jewelry, or her tears!

She dressed and immediately went to report the theft. The officer shrugged and said there was nothing he do, she should have kept the jewelry on her person. That was the end of the engagement ring from Dad and the brooch from her brothers.

On our way upstairs she met another ship's officer and related what happened. He too shrugged his shoulders in indifference and said, "There is nothing we can do. You should have kept these on your person."

His attitude caused Mother to say, "I'm sorry I spoke." It did seem that this was an ill-fated journey no matter from what angle it was surveyed. But more yet was to happen, causing Mother to forget these other "lesser" things.

As our last night was finished in this awful cabin, we took all our belongings up with us. We had only two small suitcases in the cabin, two large suitcases, and a bundle of blankets and bedding that was checked in the baggage room. We stepped out on deck to find people already lining the rail. The morning[2] was gray and misty and rather unpleasant. There in the distance was New York.

What would our next adventure be, I wondered?

---

[2] This should now be Friday 23rd July 1920.

Chapter 29

Arrival in America

Mother had her suitcase with her and we each carried our coats for we had no need to return to that cabin again. This was our last day on board. The misty morning matched the gloom we all felt at Mother's loss. Thankfully we buttoned our coats and went to our usual place, but soon there were loud cries and almost everyone rushed to one side of the ship. "There she is, there is the Statue of Liberty." Many got to their knees, handling beads and making gestures over their faces. Never having heard of the Statue of Liberty nor what it stood for, I could not understand why people seemed so excited over seeing it. I could not see over the heads and, because I had not hurried behind Mother, retreated to our place of waiting. I knew what she would do when she missed me; besides, I did not want to fall into the water when the boat tipped over! I had no understanding of how a ship stayed afloat, and with all the people on one side I fully expected to be safe where I was.

As the fog lifted, our first experience with this low-lying cloud, the sun shined and joy was everywhere present for all were tired of the confinement and the dreariness of our surroundings. It was then we noticed the ship was no longer moving. A smaller boat, bearing a number of Customs officers, was approaching to check first- and second-class passengers who would be the first passengers to disembark. They did not have to go through Ellis Island as we steerage people had to do. After a long wait these men came to our deck. It took a long time, because many foreigners could not understand what was required.

Mother was told that we three children would have to be vaccinated. After this was done, she was also told that we would have to pass the medical authorities, because we were in steerage.

This meant a stay at Ellis Island, a consequence that meant nothing to us just now. Only later did we learn how gruesome that experience would be.

As Mother moved away from the Customs officer, one of the ship's officers approached and drew her into a less crowded area. Surprisingly, he said, "Mrs. Walker, I advise you to suck all that serum from the arms of your children. If they should have even a small reaction, you will be detained at Ellis Island until the vaccinations heal. I will stand watch while you do this." He handed her a small bottle that said Mouth Wash on the label. "Use this to rinse your mouth and here's a tin to spit in," he said, handing the latter to me to hold for her. As she finished sucking out the serum from all of us children, he said, "I should not be seen here, but I also wanted to give you this tin of biscuits. It will be a long time before you will get a meal. I wish you well." He touched his cap with his forefinger and left. Mother was touched by his thoughtfulness and remarked about it later.

We stood in line a long time as the small boat left with the Customs personnel and the *S.S. Lapland* began to maneuver toward its docking place before a long low building. After the gangplank was put down and secured, one by one again the steerage passengers followed each other onto the dock. It was a slow, tedious progress but finally our turn came to step down.

In this long building were medical men who looked carefully at each immigrant, examining papers and handing them on to the next person. This person looked into our eyes, examined the medical sheet, handed us on until our ears, head, heart, and just about everything else were all examined. Each time the examiner put a check or written comment on the medical paper. As my turn came, I am sure that Mother became apprehensive when one of the medical team questioned her. I was no larger than Jessie even though I was eleven years old and I was obviously sickly. As we passed the line of medical examiners, the last person was a nurse. She looked at the papers, looked at me, and said, "This child must come with me." Mother turned to go with us but the nurse said, "No, you cannot come. Go into that door and wait." I followed the nurse into a room that had tiny individual dressing rooms. Pulling back the curtain, she said, "Go in there and take off all your clothes, The doctor will be in shortly."

I obeyed, quaking at the word "doctor," and wishing that Mother was with me. I folded my clothes carefully, then sat on them with my feet up on the seat, my arms around my knees. As I waited impatiently, I suddenly heard Mother's voice. "I must find my child before I can go farther. Please, Sir! I must wait for my child!"

Quick as a flash I dressed, then looked to the right where I had seen the nurse go. I saw no one. I got on the floor and looked underneath the partitions to my left. Some distance away I saw a door that, for some reason, was open. I crawled under the partitions of five other dressing rooms, fortunately unoccupied, and quickly ran though the door into the large room,

"Mother! Mother, here I am!" I ran quickly toward her and threw my arms around her, ignoring the man who was holding a gun pressed against her side. At my cry he turned around and stared down at me, while Jessie and Leonard hugged me. He looked up into Mother's face, "So you do have another daughter," he said, putting his gun away. "I'm sorry, Ma'am, if I seemed rough and rude, but I have to follow orders. I did not believe you, because we have many who say odd things to get out of here. Now you may go, but please turn around and go through that doorway. You will wait there until your name is called."

Mother, too, put her arms around me and kissed my forehead, then we entered the room the officer told us to go into. We stood in consternation! The room was filled with hundreds of people—and noise! It was unbelievable. There were children crying, women weeping, and men seemingly in deep despair. Mother turned to a woman who, fortunately, had some knowledge of English. "Why are all of you here?"

"We are all hoping to leave today. We have to wait until the judge comes back. He left for lunch. Some of these people were here from yesterday."

"Why are they here so long?" Mother looked puzzled.

The woman looked sad, "Most of them are not used to having their names pronounced American fashion. The judge calls a name only twice. If you don't hurry to the front, you wait until the next session. Here he comes now."

Mother looked at the many people before her and knew it would be a long time before our turn came. It was now 1:30 in the afternoon and we had not eaten yet. She opened the tin of biscuits so thoughtfully provided by the ship's officer and gave us each two. Then she realized she could not feed her children and see hunger in the eyes of so many others. She passed the tin around. The parents were grateful but refused to take any for themselves and gave only to their children. Soon the tin was empty. The people were so grateful that they motioned Mother to go ahead of them. After a bit of protesting, she did so. This was fortunate because it meant we were near the middle of the big room and enabled her to see the two young men, Mr. Green and Mr. Graves, ahead of us. They had picked up Mother's one large suitcase and our bundle of bed clothing when we came to the place where baggage was placed for the passengers to pick up. They had been near us all the time until I was separated, and in looking for me Mother was separated from them.

For some unknown reason, she was carrying their straw hats. I often wondered why they had not worn them. Now the two men's names were called and, of course, there should have been nothing further to detain them. All around the judge and against the walls across the front and back entrance were soldiers with fixed bayonets. It had been only a short time since the World War I armistice had been signed and soldiers were present to keep order. The two young men were having a problem with two soldiers who did not want them to leave Mother's baggage behind. The judge, becoming aware of this, asked for an explanation. Mr. Green spoke, then pointed toward the gathered crowd and Mother raise her hand and waved it. The judge peered and finally satisfied, gave permission for the baggage to be left behind.

Mr. Green then pointed to his head. Mother suddenly called out, "Here are your hats!" and neatly spun one through the air over the heads of the astonished people, then the second one. Everyone was delighted and there was much laughter as each man caught his hat. It was a brief moment of respite for the unhappy, waiting people. Then the judge pounded for "Order."

Names continued to be called and it was near 4:30 p.m. when

"Walker, Ivy" was called at last. Followed by us children, Mother went joyfully forward, thinking the ordeal was almost over, knowing our papers were in order. But it was not over yet. The judge said, "You will be detained, Mrs. Walker, because you have insufficient funds for entry. You need one hundred dollars for each of you, and you have only one hundred for yourself." Mother stared at him, then broke into tears. "What will I do?" she finally asked, wiping her eyes.

The Judge called a deputy and told Mother to follow him. The deputy picked up the heavy bags and led us from the room, not through the door our friends had taken, but to one that led down a flight of stairs into a room where another officer was seated. He put the bags down and left, as Mother thanked him. The officer read Mother's papers, including the one written by the judge. He reached for paper and pencil and said, "We will send a telegram to Mr. Walker requesting further funds. You will be detained until such funds are in our hands. Because this is Friday,[1] the banks in Omaha will be closed so it will be Monday at least before your husband can get money sent here." Calling another man, he said, "Follow this man and he will lead you to where you will stay."

As we went through a door, along a corridor, then through another door, the man said, "We will keep your baggage until you are ready to leave. Here is a receipt that will entitle you to receive it later." He pulled a small receipt book from his pocket, wrote out a receipt, handed it to Mother, then ushered us out.

As the door closed behind us, we stared in unbelief. We were in a large open space, hemmed in by very high walls, and all about were people. Some were standing, most were sitting on the ground. Nearby was a cement bench not being used and Mother sat down, with us children huddled close to her. Suddenly, to our consternation, she began to cry and she wept and wept, totally out of control. We stood silently, not knowing what to do nor how to comfort her.

Soon a man and a woman were standing near us. The woman reached over and touched Mother on her shoulder and said in a

---

[1] Because of the 15th July departure from Southhampton and because this must be Friday 23rd July, the ocean passage must have been a nine-day journey.

gentle voice, "Are you newly arrived?" Mother nodded and tried to stop crying. "I am Mrs. Davis and this is my husband. We can sympathize with you, whatever your problem. We will be your friends and we'll do whatever we can to help you. We too are detained here."

Mother said, "I simply cannot bear the idea of being detained. I cannot bear to be treated like an animal." Tears flowed anew.

Soothingly, Mrs. Davis said, "Oh yes, you can. You have to for the sake of your children. Even as we have to for the sake of our child." Mother looked around, then asked, "Where is your child?"

Mrs. Davis shook her head. "We don't know. Our little girl is only a year old and was taken from us because she was ill. They put her in the infirmary and we have not seen her for two weeks. We cannot get any information, and no one will help us. We just wait and wait. If we can do it for two weeks or longer, you can too."

"Oh, you poor woman," said Mother, trying to control her crying. "How can you stand it?"

"We have to," said Mrs. Davis quietly. "May we sit here with you?" Mother nodded and moved over, and both sat down. Mr. Davis asked about her husband and Mother explained that we were traveling to meet him in Omaha, Nebraska, that we had come from South Africa. "Oh, what a long journey," said Mrs. Davis, "You must be worn out. But now we must tell you about eating here. It will soon be time for the evening meal and you will find it a disaster if you do not know how to go about it. After two weeks, we have learned."

Mr. Davis was trying to make friends with Leonard, but the latter was holding back. Mrs. Davis pointed to a big doorway. "We will stand in line in front of that double doorway near here. It is best to get there early, as the people are like animals and the stampede is terrible when the doors open. We will try to be with you every meal time. My husband will carry the little boy, you hold onto one girl's hand and I will hold onto the other one. Stay as close to the side of the stairway as possible so you can be protected by the wall. The moving crowd could crush you. Try not to be shoved into the center of the stairway. If you fell there you would be trampled."

Mr, Davis said, "I think we had better get in the line now

because new arrivals do not know how to handle this." He stood up and lifted Leonard to his shoulders. Mother took Jessie's hand and Mrs. Davis held my hand. Six people stood in front of us, three abreast. We waited there about thirty minutes before the stampede started.

And it was a stampede! Two guards, opening the big double doors, had to shout to be heard. "Walk, everyone! Don't rush! You have plenty of time."

It was fortunate that Mr. and Mrs. Davis had advised us. The former reached the stairway, with all of us behind him, just ahead of the thundering herds. Leonard, sitting high on Mr. Davis' shoulder, seemed to be beyond words at all the confusion. Long, narrow tables were in front of us as we entered the dining room, and by following Mr. Davis we were able to be seated at the second table. We surely had to move fast. Manners completely disappeared in this crowd as hands reached rudely across the table to snatch the bread. We dared not put a slice down or it would be grabbed. This was our first lesson.

Two women, one on each side, walked down the length of the table, ladling out a dipper full of stew onto each plate. Others followed with large coffee pots of coffee and poured into each thick-rimmed mug. Place settings consisted of a dinner plate, a cup, and a spoon. One spoon only per setting. For breakfast we had a bowl instead of a plate to hold cooked rolled oats. After each meal the guards told us to follow the arrow to leave from the stairway in front of us. This led us to the area called the compound, the space we had first seen. Here we had to stay until time for another meal or until time to go to bed.

The Davis's stayed with us through this waiting period until time to retire. This time Mr. Davis had to go into the men's section, so Mother had to carry Leonard who was too little to climb stairs in a rush. Mrs. Davis held Jessie's and mine, as we hurried up two flights of stairs, where we turned right. Mrs. Davis had already explained to Mother the necessity of turning right instead of left. She had turned left her first night and stepped into a very dirty room where vermin bit her all night. The room on the right was clean, the only clean room there was.

When we entered this big room, Mrs. Davis led us quickly

into the first cage. Yes, indeed, cage! We did not stand and look around until we were safely in this space. It had six bunk beds with thin mattresses but no pillows or other coverings. Mother and Leonard occupied one, Jessie and I another, Mrs. Davis a third, and the other three were filled by other women. As soon as the six bunks were occupied a matron came and padlocked us in! This seemed such an unnecessary procedure, as the walls were at least twenty feet high, with tiny windows at the top, and only one entrance. We glanced around and saw all the cages filled with women and children, all locked in. Men were not with their families, because they were in a different section, although on the same floor. We slept in spite of ourselves. I am sure that many tears were shed not only by Mother but by many of the other women.

Morning finally arrived and we were awakened by a woman's strident voice, saying, "Get up! Get up at once!" She slammed a long stick against each cage as she spoke. Following Mrs. Davis' whispered instructions, we got up quickly and dressed, then stood by the door, waiting for the matron to unlock it. We hurriedly went down some steps and once again were out in the compound. Because we were almost the first out, we were able to get a bench to sit on. Once we had it, we hung onto it dearly, otherwise we would have to stand or sit on the ground. It was only five o'clock in the morning, with a chilling mist falling, and we sat and waited until 7:30 before the doors would open for another stampede for breakfast.

Our first breakfast was a revelation in food serving. A large bin was on either side so that people had to get into single file. A man gave us each a big hunk of bread—not a slice, but a hunk—and another man gave us a hard boiled egg. When we reached the table there were saucers of jam, but for our first breakfast we had to forget the jam, as we were not quick enough to grab the way other people did. Coffee was poured for adults and milk for children, a pleasant surprise. We all went downstairs again after breakfast, as we would do after each meal. Now we found the sun shining, a blessed relief after our cold waiting earlier.

After a few days we learned that the only variation for meals would be at noon, when an ethnic food was served. One noon we sat at a table almost in the rear of this large area. Across from us was a very large Italian woman with three children. Although she spoke no

English, she was friendly, and pointing to each of her children she named them, ending with "my bambino," the only words I understood. That day we were served spaghetti, the first time any of us had seen such a food. I can yet see that woman in my imagination. She raised her eyes, smacked her lips, put her palms together in a prayerful attitude, and then began to eat. In fascination, we watched her.

Neither the Davis's nor Mother nor we children ate our spaghetti. One taste proved too overpowering because it was highly seasoned. The Italian woman made us understand that if we were not going to eat ours, she would be happy to. Could she have it? She ate four of our six servings! No wonder she was so fat; at that time, she was the largest woman I had ever seen.

Each morning around ten o'clock and each afternoon at two, several men would come onto a platform and make the announcement that those qualified to leave would have their names called. Each name would be called twice and only twice, and everyone should respond immediately because there was no time to waste. The room became quiet as every person listened breathlessly.

So many names were not responded to and Mrs. Davis said sadly, "Many of these people do not understand the American pronunciation of their names. I wish there was some way to help them."

On Tuesday[2] Mother's name was called. How happy she was! She took time to hug and kiss a couple with whom she had become friendly as we walked to the stand. Then we passed quickly through a door, only to find a disappointing situation. Dad had sent a telegram to a friend, Mr. McIntosh, in New York, an attorney who had travelled to Scotland with him in 1914. He produced the telegram and could prove his identity. But Mr. McIntosh's credentials did not help in this case. We were not allowed to leave with him. Mr. McIntosh was ushered out and we were ushered back! Again Mother was in tears, "Oh, why doesn't Sid send the money? I never can depend upon him. He told me that one hundred dollars would be enough. He must have thought that was enough for our whole family, but it is one hundred dollars per person, which he should have known. I do have that one hundred dollars but it just is not enough." She cried harder. "What will happen

---

[2] This now would be 27th July.

to us if he does not send the money?" She continued to weep. Now, however, there was no Mrs. Davis nearby to comfort her.

Our routine went on the same, except that Mother thought we had to have something different to eat. She found a commissary but found that things were much too expensive. We had to be satisfied with what food was offered. The next morning Mother was again disappointed because her name was not called. Mrs. Davis said, "Your money should be here today. If that happens we may not see you again because we are to see the doctor about our child. Perhaps we should wish each other well instead of goodbye. I'm so glad we met and that my husband and I could help you."

Mother expressed her gratefulness and they embraced. We never saw them again and never learned how they got along. Each had forgotten to exchange addresses.

The next morning we were standing again before the judge as a silence settled over the crowd. Wonder of wonders! The third name called was "Walker, Ivy," and Mother hurried forward with her hand up and waving. "Here I am! Here I am!" We children followed close behind her. This time it was good news. She was given the papers and we went through that door to freedom!

Mother was surprised that our baggage was by the door leading to a gangplank. We had to walk down this to get into a boat that would take us onto the mainland. We were taken to a railroad station where Mother learned that a train was going west at six o'clock in the evening. This meant we could get into the washroom and get cleaned up. Mother was grateful for this, because we had not been able to clean properly since leaving our helpful 'Arry in Southampton almost two weeks earlier. There had been no decent washing facilities on the *S.S. Lapland* and we had had no change of clothing at all on Ellis Island. We all felt better after our needs were taken care of in that train station washroom.

Our tickets were bought and our larger baggage checked, so now it seemed that nothing more could worry Mother. Was "a brighter tomorrow" indeed arriving?

Next we heard a voice exclaim, "Why, Mrs. Walker! Is it really you!" Turning, we were astonished to see Mr. Harry Green whom we had met on the *S.S. Lapland* and who had been so kind. It was such a surprise for both Mother and him that they hugged each other, laughing and crying—at least Mother cried. She had been through so much, it was unsettling to see a friendly face. We children were almost as happy to see him as he hugged all of us.

"I thought you were visiting here in the East," Mother said. "I did visit," he said, "but I have had a position offered to me in Chicago and I am taking the six o'clock train."

"The same one we are taking." Mother looked pleased, then she told him how we had been detained those five awful days at Ellis Island, and now at last were taking the train to Omaha to meet her husband. We, however, were going by coach, not on something Mr, Green called a sleeper as he was doing.

Perhaps Mother profited by the error in not obtaining the address of Mrs. Davis. She asked him for his address and he gave her his sister's, saying that she would always know where to reach him. Later both Harry Green and George Graves would visit us in our home in Omaha many times.

At last our train arrived and we separated, each of us going to our designated coaches. Our long journey on a coal-stoked train on a hot summer day in late July 1920 had begun. We were on a train on which all windows were kept wide open because it was too hot to close them, a train that stopped at every small town. We children were enchanted because we were seeing surprising sights along the way. These were sights such as chickens in cages waiting on the platforms to be shipped and people carrying strange types of purses and wearing what we considered odd garments. At every stop a newsboy, a new idea to us, was yelling, "Paper! Paper here! Read all about it!" Young boys with baskets of fruit, cookies, and something they called candy bars were everywhere. When I heard the words, "Hershey Bars! Hershey Bars!" I remembered my long ago little friend Christine and how she refused to let me taste hers.

"Hershey Bars!" I exclaimed. "Oh, Mother, please could we get a Hershey Bar?" This was the first time I had asked for something for myself. Mother asked the price and bought two, dividing them so we each had half a bar. It was delicious. She said it was also her first taste of such a delightful bit of candy.

Our journey was getting tiresome. We were at last nearing the end of nearly seven weeks of traveling. With the open train windows, we were now dirtier than we had been at the end of our

Ellis Island experience. Everyone seemed to have black smudges on faces and hands. There was water in the little washroom, but not enough to do more than wash hands and wet a cloth for our faces. "I must keep you clean for your father," said Mother. "I want him to be proud of you. It's been a long time."

I wondered what our reception would be. Would he be a kinder, a nicer daddy than when we had seen him last? Would we be happier? Only time would tell.

We were fortunate during the latter part of our train trip to have a conductor who was good about telling us what to expect, what to see, and where we were. One early evening we were passing over a bridge that spanned a wide river. "This is the Mississippi River," he said, "and when we get across we will be in the city of Rock Island." Then he pointed. "There is what is called the Rock Island Arsenal. It was a prison camp during our Civil War days from 1861 to 1865."

Finally at almost midnight the conductor came to Mother, saying, "Our next stop is Omaha. I'll take your baggage to the end of the car."

Mother soon had us children ready, saying, "Maybe it is a good thing it is dark. We are so dirty from all that soot, your father will think we are strangers. I'll be glad to get cleaned up. I hate to have him see us like this but it will be good to reach the end of our journey."

The train pulled to a stop. We were the only passengers to get off and as it was midnight it was hard to see whether anyone was around. It was an eerie feeling and we children stayed close together behind Mother, each carrying something clutched tightly in our hands.

Then I noticed a man standing in the shadows, hat pulled over his eyes, hands in pockets. I blurted out and pointed. "Daddy is standing over there."

Mother said carefully, "Sid, is that you?" He came over slowly and his greeting was very perfunctory, considering he had not seen Mother, Jessie, nor me for six years and had never seen his son Leonard who was born after he left. He called a taxi and we then rode what seemed a long way to the home that he had prepared for us in North Omaha. After we got in the house, he took a good look at us and exclaimed, "Thank goodness, you arrived at night so none of my fellow workers could see you! I would have been ashamed of the way you all look, just like a bunch of refugees!"

More than once we had felt exactly that—a bunch of refugees!

If his greeting was not as warm as Mother would have liked, at least our life in this new home began the next morning on a note of hilarity. Very unexpectedly, Dad prepared our first breakfast as Mother got us children ready for the day. When she shepherded us into the kitchen, she suddenly stopped, looked startled, and pointing toward the table exclaimed, "Sid! Are you wanting to poison all of us.?"

It was his turn to look surprised. "Why, Cook (he still called her that!), what in the world makes you say that?"

Mother stepped to the table and lifted up one small plate on which was a half a grapefruit. "This! This fruit is poisonous! My father uprooted such a tree from his garden when he found it growing among the oranges. No one knew what it was and finally someone told him it was poisonous. I am not allowing the children to eat this!"

She sat down the plate, then picked up a package, labeled Corn Flakes. "Good heavens! Sid, do you think the children are animals? Cows and pigs eat corn."

At first Dad had an odd expression on his face, then he started laughing. "Why, Cook, the fruit is as good as any orange! We eat many grapefruit in this country and no one has died yet from eating them. Someone must have been spoofing your dad. And a box of Corn Flakes is a breakfast cereal here. Come! Try them! Sit down, children, and eat. You too, Cook."

We finally obeyed, keeping an eye on Mother, while Dad poured the coffee and milk. She waited while Dad calmly ate his grapefruit. If it did not hurt him, it would not hurt us, so we began to eat ours. It was more tart than an orange, but I liked it—sort of.

At last Mother picked up her spoon and cautiously ate this strange fruit for her first breakfast in her new home. This was the only breakfast I can remember my dad ever preparing for his family.

And so our life in this land so far from our birthplace began. Jessie was nine years old; Leonard would be six in two months; I was eleven and a half. We children all had many years ahead of us, sometimes good and sometimes not so good, in our bright new country of the United States of America. Mother had expected and hoped for some peace of mind and for someone else to bear the burdens with her. She had them all alone for so many years. In this hope, she was to be bitterly disappointed, though she never complained.

Dad would leave us in March 1921, only eight months after our arrival. Once again Mother would be the burden-bearer alone. This time, however, there was no brother Sid to talk to, no sisters, nor any relatives to help; only a few neighbors cared. The adjustments in a new land, without friends or family, only three children, were difficult. Her motto in life was, as she so often said to all of us, *Alles sal reg kom, os elkeen ny plig doen*, which translated from the Africaans means, "Everything will be all right, if everyone does his duty."

Truly she did her duty in all the vicissitudes of her life's responsibilities, to her children first, then to her partner, and most importantly, to herself. Dad left us to work in another state, less than ten hours journey from Omaha, but not once did he give Mother the support she needed. He was absent when four months later I was stricken with a massive mastoid infection and spent weeks in the hospital, on the critical list. I would add, in fairness, that he did manage to visit us for three weekends during the next five years.

In our several discussions, I often asked Mother about her feelings in this situation, namely, his obvious uncaring about us. "Well, Edna, he had no choice. He had to send for his family in order to save himself from deportation. He could not return to South Africa, for there was no possible chance for his employment because of his strike organizing activities."

No matter how often I broached this subject, she never once condemned him to me. These conversations always ended with her resorting to a phrase in the Bantu, *Uzelilele ngomso*, "there is always a brighter tomorrow." This is the philosophy by which she lived. She was, to me, "A diamond in the rough!"

Epilogue

by Andrew MacAoidh Jergens

Edna May's wish was to provide for her family and friends the memories of her young life in a country so far away from the one in which she spent most of her life. Consequently, her own story ends with her arrival in Omaha, Nebraska, seventy-three years before she died. To flesh out the story of those seventy-three years would overshadow her tale as she presents it and I do not plan to do much more than touch some highlights.

I read with some sadness her comments in Chapter 7, wherein somewhat wistfully she alludes to the several divorces she would experience. Indeed, if there is a summary comment to make about her life it is that her success in relationships with men was unfortunate. We have read throughout her own story her distance from her father, a man with whom she had only little contact as a child. Even worse, the little contact that there was seemed only to provide memories of sternness, discipline, and anger. The facts seem to indicate that he left the family in the early months of 1914 and was not seen again until the night at the end of July 1920 at the railroad station in Omaha. By the spring of 1921 he was gone again, for the most part never a presence in the family again. Edna May related a story of some later years when she saw her father on a local street. As she tried to acknowledge him, it seemed clear that at best he did not know who she was, or at worst chose deliberately to avoid her. Edna May's mother Ivy eventually divorced Sidney in 1930 and married a John Szibel. Sidney himself remarried Hannah Knox in Canada and lived ultimately in Saskatoon, Saskatchewan, for the remainder of his life.

Edna May met Archie Charles Richardson at a church in Omaha sometime in the mid 1920's. On 1st June 1927 they married in the Asbury Methodist Church in Omaha. To them was born on 13th March 1930 a son, Leonard Charles Richardson. By June 1932, however, Edna May divorced Archie and she moved to

Milwaukee. There in the depths of the Great Depression she met my father, Alfred William Roghan. When after some months she told him that she was pregnant, he revealed at last that he was in fact already married and the father of several children. She returned to Omaha where I, her second son, was born on 16th July 1935. The difficulties of finding employment and supporting two children proved to be too overwhelming for her. After great soul-searching, Edna May determined that the only path for her to follow was to place her infant for adoption. She traveled to Evanston, Illinois, and there placed her infant at The Cradle. Her own painful story of her separation from him emphasizes that by now she was separated from three or four of the significant males of her life.

This separation was unfortunately to continue. In order to provide for her son Leonard she placed him at the Wisconsin Home and Farm School, Dousman, outside Milwaukee. In years to come he would find himself estranged from his mother, remembering those years as times that she had rejected him by sending him away. There followed three more marriages, each ending in divorce. The last was on 1st December 1955 in Portland, Oregon, to Kay Cecil Booth, whose surname she was to retain until her death. It is reflecting upon these failed relationships that Edna May "felt a kinship with this great-grandmother, whom I never met, because I was pleased to know she had these multiple marriages. . . . Losing husbands through death, however, seems less demeaning than losing them through the divorce courts!"

Lest this all seems too depressing, I add that Edna May experienced several triumphant events in her life as well. Perhaps inheriting a gene from her absent father, she was a capable and competent Multilith, Multigraph, and Graphotype operator, important as a trainer to several of her employers. She worked four years for The Boeing Company in Seattle as a secretary in the Space Physics Section, being responsible for highly technical information classified Secret, Confidential, or Top Secret. She concluded her active employment with ten years as a secretary for the Seattle-King County Department of Public Health.

In 1951 she won a gold trophy, a Dale Carnegie Club International Award given for winning a speech contest in the region of Washington, Oregon, Idaho, and British Columbia. Her prize meant she was the best of the 56 who competed. She also brought home with her, as she was to relate, "a wealth of information, the good feeling of having met many fine people, the wonderful experience of competition, and the sense of pride in belonging to an organization that is trying to better human relations everywhere." She was interested in metaphysics, religious science, and astrology and was awarded a Bachelor of Metaphysics (B.Ms.) and later, in December 1965, a Doctor of Divinity (D.D.) by the Academy of Universal Truth, Seattle, Washington.

It may be, however, that a very joyous event in her life occurred in May 1989 when she and I were reunited after a 54-year separation. My name comes from my being the adopted son of Andrew Nicholas Jergens (who died in 1967), an adoption I knew of since I was twelve years old. As he had divorced his wife, the woman who was my adoptive mother, when I was three, I grew up as a youngster without a mother until he remarried when I was a young teen. Three decades passed before, beginning about the end of the 1970's, I spent almost ten years in amateur detective work, seeking to contact a birth mother whom I knew only by the name of Edna Richardson. As I had grown up with only a father present in my life—a father to whom I am grateful for giving me the ability to have a flexibility and freedom to my life—it became nonetheless also important to find that incomplete part of myself.

In 1959 the US Army assisted me in my search through an error in my records such that I needed a birth certificate to effect the correction. Along with the birth certificate came my adoption papers. I have wondered whether the attorney who provided them, the attorney who was present at the adoption, was preparing for his retirement and found a convenient way to clean out his files. These papers gave me a very important piece of information, a *name*. Edna Richardson was my mother, said the decree. During my search The Cradle had provided various non-identifying pieces of information: mother was 4' 11" tall, of Scots-English descent. But a name alone and non-identifying information are not enough and in order to find someone, one needs a place and a time. A variety of ads in genealogy society periodicals and several experts were unable to help me on the basis of this name alone. I began to suspect that mother's surname, Richardson, was an alias, or at least that remarriage had resulted in new names I could never trace.

We all, however, leave public traces of ourselves. City Directories are of great help to historians, genealogists, and biographers; ultimately they would give me what I was looking for. My continued prodding eventually resulted in The Cradle's giving me a clue that would make the difference—although luck and imaginative thinking was still necessary. Correspondence that The Cradle had with my mother fifty years earlier was to an address in a "city near Chicago," the social worker told me. Further, she disagreed that the name I was seeking was an alias, for her correspondence made it clear that Mother lived with her mother and talked to her older child about me. A map showed all the cities near Chicago and made it clear that there was much work to be done. I was *very* fortunate—some would say it was clearly meant that I should be reunited with my mother—and greatly blessed through the result, for I started in the north. Certainly, Milwaukee was a city near Chicago! City Directories for Milwaukee showed that an Edna Richardson lived at 3747 North Port Washington Avenue from 1934 through 1940! At the same address was an Ivy Walker and a child Leonard. I was on the track at long last, this being now October 1988.

I am tickled with myself over the next development that occurred, as I remember, in the shower stall one evening. If I had an older brother, and if he was in Milwaukee in 1940, as the City Directory said, he had to be in school! And schools keep records. Indeed they did, even from fifty years ago. The local public school record gave me his date of birth, 1930. Now, I missed Korea by two years and a brother five years older might well have served there. Many perished in Korea, as we know so well. The records gave his birthplace, Omaha, Nebraska, the same as mine. A letter to the proper Vital Statistics bureau produced his birth certificate. Now I knew his mother was Edna May Walker and I knew Leonard's father's name—Archie Richardson—and his Pawnee City, Nebraska, birthplace. Directory assistance provided Richardsons to talk to there, and one of them remembered Archie and his son Leonard. Leonard went to Texas Christian University, another remembered. Alumni offices!! Don't we all know that an Alumni Office never loses track of you? And they did not lose Leonard. A few more directory assistance calls and we had a phone number for my brother Leonard Richardson. All that was left was for me to place the call and on Tuesday 2nd May I garnered the courage to do so.

As anxiety-producing as it may have been for me to make that call, I can only imagine my brother Leonard's response. For all his years he believed himself to be an only child and here was a stranger from 2,000 miles away saying he was a brother. I told him my story and he asked me to send him something in writing, but early the next morning I had a telephone call from him. He had spoken with his mother—with *our* mother!—who was over-joyed to know that I was still alive. She was 80 years old and living alone in Seattle.

That evening, Wednesday the 3rd May 1989, I made the second great telephone call of 1989—indeed, of my life—and spoke with Mother for the first time since that September day in 1935 when she had to leave me at The Cradle. It was only a few days later that my wife, Linda Busken Jergens, and I met her at the Cincinnati airport for a emotional reunion. The next day she was present at the Church of the Redeemer where it was my joy and privilege as a priest of The Episcopal Church to celebrate the Holy Eucharist and preach the Seventh Sunday of Easter, my first Eucharist with my mother present. The reception that followed the Eucharist simply emphasized the joy of Easter resurrection.

In the almost four years since that phone call and before her death, it was my great joy to become acquainted with my mother and to offer her some of the care and comforts that had not to then been her part in life. We learned to accommodate to the difficulties of a cross-continent, three-hour time difference. In January 1990 we celebrated her 81st birthday at our home, the first real birthday party she could remember having. Linda and I took her in 1991 on her last visit to her native land of South Africa, where she once again met her many relatives and introduced me to my new family. She also had a last visit with her brother, Leonard Sidney Walker, "on this side," as she would have put it.

For my part, I have also gained an older brother with whom I have enjoyed a developing relationship, again as best as cross-continent distances will allow. It may also be fair to say that with my arrival in his family Leonard may have been able to cross some of that distance separating him so long from his mother—at least that is what I want to see. And it may be that in the last years of her life, Mother at long last was able to establish a relationship with one or two of the significant men in her life.

Appendix A:

British South Africa[1]

Some historical background will be helpful in understanding why Britain decided to settle the far-away land of South Africa in the year 1820, after having shown a decided lack of interest during the years this had been suggested by her officials who were there and discerned the advantages of such a colonisation.

In the mid- to late-18th century, England had enjoyed some measure of prosperity because of the necessity for manufacturing supplies of the varied sort that war always requires. The Napoleonic wars had lasted a long time, but once they were over unemployment became the rule. Conditions became worse as soldiers and sailors returned home. They, too, desired employment, housing, and the material possessions that money could supply. Food and other necessities became scarce. Social unrest and dissatisfaction increased. A succession of bad harvests had reduced agriculture to a state of virtual deprivation.

The Portuguese had endeavored many times during the fifteenth century to find a sea route around the coast of Africa to the Indies, principally at the instigation and backing of Prince Henry the Navigator.

His nephew King John II in 1487 sent three ships under the command of Bartolomeu Dias to continue this work of exploration. As they neared the southernmost tip of Africa, a violent storm blew them off course southward for thirteen days. When again able to steer a proper course, they sailed eastward hoping to find land. Dias finally reasoned that land lay northward, so he steered his ships in that direction and on 3rd February 1488 finally sighted the shore of what is now Mossel Bay. They proceeded along the shore eastward for several days, sailed into Algoa Bay, passed a couple of islands, and then dropped anchor near the mouth of Bushman's River. It was here on 12th March 1488 that they went ashore to recuperate from their

---

[1] By Edna May Walker.

wearisome voyage.[2]

While there they erected a stone monument that would be seen over three hundred years later by the British Settlers of 1820.

Dias set sail eastward another three days' journey until he arrived at the Great Fish River where he was forced to make a homeward journey, as his crew rebelled and threatened mutiny.

He reported to King John II his findings that this was the route sought to the Indies, by way of "The Cape of Storms." Instead, the King declared it was "The Cape of Good Hope," as the "good hope" lay in the fact he was convinced that Dias had found the route to the Indies. Unknowingly, he gave a name that was to continue to this day.

Holland had also sought this route for trade in the Indies, as had both France and Great Britain. It was the Netherlands East India Company, however, that was the most persistent and that finally decided to establish "a small settlement at the Cape as a half-way house to India and in 1652 sent Johan van Riebeeck with a party of 125 persons, comprised chiefly of officials, soldiers and workmen, to build a fort and to establish a garden at the foot of Table Mountain."[3]

The sole purpose was to establish a victualling station for ships sailing between Holland and the East, to replenish them with water and food supplies.

The small population was increased in 1688 by the addition of 164 French Huguenots who fled France to escape religious persecution. There also was an influx of Germans, Belgians, and more Dutch. The amalgamation of these people gradually resulted in the development of their own characteristics that became known as the "Cape Dutch," thus distinguishing them from their parent stock.

Contrary to the wishes of the Mother-country, the settlements expanded inland and eastward, creating a sparsely populated colonial possession. This created the need to enlarge the boundary lines, resulting in yet more officials as towns grew. This in turn added to Holland's expenses and brought other pressures on the settlers. This created anger among them and was one more reason for resourceful individuals and groups to leave the closer in settlement areas.

Wars change lives of individuals and the destiny of nations. Thus it was that Holland's power began to wane as the French overran

---

[2] Harold Edward Hockly, *The Story of the British Settlers of 1820 in South Africa. Cape Town and Johannesburg,* Juta and Co., Ltd., 1948, pp 2-3.

[3] Ibid., pg. 5.

their country and by 1795 established Holland as a Dependency under the name of the Batavian Republic.

The exiled former ruler of Holland sent a letter to the Cape Governor instructing him to relinquish the country to Britain, whose soldiers arrived just in time to prevent the French themselves from taking possession. Thus, Great Britain held the Cape in trust for seven years. At the Peace of Amiens in 1802 the Cape was awarded to the Batavian Republic, a vassal state of France.

War between England and France resumed in 1806 and Britain again occupied the Cape to keep it from the French. On the defeat and banishment of Napoleon in 1815, William I, King of the Netherlands by the Treaty of Paris, formally ceded the Cape to the English for a large sum of money.

The first British Governor to the Cape was the Earl of Caledon who assumed office in 1807.[4] He quickly realized the need for protecting the eastern border of this area because of the marauding Natives. Other governors followed him in appealing to England for emigrants to fill the eastern border along the Fish River, especially after England had recalled all the troops that had protected the farmers. These troops were sent to India as England became embroiled with affairs there. Gradually no protection was possible for the settlers.

Hundreds of British people were making application to depart from England, hoping to escape the deplorable economic and social conditions under which they existed. Perhaps it was this situation, together with a number of communications from Lord Somerset—at that time Governor in the Cape—that painted so beautiful a picture of the farming land in the Zuurveld, that caused the Government of England to consider the issue. Announcements were made to that effect and rules were laid down as to how the emigration was to take place.

A group leader, who had the responsibility of deciding which applicants met the requirements of good health and ability to work, was to complete the arrangements with the Government that refused to deal directly with individuals. Free passage was to be provided, including food en route, and farming tools as soon as the people arrived in the new land.

Soon from all points in England families were saying farewells to neighbors and friends, giving up their homes, and traveling by coach or walking to their ports of departure. Twenty-one ships at different ports were being readied for this exodus of four thousand

---

[4] Ibid., pg. 12.

souls.

No one took the time or the trouble to tell any of these applicants where they would be located or what were the true conditions of the land. Glowing stories were related about the rich soil suitable for farming. Most of these people had been city dwellers, workers in factories, and knew nothing about farming. They were all destined for the area called "Zuurveld," meaning "sour land," suitable only for the grazing of cattle. But, the emigrants had no cattle!

The "Kennersley Castle," a three-masted sailing vessel, weight of 400 tons, was moored at the Port of Bristol. Aboard were 202 individuals, plus the crew, all hoping for a new life in that far-away land. They comprised six different "parties" and each had its own leader. Forty-nine individuals, known as "Southey's Party," were from Somersetshire, England. Among them were Thomas and Ann Glass with their six children, ages one to fifteen. This family is of particular significance as they are the forebears of the author, Thomas and Ann being her great, great, great grandparents.

Other shipmates on the long, cold, hazardous journey were 64 from Gloucestershire under the leadership of a Samuel Bradshaw, while another 39 from that same city were directed by a William Holder; 29 were led by James H. Greathead from Worcestershire; a Welsh party of 30 was led by Mr. Thomas Phillips of Pembrokeshire. Phillips at 44 was the "old man" of the leadership. Southey was 39; the others three leaders were 34, 30, and 24, respectively.[5]

Only in one's imagination can one anticipate the feelings of these courageous people as they stood on the ship's decks, bundled against the sharp winter air, realizing they were saying farewell to all they held dear and not having the slightest idea of what lay before them. How valiant, indeed, have been all pioneers!

Two ships were lost at sea, but the remaining nineteen that left England that cold December 1819 morning arrived safely. Most of them stopped at the victualling station established at the Cape of Good Hope by the early Dutch settlers and then traveled the same route as had Bartolomeu Dias 332 years earlier. They dropped anchor at Algoa Bay 10th April 1820, the place that would become Port Elizabeth. Other ships arrived later.

There being no pier or any other kind of landing place for ships, anchor was cropped outside the bay and small boats were loaded with women and children to be taken ashore. At low tide many of the

---

[5] Ibid., pp 257ff.

men and older boys simply waded ashore. Others were carried on the backs of those who came to welcome the weary voyagers.

Whatever their thoughts as they gazed shoreward to see nothing except sand and tents, it was a rude awakening for them. For example, they had no idea that they would have to live in tents. Those who had been city dwellers could not have known what the farm tools were used for—but they certainly would learn!

On the shore were a thousand tents standing to shelter the new arrivals until transport to their new homes could be arranged. Further, there were mounds of folded tents that would become their temporary shelters in the hinterland until they could build homes. There were also piles of farm tools and other things necessary for their new adventure.

Farmers already on the land had been asked to drive the newcomers to their allotments, some of the areas being as far as 150 miles inland. As a farmer familiar with a particular allotment area arrived, passengers for that area would climb aboard his wagon, their belongings loaded, and were driven to the locations between Algoa Bay and along the Great Fish River.

It must have been a shock when a driver stopped and said, "This is your place," and began to help the women and children down. With the help of the men he then placed their belongings on the ground. Before leaving, he advised the men to keep their guns in their hands, a friendly warning that no doubt struck terror into their hearts, as no one really understood why the farmer said it.

There was no shelter, neither a friendly greeting awaiting them. Only the sky overhead and the soil beneath their feet greeted them. With effort, these former city dwellers had to erect a tent without any real knowledge of how to do so. Wood and brush were gathered to keep a fire burning all night, as their driver would have warned them of this necessity to keep away prowling wild animals. They had seen many of these beasts during their transport to their new home. And— they had been warned to watch for snakes. Some of these perils might have been at least understandable. None, however, understood what the driver meant by his warning to keep their eyes open for Natives.

So, with determination and the need for self-preservation they wrestled with these new tasks, determined to survive. It was into this situation that the author's forebears found themselves. It is incredible that these pioneers lived to establish homes, farms, and a new nation.

Appendix B

Cullinan¹

Cullinan, a town of the Transvaal, 36 miles by rail east of Pretoria, grew up around the Premier (Transvaal) Diamond Mine and was named after Thomas Cullinan, the purchaser of the ground on which the mine is situated. This land had belonged to a Mr. Prinsloo, a wealthy Boer farmer. Because he had plenty of money, he was not interested in selling, although Mr. Cullinan had approached him several times.

Mr. Cullinan had a passion for diamonds and had enough knowledge of geology to believe this farm was a potential area for diamonds. His contemporaries made sport of the idea and wondered how anyone could be so naive to believe diamonds could be found in the Transvaal. It was a well established fact that he knew the building trade. He had foreseen the growth of Johannesburg and was a very successful builder—but diamonds! That was another matter.

The men in Kimberley who thought they knew all there was to know about diamond mining simply refused to believe Cullinan knew anything at all about diamonds. Opinions of others who professed to be more knowledgeable did not deter Cullinan. He kept his own counsel, followed his own ideas. He was a kindly man, known through all his business transactions as "Honest Tom," as he was affectionately called. He never held anyone in disfavor. It frustrated him greatly to be unable to purchase this land on which he was positive diamonds were hidden. He spent much time walking over the area, searching for the clues, a definite type of soil, and always it led to the same place, just beyond the fence into the Prinsloo farm, where he had been forbidden to go! This frustration was laid aside, as were other things, when it became necessary to leave Johannesburg because the war between the Boer Republic and Britain was commencing. The departure of the British took place in 1899 and few had any idea they were leaving homes and possessions for a long period.

---

¹ By Edna May Walker.

Mother told me many tales about that period. She said the British did not realize how determined the Boers were to keep this land from British dominance. The Boers had been toughened by travail as they left their homes years before, trekking to a place where they could live a life of freedom. They had much experience in fighting for their· lives and beliefs. They would do it again.

The Cullinan family was part of the exodus and went to live in the Cape. After his wife and seven children were safely housed with her father, Mr. Cullinan signed up with the nearest volunteer force in the Cape Colony.

The contrast between these two groups of fighters, British and Boer, portrays the difference between human values. The Boer Commandos rode through Johannesburg many times and spurned the idea of taking any of the property of their enemies. There was no looting and no deliberate destruction of homes. The British soldiers had no such honor. The farms of all fighting Boers were damaged to such an extent that the few who lived through this devastation had nothing to return to. Homes were set afire as were the fields; fruit trees were broken down and all fences destroyed. The remaining horses, all cattle, and other animals were stolen, some killed and any loyal Natives who tried to save these animals of their "baas" were shot.

The British had not expected the Boers to be so tireless as fighters. These Boers, out of necessity on treks when fighting the Natives, had learned to shoot while their horses were running. Sometimes the horseman would swing his body to the side of his horse, to have a better aim. Horse and rider became a unit. This harsh experience proved them to be more adept at some battle maneuvers. They had been used to fighting in the dark. Their horses were familiar with the least change of knee pressure or voice and cooperated instantly. For instance, they were invaluable in night raids. The British were frustrated that the war was continuing so long. They wanted a quick solution and derived at the dastardly idea of interning all the women and children of the fighting Boers. Some of the leaders were positive the Boers would then capitulate.

They did not know the Boer women! They were fighters in a different way, managing to get word to their men not to give up, declaring they were in this war too! Their stamina, courage, and fearlessness gave their fighting men more determination than ever to carry on.

The British devised a concentration camp for these families in the most inhuman and unsanitary conditions possible. This was the first time prison or internment camps came into being. There were no shelters at first so these people were exposed to all the elements. When sickness and disease from malnutrition and exposure to rain and cold commenced, a doctor and a few other men with humanitarian outlooks demanded shelter. A few tents were brought in, mainly to shelter the ill. My mother could hardly tell this story. She said that every day a few more women or children would be buried. The daily allotment of food was lessened and altogether thirty thousand women and children died from malnutrition, lack of shelter, and poor medical care. When the war was over, the few surviving Boers came home to nothing. A few loyal Natives were the only greeters at what was once a home and a good farm.

When the British were able to return to Johannesburg in 1902, they were pleasantly surprised to find their homes intact. Their Natives had taken care of their gardens and the homes were dusted and clean. When servants from an adjoining home gave up, thinking their masters were not returning, the other neighboring Natives kept up the other home. There were some exceptions, but for the most part every home was well cared for, as were the yards and gardens.

Those Natives were a proud race, and they were proud to be trusted. They were loyal, honest and had deep integrity, as shown in their actions at that time.

The once wealthy Prinsloo Family did not fare so well; after the war they found themselves totally devastated. The war had been a complete disaster for them, as it was for so many other Boer families. Mr. Prinsloo had been killed and the farm was so devastated that his daughter realized that, with no one to help, she would have to sell to survive. They simply needed the money, as did so many other once affluent families.

Thus it was that Mr. Cullinan was able to purchase this land wherein his dreams had been for so long. His "brighter tomorrow," as my mother commented, had arrived. He was soon to have the last laugh over those in Kimberley who had belittled his dreams. No one can possibly know all the feelings experienced by "Honest Tom" Cullinan at the acquisition of this property that he had sought to possess since 1898 and which was now his at last in 1902.

This was to be an open pit mine and would involve many problems and much in the way of financing. Many staunch friends, believing in the judgment of "Honest Tom," had a hand in the success of the mine, to be known as the Premier (Transvaal) Diamond Mining Company, Ltd. "(Transvaal)" was added to Mr. Cullinan's mine because another was known as the Premier.

The Cullinan home was in Johannesburg and the mine all of

thirty miles distant, on the outskirts of Pretoria. Transportation between the two points was very slow. One went by two-wheeled cape cart, drawn by a pair of oxen, later by wagon, still later by train. Cullinan made this journey at least five hundred times before he purchased a motor car.

His family saw little of him in the beginning, for he would arrive at the site of the mine early and stay late, camping out at first until he had a tent, later in a shack where he could stay. He wanted to be present at each stage of the mine-creating process. He was often invited to different homes for dinner. In this way he became better acquainted with those who worked in the mine.

I remember one time in particular when he was in our home. I must have been almost two years old or a little younger. I did not walk until I was eighteen months and I was still a bit wobbly on my feet. Evidently I was looking around, deciding where to walk next, when Mother said, "Walk over to Mr. Cullinan, Edna." I looked at Dad sitting nearby, then I looked at Mr. Cullinan.

At that moment the latter held out his arms. "Come on, little one," he said softly, "you can do it." His eyes were twinkling.

Ignoring Dad's sitting there and not saying a word, I toddled over to Mr. Cullinan, to be caught up in his strong arms and hugged. It gave me a good feeling to know someone cared.

As he put me back on the floor, again I looked at Dad, hoping he would hold out his arms as Mr. Cullinan had done. He just sat there, sort of glowering at me. My chest felt tight and I am sure my lips were trembling when I heard a voice say, "Come to Mother, Baby." I turned toward her and she was smiling. All was right with my world again.

I never forgot the contrast between the two men.

It is to be expected that Mr. Cullinan had to contend with much opposition from the other diamond mining interests and it is to his credit that he maintained his composure and integrity through it all. This mine that was so scorned as being a useless venture produced two million carats of diamonds per annum and soon proved to be one of the most profitable mines of all times.

One of the biggest diamonds ever found was found in the Premier (Transvaal) Diamond Mine on 5th January 1905, and people could not stop talking about it.

In late afternoon ". . . a black mine worker came running up the slope on which Fred Wells (the surface mine manager) was standing, crying: 'Boss must come see . . . Boss must come quick.'"

"It was most unusual for a black worker, who in those days ranked only as a 'mine boy,' to shout orders to one of the white managers . . . The man's chest was heaving. He was out of breath and sweating heavily . . . no one had seen him run before. This and the man's obvious excitement persuaded Wells that something must be wrong—a fatal accident or a fire in the mine's one shaft. So he set off at a trot to find out what had happened.

"His guide . . . led him to the excavation in which the men had been working and pointed . . . There, embedded in a bank of yellow sand that formed a small cliff face where the last blast of dynamite had cleared the way, was an object gleaming brightly.

"It was the biggest diamond that Wells had ever seen . . . . This stone was five times the size of anything that had come his way in Kimberley. . .his experienced eye told him that it must weight more than a thousand carats and that it was flawless.

"The diamond was taken to the mine office, cleaned up and then measured and weighed and weighed again . . . . It tipped the scales at 3106 carats. It was ten centimetres long, six centimetres high and five wide."[2]

Another gave this: "It was late afternoon of 5th January 1905—the day the largest diamond was discovered in the Cullinan Mine. It was clear and white: the largest of its surfaces appeared to be a cleavage plain, so that it might be only a portion of a much larger stone. It was known as the Cullinan Diamond. This stone was purchased by the Transvaal Government in 1907 and presented to King Edward VII. It was sent to Amsterdam to be cut, and in 1908 was divided into nine large stones and a number of brilliants. This was the most remarkable diamond discovery of recent years. This gem was slightly over 1 $1/3$ pounds in weight."[3]

My mother remembered that finding this unusually large diamond created a tremendous stir among the members of the mining industry. Probably those in Kimberley who knew all there was to know about diamonds felt some chagrin, especially if they recalled their scoffing in earlier days. The excitement among those connected with the Cullinan Mine can only be imagined.

Many problems confronted the owners of this huge diamond, the first being its safe keeping until it could be decided what was to be done. It was kept in the vault of a bank but it could not lie there indefinitely.

[2] A. P. Cartwright, *Diamonds and Clay*, pp. 60-61 Cape Town: Purnell & Sons S.A. (Pty) Ltd., 1977.
[3] *Colliers Encyclopedia*, 11th Ed. Vol. 8, p 163.

Who would purchase such a costly gem? Should it be cut and, if so, into how many diamonds? No individual could afford to purchase it, should it be faceted into one large gem. The next question then was to decide just how many gems could or should be cut from this oversize object. These problems and others were the center of conversation for some time.

Someone came up with the idea it should be purchased by the British people as a gift to King Edward VII who was well loved for his goodness and sympathy to his people. Another idea was that the British of the Transvaal would subscribe amounts to pay for this gift to the King. Ideas flowed and flowed. The general public desired to see this wonder also.

Eventually it was decided to put it on display, and in order to control the crowd tickets were issued by the bank in Johannesburg. Three thousand people thronged to see this huge stone! Hundreds of people were turned away. No one had anticipated that so many would be interested in this display.

Finally, it was decided that the diamond should be a part of the Crown Jewels where it could be for a whole nation, rather than be cut into smaller stones for private sales. The next problem was to decide who could or would have the responsibility of cutting and faceting this stone.

The diamond merchants of the world all offered suggestions. The final decision was that the cutting should be undertaken by one of the most renowned diamond cutting firms in the world, the Asscher Brothers of Amsterdam, and that Joseph Asscher was the man who should take the job.

After this decision was made, the next was to decide how to deliver the gem to Amsterdam. If it were known when the gem stone was being shipped, would it not alert the thieves who could scheme to rob the conveyor?

The final answer was a simple one. It ". . . was delivered in the ordinary way of packets coming by registered post. As to its transmission, it seems that it was unknown to anyone except the directors of the company in South Africa. The ordinary looking packet was handed in at the Johannesburg post office shortly before the English mail, which arrived on Saturday, left the mining center. It weighed a little over a pound, and as the charge is at the rate of a penny a half ounce and two pence extra for registration, the sum paid to the post office was about three shillings. As soon as it was stamped, the packet was placed with the other registered parcels, deposited in the mail bag and sent off to Cape Town, where it was transferred to the steamer."[4]

One can only imagine how Joseph Asscher felt when he held this great stone in his hands and how carefully he studied it to determine where the proper cleavage should be done. It was his decision how many stones to cut and how these would be faceted.

It was decided that the great diamond would be the gift to the Royal Family, not as a gift from the British Empire, but as a token of loyalty from the Transvaal Government. Strangely enough the ruling party of the Transvaal at that time was made up largely of Boers who had fought against Britain during the South African War of 1902.

"On 10th August 1907, General Louis Botha, first Prime Minister of the Transvaal under Responsible Government gave notice of motion to offer the diamond to King Edward VII, his heirs and successors. Botha's motion described the gift as an expression 'of the sentiments of loyalty and affection on the part of the people of the Transvaal toward His Majesty's person and throne.'"[5]

Sketches of the proposed cleavage and gem designs had been made and met with approval of those who were in authority for this great work. "On 10th February 1908 Joseph Asscher readied himself for the all-important operation that was to cleave the rough diamond into three portions from which were to emerge three cut and polished diamonds of immense value. They were the great Star of Africa, now in a magnificent setting in the Imperial Sceptre which Queen Elizabeth II carries on State occasions. It is the biggest cut diamond in the world and weighs 530,20 carats.

"The second of these superb jewels was the Lesser Star of Africa, 317,40 carats, which is a square cut stone, the second largest cut diamond in the world. It is set in the Imperial State Crown below the immense jewel known as the Black Prince's Ruby.

"The third great jewel, 94,40 carats, was set in the crown, called Queen Mary's Crown, which also holds Cullinan IV.

"All told the great rough stone produced nine cut and polished jewels (known as Cullinan I through IX), which, as a collection are priceless. This is not only because they include the two biggest cut diamonds in the world, Cullinans I and II, but because they are all so beautifully cut that they are the most beautiful jewels ever seen."[6]

---

[4] *75th Anniversary Cullinan Chronicle*, April 1978, p. 29
[5] Ibid., pg. 29.
[6] A. P. Cartwright, *Diamonds and Clay*, pp. 70-71 Cape Town: Purnell & Sons S.A. (Pty) Ltd., 1977.

"Grateful for the restoration of self-government, the Government of the Transvaal presented the jewel to King Edward VII on his 68th birthday. The British Liberal Government, too mean to pay the account of the Amsterdam diamond cutters who had divided it with consummate skill. . .told them to keep the chips of the diamond in payment of the work. The honest Dutch cutters declared that the value of the chips was far greater than the cost of the work. His Majesty's Government cared nothing for this, provided the Treasury was not required to foot any bill, but when the news of the transaction reached South Africa, Generals Botha and Smuts organized a public subscription to buy the chips in Amsterdam and re-present these to the British Crown. Churchill said it was the most humiliating episode in the history of the British Administration with which he had been associated . . . ."[7] The chips were made into an exquisite brooch that is also part of the Royal Jewels.

The black man who called Mr. Wells so breathlessly was given a reward of a horse, saddle and bridle, and some money so he could, upon his return to his kraal, purchase cattle and a wife or two. It can well be imagined how triumphant his return, and how many times the tale would be told, for not many of his race could have such a momentous experience.

The private thoughts of Mr. Cullinan will be forever unknown. His wife and he often had joked about his laying at her feet "the biggest diamond in the world." Now that it had been found the joke became a reality. She had been left alone so very often to be both mother and father to their nine children while he spent days at the Cullinan. Yet, she never received any part of the gem. But she at least benefited in knowing her husband's dream had materialized.

It must have been a proud moment in their lives to have had the last laugh!

---

[7] Ibid. p. 72

Appendix C:

Robert Frederick Green, Joseph H. Saunders, and Charles William Clark

Three men figure in Edna May's line of descent: in the direct line, Robert Frederick Green was her grandfather and plays a significant part in her story. Two others, Joseph H. Saunders and Charles William Clark, are men who do not appear in her story, but are a part of her family's history. Local newspaper articles about each are available and are reproduced below:

The following is the obituary of **Robert Frederick Green** from a local unidentified newspaper, perhaps the *East London Daily Dispatch*:

On January 11, 1929, there was laid to rest by the Rev. D. H. Hay, a very well-known and familiar figure in the person of Mr. Robert Green, snr., of Bulugha, district East London.

The graveside was thronged with relatives and friends to pay their last tribute of respect. The deceased gentleman, who was in his 83rd year, succumbed after a painful illness of about fifteen months. He leaves a widow, six sons and five daughters to mourn his loss. Born in Cambridgeshire, England, in 1846, he proceeded with his parents to South Africa as an emigrant, landed at Port Elizabeth, where he farmed a few years. Forty-two years ago [1877] he with his family came farther up the coast into the East London district and started fruit growing. Mr. Green can be looked upon as one of the pioneer farmers of this district. He has always been enterprising and progressive, at the same time showing a keen interest in agricultural societies. The popularity and esteem in which he was held can be seen by the beautiful floral tributes sent by: His loving Wife; Aunt Flossie; Lennie and Alice; Rob and Edith; Bert and Alice; Clem and Sophia; Florrie, Adolf and family; Sid and Minnie; Steve and Martha; Bert and Libby; Henry and Lily; Eddie, Ernie, Jessie, Olive and Bobby; Mr. and Mrs. Neumann and family; Mr. and Mrs. Kleber and family; Mr. and Mrs. J. Pachonich and family; Mr. and Mrs. E. Schultz;

Mrs. C. Sparg; Mr. and Mrs. J. Fieberger and family; Mr. and Mrs. A. Pachonick and family; Mr. and Mrs. W. F. Busse; Mrs. J. Hill and family; Mr. and Mrs. C. Sonnenberger and family; Mr. and Mrs. C. Schafli; Mr. and Mrs. W. Schwartz and family; Mr. and Mrs. R. McKenzie and family; Mr. and Mrs. F. J. Kirchoff and family; Mr. and Mrs. F. H. Kirchoff and family; Mr. and Mrs. F. Houmann and family; Mr. and Mrs. Conrad Schafli and family; Penikie and De Villiers; Mr. and Mrs. Moriarty; Mrs. A. E. Taylor and family; Mr. and Mrs. H. Flanagan; Mr. and Mrs. E. J. Page and family; Barnard and family; Mr. and Mrs. E. Muir and family; friends, 32 Hill Street; several without names.

The following is from the *Eastern Province Herald* (Grahamstown), 26th September 1935:[1]

SETTLER SON'S EXPERIENCES CHARMED LIFE IN EARLY DAYS: Adventures of Mr. J. H. Saunders

Living in Port Elizabeth at the present time is Mr. Joseph H. Saunders, probably the last of the direct descendants of the 1820 Settlers.

He has led a charmed life. When nearly 14 he ran away from home, and fended for himself in a wild and lawless country. Several times he almost died of thirst, and when perilously ill from fever complications and rheumatism at Lake Ngami his life was saved by a native doctor. He does not know the details of the treatment as he was too ill at the time to know what was going on around him. All he knows is that the treatment enabled him to recover sufficiently to leave what he describes as a very unhealthy place.

Many years ago, he told a representative of the Eastern Province Herald yesterday, about 14 direct Settler descendants gathered in Grahamstown on the occasion of the visit of the Earl of Connaught, but since then many have died and he believes that he is the only one left. His brother, John William, died in Uitenhage last August at the age of 81.[2]

Mr. Saunders has been apprentice shoemaker, butcher's boy, assistant carpenter, trader, farmer, soldier, interpreter and hairdresser and tobacconist. His has indeed been a varied career, and in a wild

---

[1] Footnotes are annotations added to Edna May's copy of this article.

[2] Dying in 1935 means he was born in 1854. Grannie was born 18th February 1853; so this John William Saunders must have been the first child after great grandma became Mrs. Saunders. This indicates that Joseph H. was the younger of the two.

country, teeming with big game and carnivorous animals, particularly lions, he has escaped unharmed. His greatest peril has been the lack of water during him many long treks. Somehow the latent dangers of the country in the form of man and beast passed him by, but nevertheless he endured the hardships inseparable from the life of an adventurous boy who developed into a young man with the constitution of an ostrich.

To-day is 77 years of age.[3] Tall and built in proportion, keen of eye and mind, the years have dealt lightly with him, aided by his love of walking and the beneficial effect of an outdoor life.

A "RICH" Man His father,[4] John Saunders, landed with the Bailey party from the Chapman, the first ship to arrive in Algoa Bay in 1820. John Saunders, aged 23 at that time, was a single man, and married late in life, dying in Port Elizabeth in 1863.

Mr. Joseph Saunders was born in Uitenhage in 1858. Apprenticed in his 13th year to his half-brother[5] in Colesberg, he ran away on foot, meeting a wagon expedition which took him to the diamond fields. No whit abashed in his rough surroundings, this venturesome youngster earned 10s. a week as a butcher's boy and considered himself a rich man when his earnings as a carpenter's assistant were increased by five shillings a week. At nights, for the fun of the thing, he assisted in a humble but useful capacity in diamond mining operations, and on one occasion was stunned by a falling rock. This is the only untoward incident he can recall in a very rough and ready settlement.

But the larger world beckoned, and after 12 months' experience of the rough and tumble of the diamond fields he went to the Pilgrim's Rest gold-fields. There followed a life of wandering in the Transvaal during which he acted as an interpreter for the Dutch, until in 1876

---

[3] He was born then in 1858. His death date is unknown.

[4] This is the Saunders who became Grannie Green's step-dad. British Settlers book lists him as being age 22 and maybe from London, as the Chapman sailed from London. So he must have been born in 1798, died in 1863 only 65 years old. He was killed in a kaffir skirmish, I believe. So he and great grandmother Elizabeth Brown Nash Saunders were married about ten years. See above, "married late in life"?

[5] I wonder who the "half-brother" was? A Nash? Must have been Grannie Green's brother, as it would have had to be a person older than he. The word "half-brother" would not be used if it had been a Saunders, and any boy by the McMullen name would have been too young to be in business. I conclude, then, that Grannie must have had a brother—one of the Nash name, for the word "half-brother" to be used.

he left for Khama's station, Pamangwato, and in the same year went to Lake Ngami. Further travels, accompanied by a Native, followed by day, as it was too dangerous to travel at night on account of the prowling lions which were so numerous at that time. During an eight-day journey on foot, partly through the Kalahari Desert, the Natives told him he would die of thirst, and their prediction was almost fulfilled. He was fortunate, however, in finding two water holes.

He ventured on this journey unarmed in a vain search for a man in Matabeleland who had promised him a job. A trading post at Lake Ngami was offered to him, however, and he accepted. For three years he lived in this fever-stricken place with two other while men, the round of life being occasionally relieved by the visits of traders who came to barter with the Natives. Fever, complicated by the effects of an unwholesome diet of goat's meat, game and Kafir corn broke down his health, and his life was despaired of by a Native doctor called to his assistance by one of the Native chiefs, but nevertheless this primitive physician, aided by the ostrich-like constitution of this hardy Settler's son, worked sufficient good to enable him to trek again for more civilised parts.

During this journey he met the famous big game hunter, F. C. Selous, who mentions this meeting in one of his books.

On recovering his health he joined the Border Horse and took part in the Zulu War of that time, when Sir Garnet Wolsey was in command.

Mr. Saunders was one of the party which escorted the captured chief Sekukuni to Pretoria in '79. Later he persuaded Chief Ekalafini not to join forces with the Boers, and when the latter regained possession of the Transvaal Mr. Saunders returned to Port Elizabeth, further adventures having occurred in the meantime.

Then followed a peaceful period of business life in Grahamstown for 48 years as a hairdresser and tobacconist. After wandering in Australia with Mrs. Saunders, whom he married in Grahamstown, Mr. Saunders returned to South Africa and has lived since a life of retirement.

The following is from the *East London Daily Dispatch*, 9th April 1966:

Colourful history of family farm

When Charles William Clark was a boy, the Port Elizabeth farm, Buffelsfontein, where three generations of his family have lived, teemed with snakes. The children were trained "to look where you walk."

For the young Charles this watchfulness paid dividends. He picked up many coins, Strandloper relics and shells that are now museum pieces.

The coins are relics from the colourful history of the family farm which has supplied vegetables to Port Elizabeth since the early days.

Even today Mr Clark's two sons, Billy and Ivor, carry on their third-generation task which the Clarks of Buffelsfontein set for themselves—supplying vegetables for the tables of Port Elizabeth.

Queen Victoria Mr Clark's coins range from a Spade Guinea circa 1790 to a small 1 ½ d piece of 1843, half the size of a tickey. There are coins from George IV to Queen Victoria's reign, plus some St Helena and Mauritius coins.

These he picked up on the land. Miss Wood, whose father owned the farm previously, told him that there was an old double-storey building on the farm which has since been demolished.

The loft of this building was used as a recuperation centre for sailors sick with scurvy who were put ashore from sailing ships calling in the bay. These sailors, while regaining health in the fresh air and by eating fresh vegetables, probably dropped the coins.

Mr Charles Clark was born on the farm Buffelsfontein in 1887. Seven of his nine children were born there.

His life is bound to the land. Not for him the bright lights and fleshpots. Buffelsfontein, on the outskirts of Port Elizabeth, has meant peace, pleasure and permanence for him.

The farm reaches back into history. It was first granted to Theunis Botha d'Oude in 1776. Botha was one of the insurgents arrested with Van Jaarsveld during the troubles at Graaff-Reinet.

He later died in prison at the Castle. Van Jaarsveld was hanged and the others released when the Batavian Government took over after 1803.

Died of smallpox Theale, the noted historian, writing of this, identifies Botha and Buffelsfontein. When the British troops landed at Zwartkops Bay, Botha "who had his farm situated near the sand bay (Sardinia Bay) sent intelligence thereof by an express. . .stating "Dear brother, come quickly the English are arrived at the Bay and intend to apprehend all the inhabitants'.""

A hundred years later the Clarks came to Buffelsfontein. Mr Clark's father, aged about 18, was brought to the Kragga Kama area by his mother after her husband had died of smallpox at Cambridge, England. He worked for H. P. Christian growing vegetables.

An uncle, Robert [Frederick] Green, hired Buffelsfontein but in 1887 trekked to East London by oxwagon to farm at Bulugha [Smiling Valley Farm]. Mr Clark's father then rented the farm for 35 years before buying it.

Charles was over eight before he went to school at St Paul's with the Rev. Mr Brooke, who had married his parents and christened him. His schooling was cut short by the death of his father in 1899. He then took over the farm.

During the South African War, Mr Clark drove an oxwagon laden with vegetables for John Fox Smith who was the buyer for the Concentration Camp for Boer women and children.

Barbed wire This camp situated "at the very outskirts of town" was where the Provincial Hospital now stands. The camp was enclosed with barbed wire.

He drove through the gates past the sentries to the kitchen. This had a row of stoves down the centre. From the beams hung sides of bacon, meat, sausages and biltong.

In 1915 he married Ethel Florence Beckley. They lived in a cottage on the farm while his mother occupied the homestead.

This house with 3ft-thick walls, yellowwood floors and beams, a low loft, with many features of a bygone age architecture, is still sound and well-kept. In the livingroom, old fashioned candle brackets are still screwed into doorframes. Electricity came to Buffelsfontein only about three years ago [1963].

As a small boy he used to go out with Mr Guthrie who drove the "Driftsands Special" through Humewood. This train carried the town's rubbish to the sand-dunes.

Mr Clark was surprised one day when he was given a basket and told to go and pick some tomatoes. Sure enough, all the compost worked into the sands had borne fruit—there were melons, cucumbers, pumpkins, tomatoes growing in profusion on what was just barren sand.

Sunken gun Though Mr Clark modestly disclaims, "I am no historian," he had assimilated much history of his land. A few years ago he and his sons took part in the salvage of a 17th century naval gun submerged in Sardinia Bay.

This gun now guards the entrance to the Museum and is called the "Harraway Gun" for the part Mr Lal Harraway played in its preservation.

His two sons Billy and Ivor carry on the third generation task the Clarks of Buffelsfontein set themselves—supplying vegetables for the tables of Port Elizabeth.

Appendix D:

Genealogy

Edna May Walker was born 4th January 1909 at the Premier Diamond Mine, Cullinan, the Transvaal, in southern Africa.[1] She was the eldest of the three children of Sidney Arthur Walker and Ivy Green Walker. She was baptized at St. George's Anglican Church, Cullinan, Diocese of Pretoria, on 14th February 1909, by the Revd J.H. Boyd, M.A., Rector. She married Archie Charles Richardson 1st June 1927 and bore him Leonard Charles Richardson. Following the failure of that marriage she bore Andrew MacAoidh Jergens to Alfred William Roghan.[2] She died on 7th January 1993 in Seattle, Washington, three days following her 84th birthday, and is buried in the Joseph of Arimathaea Columbarium at the Church of the Redeemer, Cincinnati, Ohio.

Jessie Walker, Edna's sister, was born 30th March 1911 at the Premier Diamond Mine, Cullinan, the Transvaal, Union of South Africa. She emigrated to the United States with her mother and siblings in June-July 1920. She married Hans Widding and bore him George Clarence Widding and Edward Paul Beck. After Widding's death she married Herbert Beck on 30th May 1942 and bore him Sharon Paula Beck Cohran. She lives in Mt. Airy, Georgia.

Leonard Sidney Walker, Edna's brother, was born 4th September 1914 at Smiling Valley Farm, Bulugha, East London District, Union of South Africa. He emigrated to the United States with his mother and siblings in June-July 1920. In 1935 he returned to South Africa and on 7 October 1939 married Joyce Cecil Heathcote

---

[1] It would not be for more than another year, until 31st May 1910, that the Transvaal became a province of the Union of South Africa. It was yet another 31st May, this of 1961, that the Union became the Republic of South Africa.
[2] See Epilogue.

who bore him Jennifer Ann Walker Conderan, Sally Elizabeth Walker Abbott, and David Cecil Walker. He lives in George, Cape Province, Republic of South Africa.

Sidney Arthur Walker was born 10th July 1886 at Uitenhage, Cape Province, and was the twelfth and last child of Alexander Walker and his wife Catherine Ann Robinson MacKay. He was Dedicated to God on 22nd October 1886 at the Baptist Church worshipping at Queen Street, Port Elizabeth, Cape Province. He was baptized 27th March 1949 at St. John's Anglican Cathedral, Saskatoon, Saskatchewan, Canada. He married Ivy Green on 5th March 1908. He served as a Private in the 6th Battalion the Kings' Own Scottish Borders, No. 34408, April 1918 to March 1920, being awarded the British War Medal and the World War I Victory Medal. He died 18th February 1962 in Saskatoon, Saskatchewan. He is buried in the Soldiers' Field of Woodlawn Cemetery in that same city.

Alexander Walker, born 18th February 1839, likely in the croft known as Briarbank, Balfreishal, Fort Augustus, Scotland. He was the elder of a son and daughter of Corporal Alexander Walker and Ann Lawrence Walker. He was baptized 23rd March 1848 at Fort Augustus by a military chaplain. He married Catherine Ann Robinson MacKay about 1867 in South Africa. He died 26th August 1903 in Port Elizabeth and is buried at the North End Cemetery, Port Elizabeth.

Corporal Alexander Walker at the age of 16 years five months at Belfast, Ireland, enlisted in the 74th Regiment (Highlanders) as No. 1123 on 15th October 1834, his height given as 5'7". We have not yet found a record of his birth, which must have been in May 1818, place unknown. Having served with the Regiment in Ireland, the West Indies, Canada, England, and Scotland, Corporal Walker arrived at Cape Town in South Africa with his regiment on 11th May 1851. He was killed in action six weeks later on 26th June 1851 at a battle with the natives in the Amatola Heights, now the Ciskei. He left his thirteen year old son and pregnant widow who that August bore his daughter, Agnes Walker. He is buried in an unmarked soldier's grave on the Amotola Heights.

Ann Lawrence Walker was born between 1817 and 1821 in Boleskine Parish, Fort Augustus, Inverness-shire, Scotland. This birth is dated by the 1841 Census of Fort Augustus, which lists "Ann Walker, age 20, nurse, born in the county, living in the household of Francis Cowell." She was the daughter of James Lawrence, a former soldier of the 6th Royal Volunteer Battalion, and Marjorie "May" Morrison, who were married 21st June 1806 in the parish of Boleskine and Abertarff, Inverness-shire, Scotland. They had an earlier daughter, undoubtedly died in infancy, by the name of Ann who was baptized in the parish 23rd July 1811.

Catherine Ann Robinson MacKay was probably the seventh and last child of James MacKay and Christian Clarke Robertson MacKay. She was born about September 1845, most likely in Buenos Aires, Argentina. She died 12th February 1892 in Port Elizabeth.

James MacKay, her father, was baptized 6th April 1795 in the parish of Durness, Sutherland, Scotland. His parents were Seoras MacIainbhain MacKay and Catriona Nic a'Ghobhainn (Gow) MacKay.[3] He may have been a victim of the early 19th century Highland Clearances. He was married in Glasgow to Christian Clarke Robertson[4] of Glasgow, Scotland, on 25th January 1825 by Mr. Robert Clark, the Gaelic speaking minister in Glasgow. The family soon emigrated to Buenos Aires where seven chidren were born. The family emigrated to South Africa by 1846. He died at the age of 71 on 14th January 1866 somewhere in the Cape Province, South Africa.

Christian Clarke Robertson was the daughter of Donald Robertson and Agnes "Ann" Sutherland Robertson of Perthshire, Scotland. She was born 12th January 1809 in Glasgow; she died 4th December 1876 in Johannesburg, the Transvaal, South Africa, at the age of 77.

Ivy Green was the ninth child, the fourth daughter, of the fourteen children (nine sons, one died an infant, one died a youth; and five daughters) of Robert Frederick Green and his wife Louisa Jane Nash Green. She was born 19th October 1885 at Bufflesfontein. She married Sidney Arthur Walker on 5th March 1908. In addition to Edna May, her children were Jessie, born 30th March 1911, and Leonard Sidney, born 4th September 1914. She emigrated from South Africa to the United States in June 1920, being the only member of

---

[3] As these were Gaelic speaking people, their Christian and family names are given in the Gaelic. The surname, in the Gaelic "MacAoidh," is in the English spelling.

[4] The Scottish surname, "Robertson," seems later to have been translated into the English form, "Robinson" in the Walker family.

her family to leave South Africa. She died 5th April 1973 at the age of 87 years in Atlanta, Georgia.

Robert Frederick Green was born 23rd March 1846 in Bottisham, Cambridgeshire, England. He was one of at least four children of William Green and his wife Suzanna Clark. In the early 1850's the family emigrated to the Cape Province. He died 10th January 1929 at Bulugha, East London District, Union of South Africa. He is buried at the Gonubie Cemetery, East London District.[5]

Louisa Jane Nash was the great granddaughter of Thomas Glass and Ann Foricker Glass, both of Wellington, Somersetshire, England. The Glass's sailed from Bristol with Southey's Party of the Settlers and arrived late April or early May 1820.

Their daughter, Elizabeth Ann Glass, married a Henry Brown; their daughter Elizabeth Ann Brown, who survived the death of her mother at childbirth, married William Nash of Bambury Court, Yorkshire, England. Louisa Jane was born 18th February 1853 at Port Elizabeth and married Robert Frederick Green 18th November 1870 at the age of seventeen years, nine months. She died 8th March 1935.

Note: Several pages of charts will follow.

---

[5] See Appendix C for his obituary.

Forebears of Robert Frederick GREEN, 1846-1929

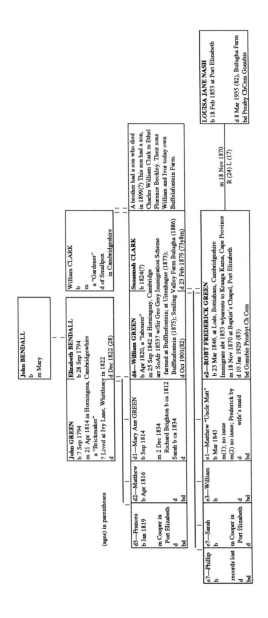

John BENDALL
b
m Mary

Elizabeth BENDALL
b 28 Sep 1794, Cambridgeshire
? Lived at Ivy Lane, Whittlesey in 1822
d Dec 1822 (28)

John GREEN
b 7 Sep 1794
m 21 Apr 1814 in Horningsea, Cambridgeshire
a "Brickmaker"
d

William CLARK
b
m
a "Gardener"
d of Smallpox in Cambridgeshire

(ages) in parentheses

d1—Mary Ann GREEN
b Sep 1814
m 2 Dec 1834
Richard Brighton b ca 1812
Sarah b ca 1834
d

d2—Matthew
b Apr 1816
m Cooper in Port Elizabeth
d
bd

d3—Frances
b Jan 1819
m Cooper in Port Elizabeth
d
bd

d4—William GREEN
b Apr 1820, a "labourer"
m 25 Sep 1842 at Horningsay, Cambridge
arr SoAfr 1853? w/Sir Geo Grey Immigration Scheme
farmed at Bufflesfontein; at Uitenhague (1873);
Bufflesfontein (1875); Smiling Valley Farm Bulugha (1886)
d Oct 1901(82)

Susannah CLARK
b 1824(?)
d 23 Feb 1879 (73y8m)

A brother had a son who died in 1899(?) This son had a son, Charles William Clark m Ethel Florence Beckley. Their sons William and Ivor today own Buffelsfontein Farm.

LOUISA JANE NASH
b 18 Feb 1853 at Port Elizabeth
d 8 Mar 1935 (82), Bulugha Farm
bd Presby ChCem Gonubie

e1—Matthew "Uncle Matt"
b Mar 1843
m(1); no issue
m(2) no issue; Frederick by wife's maid
d
bd

e2—ROBT FREDERICK GREEN
b 23 Mar 1846, at Lode, Bottisham, Cambridgeshire
Immigrate abt 1853 w/parents to Kraaga Kama, Cape Province
m 18 Nov 1870 at Baptist's Chapel, Port Elizabeth
d 10 Jan 1929 (83)
bd Gonubie Presbyt Ch Cem

m 18 Nov 1870
R (24), L (17)

e3—William
b
d in Cooper in Port Elizabeth
bd

e7—Sarah
b
records lost
d
bd

e?—Phillip
b
d
bd

Forebears of Louisa Jane NASH, 1853-1935

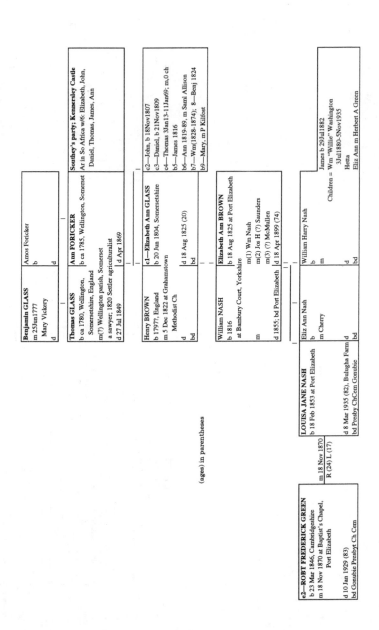

(ages) in parentheses

The Children of Robert Frederick GREEN and Louisa Jane NASH

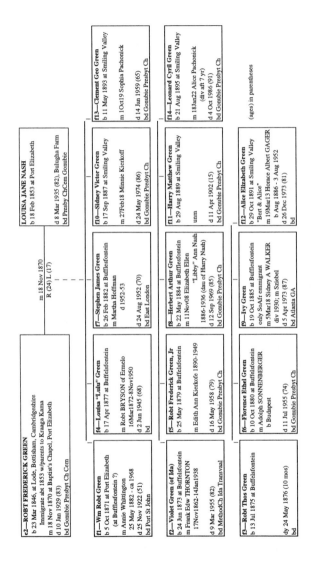

c2—ROBT FREDERICK GREEN
b 23 Mar 1846, at Lode, Bottisham, Cambridgeshire
Immigrate abt 1853 w/parents to Knaga Kama
m 18 Nov 1870 at Baptist's Chapel, Port Elizabeth
d 10 Jan 1929 (83)
bd Gonubie Presbyt Ch Cem

m 18 Nov 1870
R (24) L (17)

LOUISA JANE NASH
b 18 Feb 1853 at Port Elizabeth

d 8 Mar 1935 (82), Bulugha Farm
bd Presby ChCem Gombie

f1—Wm Robt Green
b 5 Oct 1871 at Port Elizabeth
(at Buffelsfontein ?)
m Annie Whittington
25 May 1882 - ca 1968
d 25 Nov 1922 (51)
bd Port St John

f2—Violet Green (of Ida)
b 24 Jun 1873 at Buffelsfontein
m Frank Edw THORNTON
17Nov1862-14Jan1938
d 9 Mar 1955 (82)
bd MethodCh Ida Transvaal

f3—Robt Thos Green
b 13 Jul 1875 at Buffelsfontein
dy 24 May 1876 (10 mos)
bd

f4—Louisa "Lulu" Green
b 17 Apr 1877 at Buffelsfontein
m Robt BRYSON of Ermelo
16Mar1872-8Nov1950
d 2 Jun 1945 (68)
bd

f5—Robt Frederick Green, Jr
b 25 May 1879 at Buffelsfontein
m Edith Ann Kierkofe 1890-1949
d 16 May 1958 (79)
bd Gonubie Presbyt Ch

f6—Florence Ethel Green
b 10 Oct 1880 at Buffelsfontein
m Adolph SONNENBERGER
b Budapest
d 11 Jul 1955 (74)
bd Gonubie Presbyt Ch

f7—Stephen James Green
b 26 Feb 1882 at Buffelsfontein
m Martha Hoffman
d 1952-53
d 24 Aug 1952 (70)
bd East London

f8—Herbert Arthur Green
b 22 May 1884 at Buffelsfontein
m 11Nov08 Elizabeth Ellen
"Libby" Ann Nash
1886-1936 (dau of Harry Nash)
d 12 Sep 1969 (85)
bd Gonubie Presbyt Ch

f9—Ivy Green
b 19 Oct 1885 at Buffelsfontein
only SoAfr emmigrant
m 5Mar18 Sidney A WALKER
div 1930; m Sziebel
d 5 Apr 1973 (87)
bd Atlanta GA

f10—Sidney Victor Green
b 17 Sep 1887 at Smiling Valley
m 27Feb18 Minnie Kierkoff
d 24 May 1974 (86)
bd Gonubie Presbyt Ch

f11—Harry Matthew Green
b 29 Aug 1889 at Smiling Valley
unm
d 11 Apr 1902 (15)
bd Gonubie Presbyt Ch

f12—Alice Elizabeth Green
b 29 Oct 1891 at Smiling Valley
"Bert & Alice"
m 19Mar13 Horace Albert GAGER
b Aug 1886 - 3 Aug 1952
d 26 Dec 1973 (81)
bd

f13—Clement Geo Green
b 11 May 1893 at Smiling Valley
m 1Oct19 Sophia Pachonick
d 14 Jan 1959 (65)
bd Gonubie Presbyt Ch

f14—Leonard Cyril Green
b 21 Aug 1895 at Smiling Valley
m 18Jan22 Alice Pachonick
(div aft 7 yr)
d 4 Oct 1986 (91)
bd Gonubie Presbyt Ch

(ages) in parentheses

Descendants of f1—William Robert GREEN, 1871-1922

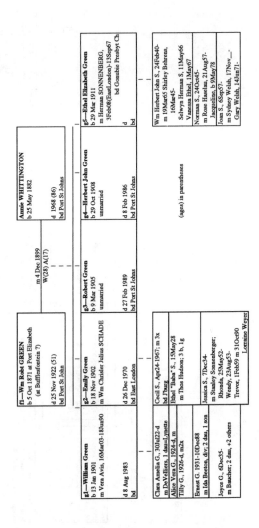

f1—Wm Robt GREEN
b 5 Oct 1871 at Port Elizabeth
(at Bufflesfontein ?)

d 25 Nov 1922 (51)
bd Port St John

m 4 Dec 1899
W(28) A(17)

Annie WHITTINGTON
b 25 May 1882

d 1968 (86)
bd Port St Johns

---

g1—William Green
b 13 Jan 1901
m Vera Avis, 16Mar03-18Jun90

d 8 Aug 1983
bd

g2—Emily Green
b 18 Nov 1902
m Wm Chrisler Julius SCHADE

d 26 Dec 1970
bd East London

g3—Robert Green
b 9 Mar 1905
unmarried

d 27 Feb 1989
bd Port St Johns

g4—Herbert John Green
b 29 Oct 1908
unmarried

d 8 Feb 1986
bd Port St Johns

g5—Ethel Elizabeth Green
b 29 Mar 1911
m Herman SONNENBERG,
3Feb08(EastLondon)-13Sep67
bd Gonubie Presbyt Ch

d
bd

Clara Amelia G., 30Jul22-d
m DeVelliers, 1 dau=Lynette
bd P'burg

Alice Vera G., 1924-d, m

Tilly G., 1926-d, m2x

Cecil S., Apr24-1967; m 3x
bd P'burg

Ethel "Baba" S., 15May28
m Thos Hudson; 3 b, 1g

Wm Herbert John S., 24Feb40-
m 19Mar65 Shirley Behrens,
16Mar45-
Selwyn Herman S, 11May66
Vanessa Ethel, 1May67

Ernest G. 1931-10Dec88
m Ida Beeton, div; 2 dau, 1 son

Joyce G., 6Dec35-
m Baucher; 2 dau, +2 others

Jessica S., 7Dec34-
m Stanley Sonnenberger;
Rhonda, 25May52-
Wendy, 23Aug53-
Trevor, 1Feb59 m 31Oct90
          Lorraine Weyer

(ages) in parentheses

Norman S., 24Oct45-
m Rose Haselau, 21Aug57-
          Jacqueline, b 9May78

Joan S., 6Sep57-
m Sydney Welsh, 17Nov__-
   Gary Welsh, 14Jun71-

Descendants of f2—Violet GREEN, 1873-1955

f2—Violet GREEN
b 24 Jun 1873 at Buffelsfontein
d 9 Mar 1955 (82)
bd Method/Ch: Ida Transvaal

m 23 Dec 1889
F(27) V(16)

Ely THORNTON
b Manchester, England
d 1915, East London
bd East London, RSA

Mary Jane Bletcher
England
d 1919, Salisbury, Rhodesia
bd Umtali, Rhodesia

Frank Edward THORNTON
b 17 Nov 1862 Manchester Engl
d 14 Jan 1938
bd Methodist Ch, Ida, Transvaal

---

g1—Violet Louisa "Louie"
b 29 Sep 1890
m Edgar J CUMMING
d May 1952, Lydenburg TVL
d Jan 1952
bd

g2—Arthur Edward
b 28 Aug 1892
m Elsie Page
d May 1971, Cape Town
bd

g3—Dorothy Mary "Dot"
b 6 Nov 1894
m Harry J Clark, 13Jul87-Jul53
d 31 Aug 1971
bd 3 Sep, at Port Elizabeth

g4—Eric Ronald Francis "Bob"
b 31 Mar 1896
m Mary Ewing, div
m Rita Simpson: Ronald
d Jul 1965, Johannesburg
bd

g5—Herbert Gordon
b 7 Apr 1899
m Gladys Horingold
d 1985?
bd

g6—Marjorie Edith "Madge"
b 26 Aug 1900
m Clement E Whittier
d Mar 1978
bd

Descendants of g1:
Leslie Cumming
b 24 May 1918
m Hazel
dau Gillian; son Alan

Joan Thornton, b 1927
m Ian Echard
son Christopher, b 1955
David, b 1933, m Rosemary

Descendants of g3:
Herbert Clark 1924-1974
m Marjory Coleman
Peter, Jennifer, John,
Sheila, m Glen du Toit
2 son, 1 dau
Dennis Clark
m Lucille Lusan; 1 dau, 1 son

Descendants of g4:
from 2m, Ronald Thornton

Frank Thornton
Errol, m Helen Thorpe;
2 sons
Derek, m Rosemary Williamson
m Bronwyn. 1 son 1 dau

Descendants of g6:
John Ernest Whittier
b 30 Nov 1925
m Eileen Bennetts; Jeanetter,
Michael, Brian, Pamela, Graham
Austen Whittier
b 29 Jun 1927
m Mary Tingley; John, Stephen
m Cynthia, Ann

---

g7—Millicent Amy
b 21 Aug 1903
m Eugene Cloete;
d 27 Dec 1978
bd

g8—Ernest Harry
b 17 Jul 1905
d 2 Mar 1919
bd

g9—Joyce Muriel
b 6 Jul 1908
m Cecil Whittle,
d 28 Mar 1947
d 9 Oct 1978
bd

g10—Donald Edgar "John"
b 28 Mar 1911
m Verna Whittle, d 18 Apr 1980
d
bd

Descendants of g7:
Eugene Thornton Cloete
b 1927; m Barbara Skinner
Michael, Bernard, Cheryl
Donald Thornton Cloete
b 1929; m Elaine Sills
Claude, Bridget, Andrew
Henry Thornton Cloete
b 1934; m Margaret Cotterell
Sallyanne, Peter, Alison, Lynda
Jillian Dora Thornton
b 1943; m Glenn Cotterell
Bernard, Eugene, Ashley, Jessica

Descendants of g9:
Shirley Whittle
m Vivian Malony
Stewart, Annemarie, Tracey
Margaret Whittle
m William Spalding
Sandra, Brigdet, Deborah
Lynette Whittle
m Ivan Boucher
Gregory, Kim
Ronald Whittle
m Lola Schaffer
Caroline, Lon

Descendants of g10:
Athole Thornton
m Ben Botha
Susan
Rosemary Thornton
m Rodney Dewberry, div
Wendy, Joananne, Caroline
Donald Thornton
m Jennifer Boucher
Dale, Gavin, Melanie
Irene Thornton
m Roy Armour
Mark, Simon

Descendants of f4—Louisa "Lulu" GREEN, 1877-1945

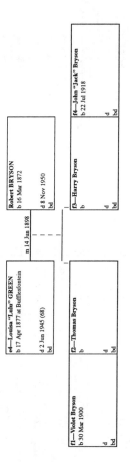

Descendants of f5—Robert Frederick GREEN, Jr, 1882-1922

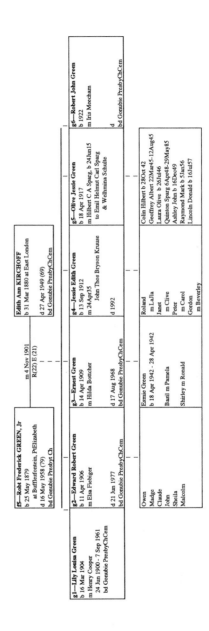

f5—Robt Frederick GREEN, Jr b 25 May 1879 at Bufflesfontein, PtElizabeth d 16 May 1958 (79) bd Gonubie Presbyt Ch	m 4 Nov 1901 R(22) E (21)	**Edith Ann KIRCHOFF** b 31 Mar 1880 at East London d 27 Apr 1949 (69) bd Gonubie PresbyChCem	

g1—Lily Louisa Green	g2—Edward Robert Green	g3—Ernest Green	g4—Jessie Edith Green	g5—Olive Jessie Green	g6—Robert John Green
b 16 Mar 1904	b 11 Apr 1906	b 14 Apr 1909	b 13 Sep 1912	b 18 Apr 1917	b 1922
m Henry Cooper	m Elsa Fiebiger	m Hilda Bottcher	m 24Apr35	m Hilbert C A Sparg, b 24Jun15	m Iris Meecham
24 Jun 1900 - 7 Sep 1961			John Thos Bryson Kruuse	to Emil Helmut Carl Sparg	
bd Gonubie PresbyChCem	d 21 Jun 1977	d 17 Aug 1968	d 1992	& Welhmina Schulte	d
	bd Gonubie PresbyChCem	bd Gonubie PresbyChCem			bd Gonubie PresbyChCem

Owen	Ernie Green	Roland	Colin Hilbert b 28Oct 42
Madge	b 18 Apr 1942 - 28 Apr 1942	m LaJla	Geoffrey Albert 22Mar45-12Aug45
Claude		Janet	Laura Olive b 26Jul46
John	Basil m Pamela	m Clive	Quinton Sparg 6Apr48-29May85
Sheila		Peter	Ashley John b 16Dec49
Malcolm	Shirley m Ronald	m Carol	Raymond Mark b 5Jan56
		Gordon	Lincoln Donald b 16Jul57
		m Beverley	

Descendants of f6—Florence Ethel GREEN, 1880-1955

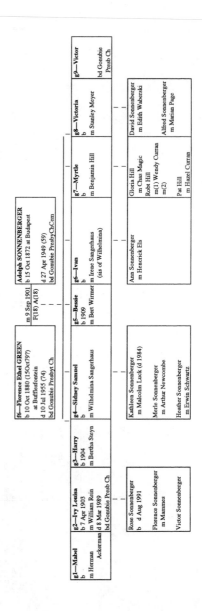

f6—Florence Ethel GREEN
b 10 Oct 1880 (15Oct79?)
at Buffelsfontein
d 10 Jul 1955 (74)
bd Gonubie Presbyt Ch

m 9 Sep 1901
F(18) A(18)

Adolph SONNENBERGER
b 15 Oct 1872 at Budapest
d 27 Apr 1949 (59)
bd Gonubie PresbyChCem

g1—Mabel
b
m Herman Ackerman

g2—Ivy Louisa
b 7 Apr 1903
m William Rein
d 8 Mar 1989
bd Gonubie Presb Ch

g3—Harry
b 1904
m Bertha Steyn

g4—Sidney Samuel
b
m Wilhelmina Sangerhaus

g5—Bessie
b 1909
m Bert Wirmer

g6—Ivan
b
m Irene Sangerhaus
(sis of Wilhelmina)

g7—Myrtle
b
m Benjamin Hill

g8—Victoria
b
m Stanley Meyer

g9—Victor
bd Gonubie
Presb Ch

Rose Sonnenberger
b   d Aug 1991

Florence Sonnenberger
m Mammes

Victor Sonnenberger

Kathleen Sonnenberger
m Malcolm Luck (d 1984)

Merle Sonnenberger
m Arthur Newcombe

Heather Sonnenberger
m Erwin Schwartz

Ann Sonnenberger
m Hencrick Els

Gloria Hill
m Chas Magic
Robt Hill
m(1) Wendy Curran
m(2)

Pat Hill
m Hazel Curran

David Sonnenberger
m Edith Waberski

Alfred Sonnenberger
m Marian Page

5/8/94

Descendants of f7—Stephen James GREEN, 1882-1922

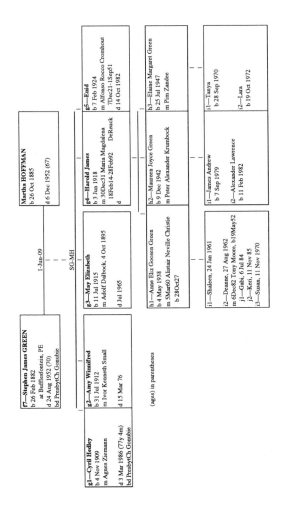

f7—Stephen James GREEN
b 26 Feb 1882
at Bufflesfontein, PE
d 24 Aug 1952 (70)
bd PresbytCh Gonubie

Martha HOFFMAN
b 26 Oct 1885
d 6 Dec 1952 (67)

1-Jun-09

SG-MH

g1—Cyril Hedley
b 4 Nov 1909
m Agnes Ziemann
d 3 Mar 1986 (77y 4m)
bd PresbytCh Gonubie

g2—Amy Winnifred
b 31 Jul 1912
m Ivor Kenneth Small
d 15 Mar 76

g3—May Elizabeth
b 11 Jul 1915
m Adolf Dalbock, 4 Oct 1895
d Jul 1965

g4—Harold James
b 3 Jun 1918
m 30Dec31 Maria Magdalena DeReuck
18Feb14-28Feb92
d

g5—Enid
b 7 Feb 1924
m Alfonso Rocco Cromhout
7Dec21-1Sep51
d 14 Oct 1982

(ages) in parentheses

h1—Anne Eliz Goosen Green
b 4 May 1938
m 5Mar60 Alistair Neville Christie
b 28Oct27

h2—Maureen Joyce Green
b 9 Dec 1942
m Peter Alexander Krumbock

h3—Elaine Margaret Green
b 25 Jul 1947
m Pim Zandee

i1—Shaleen, 24 Jan 1961

i2—Deanne, 27 Aug 1962
m 6Dec82 Tony Moore, b19May52
j1—Gabi, 6 Jul 84
j2—Keri, 11 Nov 85
i3—Susan, 11 Nov 1970

i1—James Andrew
b 7 Sep 1979

i2—Alexander Lawrence
b 11 Feb 1982

i1—Tanya
b 28 Sep 1970

i2—Lara
b 19 Oct 1972

321

Descendants of f8—Herbert Arthur GREEN, 1884-1969

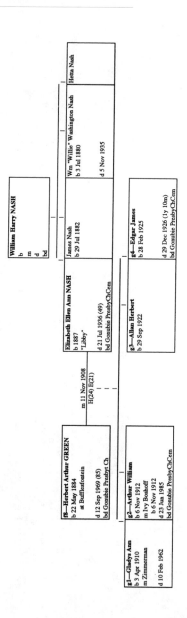

William Harry NASH
b
m
d
bd

Elizabeth Ellen Ann NASH
b 1887
"Libby"

d 21 Jul 1936 (49)
bd Gonubie PresbyChCem

James Nash
b 29 Jul 1882

Wm "Willie" Washington Nash
b 3 Jul 1880

d 5 Nov 1935

Hetta Nash

f8—Herbert Arthur GREEN
b 22 May 1884
at Bufflesfontein

d 12 Sep 1969 (85)
bd Gonubie Presbyt Ch

m 11 Nov 1908
H(24) E(21)

g2—Arthur William
b 6 Nov 1912
m Ivy Boshoff
b 6 Nov 1912
d 23 Jun 1985
bd Gonubie PresbyChCem

g3—Allan Herbert
b 29 Sep 1922

g4—Edgar James
b 28 Feb 1925

d 29 Dec 1926 (1y 10m)
bd Gonubie PresbyChCem

g1—Gladys Ann
b 3 Apr 1910
m Zimmerman

d 10 Feb 1962

Descendants of f9—Ivy GREEN, 1885-1973
Edna May

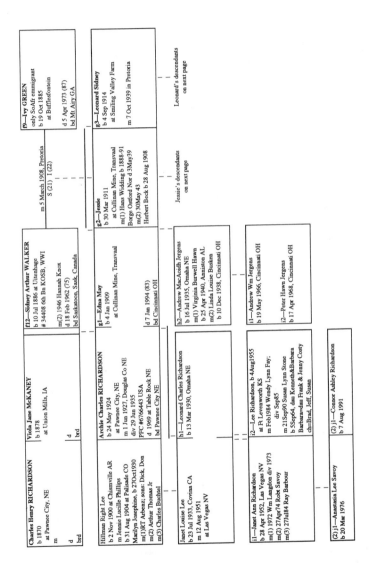

f9—Ivy GREEN
only SoAfr emmigrant
b 19 Oct 1885
at Bufflesfontein

d 5 Apr 1973 (87)
bd Mt Airy GA

m 5 March 1908, Pretoria
S (21) I (22)

f12—Sidney Arthur WALKER
b 10 Jul 1886 at Uitenhage
34408 6th Bn KOSB, WWI

m(2) 1946 Hannah Knox
d 18 Feb 1962 (75)
bd Ssakatoon, Sask, Canada

Charles Henry RICHARDSON
b 1870
at Pawnee City, NE
m

d
brd

Viola Jane McKANEY
b 1878
at Union Mills, IA

d
brd

g3—Leonard Sidney
b 4 Sep 1914
at Smiling Valley Farm
m 7 Oct 1939 in Pretoria

Leonard's descendants
on next page

g2—Jessie
b 30 Mar 1911
at Cullinan Mine, Transvaal
m(1) Hans Widding b 1888-91
Borge Oxford Nor d 3May39
m(2) 30May 43
Herbert Beck b 28 Aug 1908

Jessie's descendants
on next page

g1—Edna May
b 4 Jan 1909
at Cullinan Mine, Transvaal

d 7 Jan 1994 (83)
bd Cincinnati OH

Archie Charles RICHARDSON
b 24 May 1924
at Pawnee City, NE
m 1 Jun 1927, Douglas Co NE
div 29 Jun 1935
PFC #6766443 USA
d 1969 at Table Rock NE
bd Pawnee City NE

h2—Andrew MacAoidh Jergens
b 16 Jul 1935, Omaha NE
mt(1) Virginia Burwell Hawn
b 25 Apr 1940, Anniston AL
m(2) Linda Louise Busken
b 10 Dec 1938, Cincinnati OH

i1—Andrew Wm Jergens
b 19 May 1966, Cincinnati OH

i2—Peter Hawn Jergens
b 17 Apr 1968, Cincinnati OH

h1—Leonard Charles Richardson
b 13 Mar 1930, Omaha NE

Hillman Right Lee
b 2 Nov 1900 at Chismville AR
m Jennie Lucille Phillips
b 31 Aug 1904 at Palisade CO
Marilyn Josephine, b 27Oct1930
m(1)RT Arbenz; sons: Dick, Don
m(2) Arthur Thomas Jr
m(3) Charles Buchtel

i2—Lee Richardson, b 4Aug1955
at Ft Levenworth KS
m Feb1984 Wendy Lynn Fay;
div Sep85
m 21Sep90 Susan Lynn Stone
b 5Sep64, dau Kenneth&Barbara
Barbara=dau Frank & Jenny Costy
ch=Brad, Jeff, Susan

Janet Louise Lee
b 23 Jul 1933, Covina CA
m 12 Aug 1951
at Las Vegas NV

i1—Janet Ann Richardson
b 28 Apr 1952, Las Vegas NV
m(1) 1972 Wm Langdon div 1973
m(2) 27Apr74 Robt Savoy
m(3) 27Jul84 Ray Barbour

(2)j1—Anastasia Lee Savoy
b 20 Mar 1976

(2)j1-—Connor Ashley Richardson
b 7 Aug 1991

Descendants of f9—Ivy GREEN, 1885–1973
Jessie and Leonard

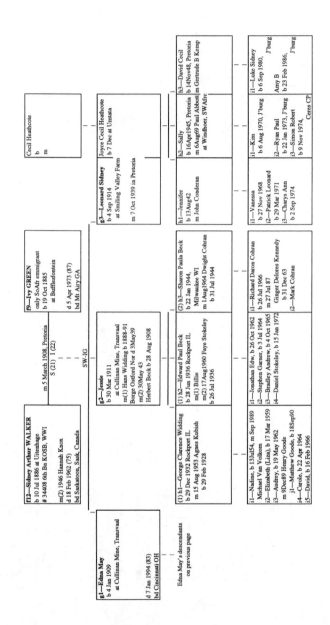

f12—Sidney Arthur WALKER
b 10 Jul 1886 at Uitenhage
34408 6th Bn KOSB, WWI

m(2) 1946 Hannah Knox
d 18 Feb 1962 (75)
bd Saskatoon, Sask, Canada

f9—Ivy GREEN
only SoAfr emmigrant
b 19 Oct 1885
at Bufflesfontein

d 5 Apr 1973 (87)
bd Mt Airy GA

m 5 March 1908, Pretoria
S (21) I (22)

SW-IG

Cecil Heathcote
b
m

g1—Edna May
b 4 Jan 1909
at Cullinan Mine, Transvaal

d 7 Jan 1994 (83)
bd Cincinnati OH

Edna May's descendants
on previous page

g2—Jessie
b 30 Mar 1911
at Cullinan Mine, Transvaal
m(1) Hans Widding b 1888-91
Borge Ostford Nor d 3May39
m(2) 30May 43
Herbert Beck b 28 Aug 1908

g3—Leonard Sidney
b 4 Sep 1914
at Smiling Valley Farm

m 7 Oct 1939 in Pretoria

Joyce Cecil Heathcote
b 7 Dec at Umtata

(1) h2—Edward Paul Beck
b 28 Jun 1936 Rockport IL
m(1) Billie
m(2) 17Aug1960 Faye Stokeley
b 26 Jul 1936

(2) h3—Sharon Paula Beck
b 22 Jan 1944,
Milwaukee WI
m 1Aug1964 Dwight Cohran
b 31 Jul 1944

h1—Jennifer
b 13Aug42
m John Conderan

h2—Sally
b 16Apr1945, Pretoria
m 6Aug69 Paul Abbott
at Windhoer, SW Afrc

h3—David Cecil
b 14Nov48, Pretoria
m Gertrude B Kemp

(1) h1—George Clarence Widding
b 29 Dec 1932 Rockport IL
m 15 Aug 1953 Agnes Kubish
b 29 Feb 1928

i1—Nadine, b 13Jul54, m Sep 1989
Michael Van Volkom
i2—Elizabeth (Liza), b 17 Mar 1959
i3—Audrey, b 19 May 1962
m 9Dec89 Henry Goode
j1—Matthew Goode, b 18Sep90
i4—Carole, b 22 Apr 1964
i5—David, b 16 Feb 1966

i1—Jonathan Edw, b 26 Oct 1962
i2—Stephen Garner, b 3 Jul 1964
i3—Bradley Andrew, b 4 Oct 1965
i4—Daniel Stokeley, b 15 Jan 1972

i1—Richard Daron Cohran
b 26 Jul 1966
m 27 Jul 87
Ginger Delores Kennedy
b 31 Dec 63
i2—Mark Cohran

i1—Vanessa
b 27 Nov 1968
i2—Patrick Leonard
b 29 Mar 1971
i3—Charys Ann
b 2 Sep 1974

i1—Kim
b 6 Aug 1970, J'burg
i2—Ryan Paul
b 22 Jan 1973, J'burg
i3—Simon Robert
b 9 Nov 1974,

i1—Lake Sidney
b 6 Sep 1980,
J'burg
Amy B
b 23 Feb 1986,
J'burg
Ceres CP

Descendants of f10—Sidney Victor GREEN, 1887-1974

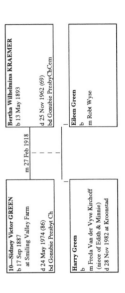

| 10—**Sidney Victor GREEN** |
| b 17 Sep 1887 |
| at Smiling Valley Farm |
| |
| d 24 May 1974 (86) |
| bd Gonubie Presbyt Ch |

m 27 Feb 1918

| **Bertha Wilhelmina KRAEMER** |
| b 13 May 1893 |
| |
| d 25 Nov 1962 (69) |
| bd Gonubie PresbyChCem |

| **Harry Green** |
| b |
| m Freda Van der Vyve Kirchoff |
| (niece of Edith & Minnie) |
| d 28 Nov 1982 at Kroonstad |

| **Eileen Green** |
| b |
| m Robt Wyse |

Descendants of f12—Alice Elizabeth GREEN, 1891-1973

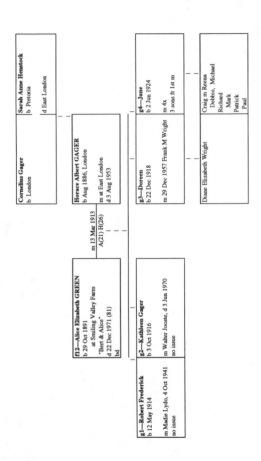

Descendants of f13—Clement George GREEN, 1893-1959

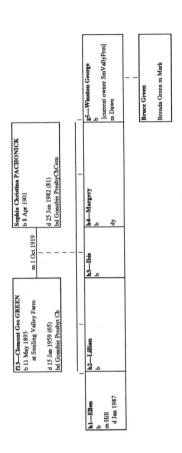

f13—Clement Geo GREEN		Sophia Christina PACHONICK
b 11 May 1893		b 8 Apr 1901
at Smiling Valley Farm		
	m 1 Oct 1919	d 25 Jun 1982 (81)
d 15 Jan 1959 (65)		bd Gonubie PresbyChCem
bd Gonubie Presbyt Ch		

h1—Ellen	h2—Lillian	h3—Ibis	h4—Margery	g5—Winston George
b	b	b	b	b
m Hill		dy	dy	[current owner SmVallyFrm]
d Jan 1987				m Dawn

| Bruce Green |
| Brenda Green m Mark |

Forebears and Sister of Alexander WALKER, 1839-1903

James LAURENCE
b
m 21 Jun 1806 in Boleskine Parish, Scotland
soldier, 6th Royal Veterans Bn
later a weaver in Fort Augustus
b
bd

Marjorie MORRISON
"May," "Mary"
b
bd

d5—Ann "Agnes" Laurence
b 1817-1821
in Boleskine Parish, Scotland
m ca 1837

Alexander WALKER
b 15 May 1818, place unknown
a labourer, 5'7", enlisted 15 Oct 1834, at Belfast
(WO 12/8104 gives his age at enlistment as 16y5m)
#1123 74th Regiment (Highlanders);
Sailed to SoAfrica on the troop ship Vulcan
kia 26 Jun 1851 on the Amatola Heights
bd Amatola Heights, Cape Prov

d1—Barbara, b Jun 1807
d2—John, b Jul 1809
d3—Ann, b ca. Jul 1811, d ca. 1816
d4—James, b 26 Jul 1813
   d 8 Jun 1885, bd Fort Augustus
d6—Margery, b ca 1825
d7—Donald, b 27 Mar 1826
d8—Catharine, b ca. 1831

e1—Alexander WALKER
b 18 Feb 1839
at Fort Augustus

m 1860? in SoAfr; a Baker
d 26 Aug 1903 (64y6m)
bd NECem PtEliz

e7—Catherine Ann Robinson MacMAY
b Sep 1845 in Buenos Aires

d 12 Dec 1892 (47)
bd NECem PtEliz

e2—Agnes WALKER
b August 1851 at Cape Town
"6 wks after her father's death"
m ca 1871

d 24 Apr 1906 at Grahamstown
bd Grahamstown

Joseph Charles ORSMOND
"Oompie"
b circa 1848 at Port Elizabeth
son of Joseph Orsmond
b 1804 d 25 Nov 1885

d 24 May 1929
bd Grahamstown

Leopold Charles Orsmond

m Alice Godfrey

Joseph "Poppity" Orsmond
b 1872

m Emily Jane Patrick
1870 - 1927

d 15 Aug 1941, Grahamstown
bd Grahamstown

Maud Victoria
Jos Chas m Adeline Granger Gush

James Herbert
Agnes Emily
   m Frank Edwin Fellows
George William

Gladys
   m Kruger

Charles
Robert
   m Blanche
   son = RC Bp Reginald Orsmond

328

Forebears of Catherine Ann Robinson MacKay, 1845?-1892

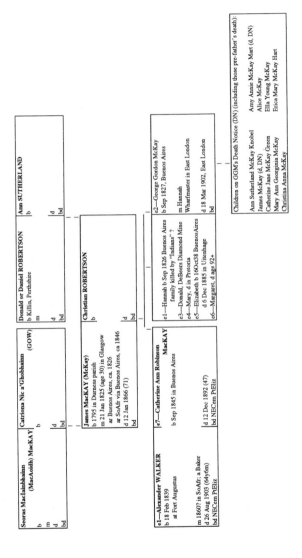

Seoras MacIainbhainn (MacAoidh) MacKAY
b
m
d
bd

Catriona Nic a'Ghobhainn (GOW)
b
d
bd

Donald or Daniel ROBERTSON
b Killin, Perthshire
m
d
bd

Ann SUTHERLAND
b
d
bd

James MacKAY (McKay)
b 1795 in Durness parish
m 21 Jan 1825 (age 30) in Glasgow
ar Buenos Aires, ca. 1826
at SoAfr via Buenos Aires, ca 1846
d 12 Jan 1866 (71)
bd

Christian ROBERTSON
b
d
bd

e1—Alexander WALKER
b 18 Feb 1839
at Fort Augustus
m 1860? in SoAfr; a Baker
d 26 Aug 1903 (64y6m)
bd NECem PtEliz

e7—Catherine Ann Robinson MacKAY
b Sep 1845 in Buenos Aires
d 12 Dec 1892 (47)
bd NECem PtEliz

e2—George Gordon McKay
b Sep 1827, Buenos Aires
m Hannah
Wharfmaster in East London
d 18 Mar 1902, East London
bd

e1—Hannah b Sep 1826 Buenos Aires
family killed by "Indians"?
e3—Donald, DeBeers Diamond Mine
e4—Mary, d in Pretoria
e5—Elizabeth b 16Oct38 BuenosAires
d 6 Dec 1885 in Uitenhage
e6—Margaret, d age 92+

Children on GGM's Death Notice (DN) (including those pre-father's death):

Ann Sutherland McKay Knobel
James McKay (d, DN)
Catherine Jane McKay Green
Mary Ann Georgnia McKay
Christina Anna McKay
Amy Annie McKay Mart (d, DN)
Alice McKay
Ella Young McKay
Erica Mary McKay Hart

The Children of Alexander WALKER and Catherine Ann Robinson MacKAY

e1—Alexander WALKER
b 18 Feb 1839
at Fort Augustus

m 1860? in SoAfr; a Baker
d 26 Aug 1903 (64y6m)
bd NBCem PtEliz

e/7—Catherine Ann Robinson MacKAY
b Sep 1845 in Buenos Aires

d 12 Dec 1892 (47)
bd NBCem PtEliz

f1—Alexander Walker
b 1860(?)

m Eliz Unkn
d 14 Mar 1955

d 1924(?); 20 Jun 1936 (?)
bd SBCem PE fr St Paul's Ch

f2—James William Walker
b 16 Sep 1863 at Port Elizabeth
bap 1 Nov63 StPaulAnglCh pg 96
m Catherine Agnes Allen
in Uitenhage

d 13 June 1921 at Johannesburg
bd Brixton Cem, Johannesburg

f3—Alice Walker
b 8 Jul 1865 at Port Elizabeth
bap 30Jul65 StPaulAnglCh pg 132
m Henry Acker

d
bd

f4—Jessie Walker, d pre-03
b 19 Oct 1867 at Port Elizabeth
f5—Robert Manville Walker
b 14 Jun 1869 at Port Elizabeth
bap 11Aug69 StPaulAnglCh pg 218

f6—Agnes Robinson Walker
b 12 Jul 1871; bap StPaul pg 267
m(1) Jon Svendsen d 1898 Rhod
ch=Agnes; Thelma&Percy dy Rhod
m(3) Alfred Wm Anderson d 1904
ch=Edith'02, Gladys'03, Alfred'04
d 26 Dec 1954D (82)
bd

f7—Geo Chas Henry Walker, d pre-03
b 28 Apr 1874 bap StPaul pg 357
d 16 Sep 1880 (6y5m) PtEliz
f8—Herbert Walker, d pre-03
b 13 Oct 1879 at Pt Eliz
bap StPaul pg 571
f9—Florence Walker, d pre-03
f10—Mabel Walker, d pre-03

f11—Ivan Lawrance Walker
b 7 Nov 1883 at Uitenhage, CP

m1 Carrie Lee; 5 children; div
m2 Ness Addison; 5 children
Secy Labor1930-1946
d 24 Sep 1961
bd Pretoria Crematorium

f12—Sidney Arthur Walker
b 10 Jul 1886
at Uitenhage
m(1) 5 Mar 1908 Ivy Green
m(2) 1946 Hannah Knox
2 yrs WWI mil; trnd in E Canada
d 18 Feb 1962 (75)
bd Saskatoon

The GREEN Family: *Back row, left to right:* Ivy (the author's mother), Herbert Arthur, Robert Frederick Jr, Louisa "Lulu," William Robert, Stephen James; *Middle row:* Alice Elizabeth, Robert Frederick Green, Clement George, Louisa Jane Nash Green, Florence Ethel, Violet; *Seated, front row:* Sidney Victor, Leonard Cyril, Harry Matthew. *Ca.* late 1901.

The font, St. George's Anglican Church, Cullinan, in which was baptized Edna May and her sister Jessie Walker.

Edna May Walker

Sidney Arthur Walker and Ivy Green Walker with Edna May, *ca.* mid 1910.

St. George's Anglican Church, Cullinan,
the Transvaal, as it appears in 1991.

332

The railroad tracks at Cullinan in which young
Jessie's foot was caught; 1991 photo.

The author on the verandah of the main house at Buffelsfontein, 1991.

Buffelsfontein Farm, a dozen miles west of Port Elizabeth,
as it appeared in 1991.

The main house at Smiling Valley Farm, East London District as it
appeared in 1991. It was built in 1909, the year of the author's birth.

Robert Frederick Green and Louis Jane Nash Green with William Robert, Violet, and probably Louisa "Lulu," *ca.* summer 1877.

Aunt Violet Green Thornton with Frank Edward Thornton,
same date as the Green Family photograph.

Uncle Robert Frederick Green, Jr., with Edith Ann Kirchoff Green,
married 4th November 1901.

Aunt Florence Ethel Green with Adolph Sonnenberger,
married 9th September 1901 (photo date, Oct. 1901).

Aunt Florence and Adolph Sonnenberger, with Mabel and Ivy, *ca.* 1904.

Adolph Sonnenberger with sons Harry, Sydney, and Ivan,
cousins to Edna May, perhaps *ca.* 1924.

The Sonnenberger daughters, cousins to Edna May:
l. to r., Mabel, Ivy, Bessie, Myrtle, Victoria, same date as the sons' photo.

Martha Hoffman Green, wife of Uncle Stephen James Green,
with Cyril Hedley and Amy Winnifred, *ca.* mid 1914.

Dorothy Mary Thornton, daughter of Aunt Violet Green Thornton,
age 18, in March 1913.

Uncle Sidney Victor Green, photo undated.

Uncle Clement George Green with Sophia Pachonick,
married 1st October 1919.

Robert Frederick Green and Louisa Jane Nash Green on their
58th wedding anniversary, 18th November 1928.

Tombstone at the Presbyterian Church, Gonubie,
East London District, as it appeared in 1991.

Robert Bryson and Louisa "Lulu" Green Bryson,
photo with "Nobby" in August 1943.

Ivan Lawrence Walker and Sidney Arthur Walker
with their father Alexander Walker, *ca.* 1900.

Tombstone at North End Cemetery, Port Elizabeth, as it appeared in 1991.

Pvt. Sidney Arthur Walker, the author's father, 6th Battalion, the King's Own Scottish Borderers, *ca.* 1916.

The passport photo, 1920: Edna May, Ivy Green Walker, Leonard Sidney, and Jessie.

R.M.S. Saxon, 12,385 tons, Union-Castle Lines, on which Ivy Green Walker with her children sailed from South Africa to England on the way to the United States.

Jessie Walker Beck and Herbert Beck, May 1987.

The author with her brother, Leonard Sidney Walker, Cape Town, 1991.